SCANDAL OF THE WEST

DOMESTIC VIOLENCE ON THE FRONTIER

R. E. Mather

with an Introduction by Louis Schmittroth

History West Publishing Company
Oklahoma City, Oklahoma 1998

In-house editing by Louis Schmittroth

Cover design by Margaret Anderson

LIBRARY OF CONGRESS CATALOGING-IN-PUBLICATION DATA

Mather, R. E. (Ruth E.), 1934-
    Scandal of the West : domestic violence on the frontier / by R.E.
    Mather ; with an introduction by Louis Schmittroth.
        p.   cm.
    Includes bibliographical references and index.
    ISBN 0-9625069-2-3 (paperback : alk. paper)
    1. Family violence—West (U.S.)—History—Case studies.
    2. Frontier and pioneer life—West (U.S.)   I. Title.
    HV6626.22.W47M37 1998
    362.82'922'0978—dc21   98-4063
                                          CIP

Printed in Canada

DEDICATION

This book is dedicated to Benjamin Eldon Tallman, who taught me how to read. I was three years old; he was thirteen and tired of reading the funny papers to a demanding little sister. His motivation, however, does not diminish the nobility of his act.

Ruth E. Mather

Contents

List of Illustrations

Acknowledgment

A special thanks is extended to Louis Schmittroth — the editor of this volume — for his encouragement and support of a project which some historians considered controversial because it presents hard truths of frontier life.

Thanks are also due the following libraries and historical societies:

Bancroft Library, Berkeley
California Historical Society
California State Archives
California State Library
The Church of Jesus Christ of Latter-day Saints Genealogical
        Library, Salt Lake City
Idaho Historical Society
Library of Congress
Montana Historical Society
National Archives, San Bruno, California
Nevada County Library, Nevada City, California
Oregon Historical Society
Oregon State Archives
Searls Historical Library, Nevada City, California
Society of California Pioneers
Stanford University Libraries
Sutro Library, San Francisco

Special acknowledgment goes to Fred Boswell for donating his photos and acting as a reader, and also to Peggy and Merrill Tallman for allowing access to their library of Western history books and contributing newspaper items.

Introduction

"History is little else than a picture of human crimes and misfortunes."- Voltaire, L'Ingenu. Chap. x. (1767.)

Crimes and misfortunes have always played a large part in the history of the West, but domestic violence, wife abuse, and child abuse have no place in the traditional myth of the western frontier, populated by noble settlers, dashing cowboys, courageous soldiers, gentle womenfolk, and sturdy children helping to forge a new society in the wilderness. But, as we learn from this fascinating account of life on the western frontier, the reality was quite different from the myth.

Using diaries, newspaper accounts, journals, memoirs, books, and reminiscences, the author cuts across decades of time and a half-continent of space to bring you a picture both grand and horrifying. You will meet a cast as varied as Narcissa Whitman, a cultured, educated, devout woman of God, to Emma LeDoux, no saint, but also much sinned against by her abusive husband. And, wherever possible, you will get the story from the words of the participants themselves.

This new book by historian Ruth Mather includes stories, case histories, and dramas as gripping as any you will find in the literature of the frontier. The author deals with universal themes, but concentrates on abuse within the family on the frontier. Although tragic, the stories are as compelling as a short story or novel. This is an important book that fills a void in the literature of the frontier.

Western history has been written primarily by men about men. Women appear in many histories as one of three stereotypes: the refined lady, the helpmate, and the bad woman—who have come to symbolize all women in the West. Ruth Mather brings us a history that includes the whole family: men, women, and children. Some suffered, some survived, some lived to tell of it, but some met a tragic end. By the time you have finished reading Mather's book, you will have gained a deeper understanding of the lives of women and children on the frontier.

This book has special significance to the history of the Montana gold camps. The author has researched the Vigilantes of Montana for more than thirty years and bases two of her case histories on players in that drama. You will meet vigilante John Grannis, who followed his wife through five states or territories after she left their abusive relationship. Another vigilante, James Williams, is shown frantically trying to complete the hanging of Joseph Slade before Slade's wife could ride to town to plead for his release. At most, Slade was guilty of disturbing the peace and bad-mouthing the Vigilantes. One of the many poignant scenes of the book is that of eleven-year-old Mollie Sheehan watching helplessly as Mrs. Slade lay sobbing on the still-warm body of her dead husband. Mollie bore the psychological scars of vigilante violence all her life. The Montana Vigilantes started a reign of terror in January of 1864, first with the object of getting rid of suspected criminals, later to silence any opposition to the extra-legal methods used. That this violence had an effect on children was of no concern to them, but had serious consequences to unintended victims: children.

An unusual aspect of the book is the inclusion of material on the life of, and abuse of, children on the frontier. You will be deeply moved by the hopelessness of the lives of some of the children you will meet in these pages. The book is worth reading for the story of the Sager orphans alone, which the author tells with understanding and sympathy. This is one area of family relations that has definitely improved. But in the attitude toward spousal abuse, I am not so sure things have changed that much, or at least we still have a long way to go.

Two women whose tragedies of domestic violence are treated in detail in the book were Californians: Lucinda Bohall Vedder, who came West with her family during the gold rush, and Emma Cole LeDoux, born in California to dirt-poor farmers, and whose "crime" was loving a man too much. Both abusive husbands were killed. The first, John Vedder, was killed by law officer Henry Plummer in self-defense. The second, Albert McVicar, was found dead in a trunk. The case of Lucinda Vedder and Henry Plummer has a special significance to Montana, since later, in 1863, he became the first elected sheriff of the region and was lynched by Vigilantes on January 10, 1864, in Bannack, MT (still Idaho at that time).

It is tempting to compare the present (1998) situation with the picture presented in these pages. Awareness of domestic violence has risen dramatically. Recently I did a search for "Domestic Violence" on the Internet and in a few minutes had the addresses of 500 web sites devoted in whole or part to the subject. I learned there is a *Violence Against Women Act of 1994* in the United States, and many states and Canadian provinces have similar laws. Police departments across the United States and Canada have training courses for officers, awareness sessions for the public, and hotlines for reporting domestic violence.

As an example, here is part of the policy statement of the Louisville Division of Police, taken from their web site:

> The Domestic Violence Squad investigates domestic-related felony assaults. The detectives in this squad have the option to call the Evidence Technician Unit, but they are also skilled in photographing crime scenes and collecting evidence. [...] The Domestic Violence Squad has also entered into a relationship with the Clinical Forensic Staff, in which an on-call clinical nurse will respond at the request of a Domestic Violence Squad detective to assist in the investigation of serious felony assault domestic violence situations. [...]

Lucinda Vedder in Nevada City, California, in the 1850s, had no such legal protection. After years of increasingly violent physical and verbal abuse, she finally summoned the courage to go to the courthouse, but could only report her plight to the clerk and recorder, who took no action. Lucinda had two strikes against her, the lack of a legal framework for assistance to victims of abuse, and the prejudice of society — women included — against interfering in "family affairs." She also had very little chance of making her own way economically, if she were to leave the abusive marriage.

In the 1990s, the situation is very different: the legal framework exists, police and social agencies have come to acknowledge a responsibility to intervene in abusive domestic situations, and many women are financially independent, or have a good chance of becoming so. However even now the system too often does not work. The *Edmonton Journal* of November 27, 1997, carried the story of a young mother, Jennifer Petruik, who had successfully extricated herself from a violent and dangerous marriage and had sought the protection of the law. Her former husband, who had recently threatened to kill her, had been convicted of carrying illegal weapons in his vehicle. In spite of this, the court released him on bail and failed to restrict his movements. He stalked her, killed her in front of their children, then took his own life. At the time of her tragic death, she had successfully carved out a career as a nurse and looked forward to raising her children.

Before you conclude Jennifer Petruik was an isolated case, consider this statistic from an impeccable source:

> Domestic violence is the leading cause of injury to women between ages 15 and 44 in the United States - more than car accidents, muggings, and rapes combined. (Uniform Crime Reports, Federal Bureau of Investigation, 1991)

In the nineteenth century, domestic violence was considered too scandalous to talk about. This has changed, and clearly for the better. But what needs work, still, are the attitudes toward domestic violence, not only on the part of the police and justice system but in the general public. One of the saddest commentaries on attitudes came during the trial of O. J. Simpson, the prohibition of allowing the jury to hear Nicole's own words describing the horrible abuse she suffered, and the fear she had up to the time of her murder. Her call to a battered women's shelter five days before her death was not admitted as evidence in the trial. Andrea Dworkin had this to say in the *Los Angeles Times* on January 29, 1995:

> Nicole's ordinary words of fear, despair and terror told to friends, and concrete descriptions of physical attacks recorded in her diary, are being kept from the jury. Insignificant when she was alive — because they didn't

save her — the victim's words remain insignificant in death: excluded from the trial of her accused murderer, called "hearsay" and not admissible in a legal system that has consistently protected or ignored the beating and sexual abuse of women by men, especially by husbands.

As you read the pages of this book, think about the similarity of the attitudes we still have toward domestic violence. Aside from being a fascinating and riveting read, this history of families on the frontier is important because it helps to fill in gaps in our history of the West.

Louis Schmittroth

Louis Schmittroth, a native of Dillon, Montana, received his doctorate at Stanford University and conducted postdoctoral work at Harvard. During his academic career, he has served as a professor at universities in Montana, Idaho, and Utah. He and his sister, Esther Mooney, are the donors of the Esther Stahl Schmittroth Collection of Western history, housed at Western Montana College in Dillon. Some of the materials in this collection are available on the World Wide Web, and Dr. Schmittroth is also the Webmaster for a site dedicated to the study of the Montana Vigilantes.

Author's Foreword

This book is a collection of stories documenting the prevalence of child and wife abuse in the Old West—roughly that period between the 1840s and the first decade of the twentieth century. While conducting research for four previous Western history books, I have collected and filed away the accounts of domestic troubles which I uncovered in early newspapers, court records, trial transcripts, diaries, journals, letters, and personal memoirs. This interest in violence within the family had grown out of my own experiences in an abusive marriage.

The stories I have selected to include in this volume unite past and present by shedding light on a problem frontier society shared with present-day society. Though some of the early narrators were of limited formal education, it is my intention to let them speak for themselves as much as possible because these voices from the past eloquently speak the truths of frontier life.

I

Child Abuse on the Western Frontier

Children's Frontier Experience

Even if there had been no child abuse in the Old West, the lot of children would not have been easy. Uprooted from their former security and thrust into a wilderness fraught with perils such as poison water, shortage of food, buffalo stampedes, flooding streams, and Indian attacks, children often had no other comfort than nostalgic memories of the home left behind. "A boy's recollections are very vivid," one Oregon settler stated in a newspaper interview, "and I can remember very distinctly how good the papaws, the persimmons, the fox grapes, the wild blackberries, and the wild strawberries tasted back in Missouri."[1]

In the midst of the westward migration, however, the children had little time for reminiscing about home. They shared their parents' excitement at making a new start in life and at the same time making history, and like their elders, they marveled at the wonders in the wilderness they were crossing. But they also faced the same problems confronting the adults, such as dangers and insufficient supplies on the trail. "Emigrants were hungry all the time," recalled Jesse Applegate, who was not yet seven when he traversed the Oregon Trail. "Children," Applegate wrote, "would enjoy themselves for hours gnawing off the fat coating from the dried salmon skins. An emigrant not hungry was thought to be ill."[2]

Thirst was another common companion on the trek West. Near Fort Laramie, an 1863 wagon train was pinned down by Indians and while under siege, depleted its entire supply of water. A seven-year-old boy "corralled" inside the dusty wagon circle with women and other terrified children later reported that the small companions languishing beside him in the sweltering confinement "were so thirsty they were crying for water."[3]

Before any deaths from lack of water occurred, the train was rescued by a troop of soldiers, but other trains were not so fortunate in combating deprivations and hazards. The overland routes were dotted with small graves of young travelers who would never see the promised land. And those who did survive, but experienced the trauma of losing a sibling to the hostile new environment, often bore emotional scars for the rest of their lives. At age eighty-eight, the previously mentioned Oregon pioneer who retained fond memories of the tasty fruits back in Missouri also harbored the tormenting vision of his six-year-old brother's death during the emigration: "My brother, George Smith Collins, was killed while we were crossing the plains, three miles from Soda Springs. He fell out of the wagon and the wheel ran over him, killing him instantly."[4]

Another Oregon trail emigrant was haunted by this final image of her younger sibling: "My brother . . . was a little chap. . . . He was playing with a rope and tripped on the rope and fell into the campfire, knocking over a large kettle of boiling water, which scalded him to death."

Likewise, young Jesse Applegate could not rejoice when the remnants of his family gathered around the fireplace of their first log cabin in Oregon's Willamette Valley. What would have been a joyous event was marred by the conspicuous absence of a brother and a cousin who during the journey West had drowned in a river. "Oh! how we could have enjoyed our hospitable shelter," Applegate lamented, "if we could have looked around the family circle and beheld the bright faces that had accompanied us on our toilsome journey almost to the end. Alas, they were not there!"[5]

Despite painful memories of the overland trek, children contributed their full share to the task of carving out new homes. This civilizing of the wilderness was a creative process: converting fields of wild grass to orderly rows of corn, constructing log cabins and furniture, and establishing schools and churches. Yet conquering the wilds also involved a certain amount of destruction: an elimination of the native inhabitants, the fauna, and the flora that had coexisted on the land before the settlers' arrival. And just as children took part in the creative projects, they also participated in the destructive processes.

In a diary kept of an 1864 expedition into Dakota Territory, Frank Myers — a young private of the Sixth Iowa Cavalry–disclosed the deprivations his company inflicted upon the native population. The cavalry was sent to the area because Sioux Indians had become disquieted over trains of gold seekers cutting through Powder River's buffalo country to reach gold diggings in Idaho Territory. Therefore, as Myers explained in his diary, the cavalry's mission in Dakota was "to protect the frontier and open up a trail through to the Yellowstone River country." During one campaign, the Private blithely reported, their troops approached a large butte "covered with Indian squaws and those not engaged in the battle." When the soldiers reached firing range of the inhabited butte, "a cannon was turned on it." Though the first shell fell short of the target, "the second one exploded on top of it," and "in a very short time the Indians were scattered in all directions." The battle yielded a "slaughter of the reds" that was "terrible," yet young Myers found it "amusing" to watch "the desperate efforts made by the Indians to get out of reach of the cannon."[6]

On another occasion, the Sixth Iowa Cavalry pursued three Sioux warriors who were fleeing on foot before the advancing soldiers. Upon catching up to the runners, the cavalrymen "killed the three Indians," Myers wrote, "cut off their heads and brought them into camp." In addition to killing the enemy, it was the cavalry's policy, after each victory, to destroy the Indians' property. Fanny Kelly, who was a captive of the Sioux during one of their defeats by Myers's company, described the results of the military's victory pillage. The Indians' village and property, she wrote, "including all the stores of provisions they had gathered for the winter were lost." And, she pointed out, "Without shelter, without food, ... death from starvation seemed inevitable."[7]

But the natives resisting the invasion of the settlers also committed their share of barbarities against the encroachers, and children of the enemy were certainly not exempt during a massacre. Typical is an 1867 incident near Forestburg, Texas–which was located close to the border of Indian Country. In a midnight raid to steal horses and other plunder, Indians attacked a farmhouse where only women and children were at home. The marauders hacked to death a widow, her two children, and two children of a second family, then smashed dishes, ripped all the cloth from pillows and beds, and retreated north to Indian Country.

A child sleeping in a trundle tucked under a larger bed escaped notice, but the child's mother was scalped while still alive. Passing travelers, who suspected trouble when they noticed a whirlwind of chicken feathers that had been shaken out of slashed pillows and bed ticks, saw the dazed housewife and at first glance thought she was wearing a red hood. They soon discovered that her head and face were "one mass of blood." In spite of her state of shock, the scalped woman had summoned the presence of mind to find the one sheet the Indians had overlooked and use it to cover the corpses of the dead children.[8]

Lifting a corner of this shroud, one of her rescuers later wrote, "I stood there looking at those pale little faces stained with blood. A sick and fainty feeling came over me." The sickened man turned away from the sight, struggling with the question of how God's design should include "that little innocent children should bleed and die to consecrate the soil to make homes for others."

Eight years earlier, Indians had attacked a small Texas settlement near Sugar Loaf Mountain. Those who came to the rescue found "mutilated bodies" and a "little babe crawling around on the ground in the blood of its father and mother." This "bloody babe of Texas" is a fitting symbol for the destruction which the two races wreaked upon each other's families.[9]

In this sanguinary feud–to which children were introduced upon being brought to the frontier—both races viewed the destruction of the other as a necessity for their own survival. Another necessity for survival on the frontier was killing the local fauna. Occasionally wildlife was shot as sport, as on the Dakota cavalry expedition, where Private Myers described soldiers killing elk and buffalo "for amusement." But more frequently, meat on the hoof—or on the wing as the case might be—was hunted for food. And, as in the aforementioned racial atrocities, children were involved in the killing.[10]

The slaughter of wildlife which children witnessed, or sometimes participated in, was often performed in a brutally primitive manner. The hunts were a blend of anxiety to relieve hunger, excitement of the chase, and pride in being the provider. These animated events could leave an indelible imprint on a young hunter's mind, somewhat akin to ancient initiation rites that employed cave paintings of animals to permanently impress a sacred concept on the novice's consciousness. "I killed my first deer with a club," Thomas C. Watts recalled of his boyhood on the Scappoose plains of northern Oregon. "I stood beside a deer trail, and pretty soon along came a deer. I . . . aimed a blow at its head, . . . but the club came down across its back and crippled it." Dragging its paralyzed hindquarters, the deer floundered about in an attempt to escape further blows, but nevertheless the boy persisted in delivering the necessary death wallops.[11]

Similar to Watts's vivid recollection of bludgeoning the injured deer to death is a description in the memoirs of Granville Stuart (who with his brother James accomplished the first gold sluicing in Montana in the early 1860s). In 1858 the two Stuart brothers and companions had set out from Montana's Deer Lodge valley to purchase supplies at Fort Bridger. Since their ration of dried moose meat was running low, one member of the party—who had a very strong hankering for fresh meat—shinnied up a cottonwood tree and attempted to reach a raven's nest. Though the two elder ravens fought desperately to save their offspring, the meat-hungry hunter finally succeeded in tossing four "half grown birds" out of the nest.

Other members of the Stuart party devoured the roasted fledglings, but Granville and James preferred to masticate remnants of the "flint-hard" moose jerky. Their reluctance to eat the ravens, however, did not stem from any revulsion generated by the pitiful sight of the parent birds futilely attempting to defend their helpless young. Instead, the two brothers rejected raven flesh because it had a "peculiar flavor and smell." The Stuarts–who as youngsters had resided in Iowa Territory and from there departed for the California goldfields–were too much the veterans of the frontier war for survival to reject food on grounds of pity for animals.[12]

Just as the Stuart boys had done in the 1830s, when their parents uprooted them from Illinois and transplanted them to a log cabin bordering bark huts inhabited by Musquawkee Indians of Iowa Territory, the children transplanted to the Far West in the 1840s, 1850s, and 1860s quickly adapted to the rigors of the new environment. Unfortunately, it was not uncommon for the value of these plucky children to be calculated in terms of the amount of labor they could produce. For example, an eight-year-old boy who lost his eyesight after contracting measles was judged "of no use" and sent to another home.[13]

The philosophy of the day was that children should work like adults, but should be seen and not heard. Also, they required liberal doses of the rod in order to improve their behavior and enhance their chances for a glorious afterlife.

As observant visitors from Europe noted, the conquering of the American West exacted a toll from the daring pioneers' progeny. John David Borthwick—a Scottish artist and correspondent who followed the gold rush to California—reported that Western children seemed to spring from the cradle directly into adulthood. A Montana homesteader confirmed Borthwick's contention, stating that in the 1860s, "10 year old girls considered themselves young women in society." And an early Oregon farmer recounted that before he was twelve years old, he had full responsibility for supporting his widowed mother and five siblings.[14]

Also in agreement with Borthwick's observation of childhood on the frontier was English author Isabella Bird, who observed that, "One of the most painful things in the Western States and Territories is the extinction of childhood." During her 1872 journey through the present-day states of California, Nevada, Utah, Wyoming, and Colorado, Bird was moved by the "wretched existence" of youngsters growing up in a society governed by the survival instinct and motivated by a burning desire for economic betterment. "Hard greed, and the exclusive pursuit of gain, with the indifference to all which does not aid in its acquisition," Bird detected, were "eating up family love and life throughout the West." Comparing the "sweet" pioneer children to "flowers in a desert," she characterized their daily family life as "work, work, work."[15]

Jesse Applegate's memoirs bear out Bird's assertion that the pioneer child's existence was dominated by labor. At school, he wrote, "I can remember no play time, no games, not even tag." And by the last day of the school term, the wheat was always ready for harvest. "My work," Applegate continued, "was to stack the sheaves into shocks. A vine known as the ground blackberry had grown with the grain . . . My poor, bare feet had to wander in thorny paths and the scratches on my hands made me forget that I was tired and hungry."[16]

As another example of lost childhood, a settler of both California and Oregon related that his school days came to an end when he turned eleven. In that year, 1856, a contentious neighbor shot the boy's father during a dispute over straying cattle. "I was the oldest boy," the settler said, "and had to do the plowing with two yokes of oxen and attend to the farm work. . . . I never had time to go fishing. . . . Whenever we needed meat I would kill a deer." He summed up his life between the ages of eleven and twenty-one by stating, "All I knew was to work from sunrise to sunset."[17]

Abuse Of Frontier Orphans

That the settlers' children performed hard physical labor was no secret; the well-kept secret of the frontier was the emotional, physical, and sexual abuse which many of these children also endured. Since early diaries and letters usually avoided such topics and since few such cases reached the courts, it is difficult to ascertain the pervasiveness of crimes committed against children in their own homes during the latter half of the nineteenth century. But judging from a series of interviews that aged pioneers granted in the 1920s, the problem was not uncommon. Especially vulnerable were the children whose parents had succumbed to the diseases and hazards encountered on the trail or in the new land.[18]

As each of the seven Sager youngsters—the best-known orphans of the frontier—could testify, no children were more at risk of abuse than those left without parents to sustain and defend them. In referring to her abuse, Matilda Jane Sager confided in old age, "I got to feeling about it as one does the winter rain—that it was inevitable and was to be borne without complaint for nothing could be done about it."

Yet when Matilda wrote her book about the notorious Whitman Massacre, she was cautioned to avoid the subject of her abuse. "If I had had my way," she insisted, "I would have told some wholesome truths." But she discovered that in 1920, wholesome truths were not welcomed; instead, domestic violence was draped in a veil of silence, serving to protect abusers from exposure to the community. Not until Matilda was eighty-two years old did she finally reveal the dark secrets of her childhood, but even then she refused to name her abuser.[19]

Story Of Most Famous Orphans Of The Old West: The Sager Children

Aside from the various instances of their abuse, the story of the Sager orphans is well known. Their parents, Henry and Naomi, had also been children of a developing frontier; born in Virginia, both emigrated with their respective parents to the Ohio wilderness and there met and married in 1830. But, their children remembered, Henry was "one of those restless men who are not content to remain in one place long," and after the birth of the couple's fourth child, he moved his growing family to Platte County, Missouri. Here Matilda and her younger sister were born, making a total of six siblings: older brothers John and Frank, followed by the four sisters, Catherine, Elizabeth, Matilda, and Louise.[20]

Catherine, being the eldest daughter, could recall life in their Platte County neighborhood, where both Henry and Naomi enjoyed "a wide reputation for ingenuity." Henry, who set up a blacksmith shop on his farm, became known as an artisan who could fashion any item in common use, ranging from a spinning wheel and loom to a horse's saddle. And when a death occurred in the vicinity, it was Henry Sager who always built the coffin. As for Naomi, who before her marriage had spent several years teaching school, "she was looked up to as an oracle." On week days, neighbors brought her their letters to be read and answered, along with any fancy work in need of embroidery; while on Sunday, they brought their children to the Sager farm for the Sabbath class Naomi taught.[21]

When in the spring of 1844 Henry again became restless and the Sager family set out for Oregon, Naomi was not only in fragile health, but also seven-months pregnant. It was the hope of both parents that when they reached the bountiful Eden on the Western coast, Naomi would regain her health and Henry would attain prosperity. In retrospect, Catherine expressed gratitude that her optimistic parents had not been able to look into the future and foresee the tragedy that lay ahead.

Matilda was only five when the family left Missouri and therefore retained few memories of the great adventure, but Catherine, age nine, vividly recalled "the bright spring morning" the family crossed the broad Missouri with their wagon and livestock. "Oh, those first encampments!"

she later wrote, "How the children did enjoy them!" Yet from the outset, the Sager family was plagued with difficulties.[22]

A diary kept by another member of their wagon train, the Reverend Edward Evans Parrish, reveals that the Sagers frequently held back their fellow travelers. From the May 16 encampment on the western side of the Missouri, Parrish wrote that the wagon train was awaiting the arrival of stragglers, causing "much uneasiness in camp and anxiety to be off." The Sagers were, in fact, one of the last of the stragglers to arrive. Then the following morning, Henry discovered his cattle had swum back across the Missouri. This time, however, the anxious emigrants rolled out as scheduled, leaving the lone wagon behind to collect livestock.[23]

Not long after catching up to the train, the Sagers caused another delay. "A frolic in Mr. Sager's family to-day," Parrish recorded on May 31; "Camped on a round hill. Much lightning, some wind and rain this evening." The reported "frolic" was the arrival of Naomi's seventh child, Rosanna. The birth was not an easy one, and the mother lying inside a wagon besieged by the elements seemed to be poised on a fine line between life and death. Sympathetic to the Sagers' plight, Captain William Shaw ordered a halt to the march. "We are camped to await the arrival of Mr. Sager whose wife is sick," Parrish noted on June 1; "Hope she will be well soon." But it was two more days before Naomi had recovered sufficiently to enable travel.[24]

From that date onward, the Sagers' luck went steadily downhill. One night the six older children–who slept in a tent beside their parents' wagon–got their blankets too close to the campfire and, Catherine related, "narrowly escaped being burned to death."

And near the crossing of the South Fork to the Platte, the Sagers' unbroken oxen left the trail and ascended an embankment, overturning the wagon. Henry, who was himself badly scraped in the accident, ripped off the wagon cover and began extracting the frightened passengers one by one. Though Catherine's dress "was torn off, leaving nothing but the waist and a strip of the hind breadth," not one of the children was seriously injured. When Henry reached his wife, however, he discovered her unconscious. Quickly, he unpacked the tent and set it up as a hospital room, and to Catherine, it seemed "a long time" before her mother at last regained consciousness and they could overtake the other wagons.

Then just outside Fort Laramie, Catherine suffered the accident that would leave her crippled for the rest of the trip. While attempting to jump from the tongue of the moving wagon, she snagged her dress hem and tumbled under a front wheel. By the time Henry was able to halt the spooked oxen, the rear wheel also had passed over Catherine's left leg. Leaping from the wagon, Henry ran to his injured daughter and scooped her into his arms. As he hurried to seize the reins of the oxen, who had taken flight, he glanced down at Catherine and observed with horror that her left leg was "dangling in the air." "In a broken voice he exclaimed, 'My dear child, your leg is broken all to pieces!'"[25]

After pausing long enough for Henry to set Catherine's broken limb, the Sager wagon proceeded on to Fort Laramie. Soon after their departure from the fort, Henry, John, and Frank came down with typhoid. Though the two boys were strong enough to dismount from the wagon from time to time and lead the oxen across a stream, Henry was confined to a bed beside his crippled daughter. His suffering was so great, seven-year-old Elizabeth remembered, that "as we jolted along the road, father begged to be taken out of the wagon and left by the side of the road."[26]

On August 27, the train crossed the Green River and commenced making night camp on the west bank. As usual, the Sager wagon was the last to ford the river and roll into camp. When Captain William Shaw visited the Sagers that evening, he found Henry "weeping bitterly" for the fate of his family. In an effort to ease the pain of the disconsolate father, Captain Shaw assured Henry that in the event of his death, Shaw personally would assist Naomi and the children. And since Naomi was still feeble, Sally Shaw, the Captain's wife, sent a young man to the Sager tent to nurse Henry.

"The sick man was either wholly or partly unconscious from high fever," the Good Samaritan recalled, "and I kept vigil all night, suffering from inability to help this life, which seemed to be burning away."[27]

As Catherine related the unfolding tragedy, "Father expired the next morning." His final words to her were, "Poor child! What will become of you?" Henry Sager, who was thirty-eight at the time of his death, was buried on the west bank of the Green River, "his coffin consisting of two troughs hastily dug out of a trunk of a tree." The following year, the Sager children would learn from the 1845 emigrants that their father's grave had been "desecrated" and his bones left "to bleach on the prairie."[28]

A few days after the brief riverbank funeral in which the Sager children had a last glimpse of their father's face, their mother also developed typhoid. Holding infant Rosanna in her arms, Naomi took her husband's bed beside the injured Catherine, and the wagon rolled onward. As her condition deteriorated, Naomi called for a young doctor traveling alone in the train behind them. Though Dr. Theophilos Degen could offer Naomi little hope of recovery, he did promise, with tears running down his cheeks, that he would look out for her children. Soon after this interview, Naomi became delirious, continually holding conversations with her departed husband as though he were still alive. Other nursing mothers took turns nourishing little Rosanna and, out of compassion for Naomi's suffering, hung a sheet over the wagon opening to shield her from the dust cloud enveloping all but the pacesetter of the moving train.

It now became the fate of Catherine, who had lain beside her father in his final days, to witness her mother's death agony: "The kindhearted women were also in the habit of coming in when the train stopped at night to wash the dust from her face. . . . As the disease advanced she became unconscious, making only a low moan. . . . Her last words were, 'Oh, Henry

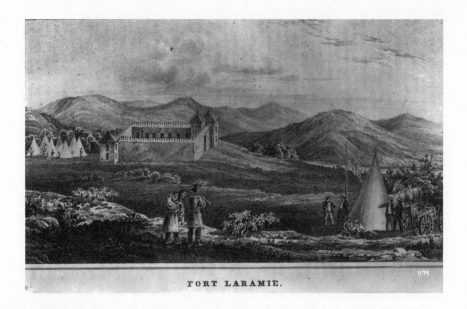

FORT LARAMIE.

FORT LARAMIE, 1843. Soon after leaving the fort, three members of the Sager family came down with typhoid. *Courtesy Library of Congress*

if you only knew how we have suffered!'" When Naomi died on the night of September 25, women of the train took the children to another wagon. "The next morning," Catherine wrote, "we were taken in to take the last look on the face of our departed mother." Then hasty preparations for the burial began.

Among the many possessions packed in their wagon, the children could not locate Naomi's best dress, so women sewed the frail, calico-clad form into a winding sheet, after which men lowered the light bundle into a shallow grave lined with willow boughs. More willows were then placed over the sheet, and with the six older children looking on, dirt was shoveled upon the willows. "We were orphans," Catherine realized, "the oldest fourteen years old and the youngest five months."[29]

Following the burial, the westward march continued. As Dr. Degen had promised Naomi, he took charge of six of the Sagers, and the mothers who had been nursing Rosanna continued passing her between them. The train was now out of flour and subsisting solely on whatever wildlife could be killed, though Catherine's younger sister Matilda did remember that members of the train "shared their last piece of bread with us."

The company was attempting to make up for lost time, but they had tarried too long and odds were not in their favor. Upon the train's departure from Fort Boise, Reverend Parrish wrote in his diary, "After a hard day's drive over hills and rocks we think it the roughest and hardest part of our journey." By the time they reached the Powder River on October 12, the mornings were "cold and frosty," while nine days later, the Blue Mountains were "white with snow."[30]

Meanwhile, the news that seven orphaned children were among a party of immigrants struggling through the Blue Mountains reached Dr. Marcus Whitman and his wife Narcissa at the Wailatpu Indian Mission, (situated a few miles west of present-day Walla Walla, Washington). Since the Whitmans routinely assisted needy immigrants who detoured to their mission, they began making preparations for the desperate 1844 party. "It is expected that there are more than five hundred souls back in the snow and mountains," Narcissa wrote her parents, and "among the number is an orphan family of seven children. . . . Application has been made for us to take them. . . . What we will do I cannot say; we cannot see them suffer, if the Lord casts them upon us."[31]

The future of the seven orphans now depended upon the decision facing the Whitmans. The decision was particularly painful for Narcissa because since coming to the mission, she had buried her only child. Like the Sager children's first mother, the woman destined to become their second mother had formerly been a school teacher. At age twenty-seven, she had married a thirty-three-year-old doctor possessed of a burning desire to bring Christianity, good health, and prosperity to the Indians of the Northwest. The day after the Whitmans' wedding (held in the Presbyterian church in Angelica, New York on 18 February 1836), the couple embarked upon a ten-month honeymoon, a journey intended to take them across the entire continent to the wilderness on the opposite coast known as Oregon Country, whose ownership was still a matter of dispute between the United States and Great Britain.[32]

Like the Sager story, the Whitmans' tragic experience in the Western wilds has been told before, but never with an eye to better understanding the problem of domestic violence on the frontier. In their westward journey, the Whitmans paused in Ohio to unite forces with a second missionary couple, Henry and Eliza Spalding. Thus, Narcissa Whitman and Eliza Spalding would be the first white women to attempt the crossing of the Rocky Mountains and the continued passage through the unsettled area on the western side.

In the journal she kept en route, Narcissa detailed the hardships encountered: the scorching rays of the prairie sun, the hazardous river crossing which soaked their precious books, the precipitous trails in mountains beyond the prairies, the attacks by mosquito swarms, and one massive flea invasion that left Narcissa badly shaken. "I cast my eyes upon my dress," she wrote in the journal, "& to my astonishment found it was black with these creatures making all possible speed to lay siege to my neck & ears. This sight made me almost frantic. . . . We brushed & shook for an hour." But still she could not rid herself of the "miserable companions" whose continual biting would not allow her to "rest for a moment in any one position."[33]

Through such moments of distress, her recurring bouts of fatigue, and her ever-present homesickness, Narcissa–who was as much the missionary as her new husband–drew strength from "sweet communions" with her Provident Maker. "The Lord provides & smooths all our way for us," she wrote, listing such blessings as feeling "the gentle breezes" that relieved the oppressive heat, drinking in the beauty of a crystal-clear spring, relishing wild gooseberries, blackberries, hazel nuts, and the crusty "mountain bread" fried in buffalo grease over a campfire, but best of all, savoring her rare moments alone with Marcus. "I have," she confided in a letter to her mother, "one of the kindest husbands, and the very best every way," and to her sister, "If you want to be happy get as good a husband as I have got."[34]

From the Missouri River to the fur-trapping rendezvous on the Green River in Wyoming, the Presbyterian missionary party traveled under protection of an American Fur Company caravan, composed of more than sixty men and four hundred head of livestock. Naturally, the two daring women accompanying the fur caravan piqued the sixty men's interest, and mountain man Isaac P. Rose made this insightful summary of Narcissa's appearance and personality: "Mrs. Whitman was a large, stately, fair skinned woman, with blue eyes and light, auburn, almost golden hair. Her manners were at once dignified and gracious. She was by nature and education, a lady, and had a lady's appreciation of all that was courageous and refined, yet not without an element of romance and heroism in her disposition."[35]

On reaching the Wyoming rendezvous, the missionaries joined a Hudson's Bay party bound for a company post at the confluence of the Columbia and Walla Walla rivers. But on arrival at Fort Boise, Marcus learned it would be impossible to cross the Blue Mountains with a wagon, and from Boise onward, Narcissa and Eliza went on horseback. On September 1, they rode into Fort Walla Walla and shortly thereafter took a boat downriver to Fort Vancouver. It was now time for the two missionary couples to part ways for their separate assignments. The Spaldings would set up their station on the Clearwater River, while Marcus Whitman departed to construct the mission of Wailatpu on the Walla Walla River.[36]

During her husband's absence–September 21 until December 9– Narcissa spent most of her time at Fort Vancouver as a guest of Dr. John McLoughlin, the chief factor of the Hudson's Bay Company. The White-headed Eagle, as local Indians called the imposing, 6' 4" Scot, was master of a vast fiefdom bounded on the west by the Pacific Ocean and on the east by the Rockies, and stretching north as far as Alaska and south to what is now California. Since McLoughlin's accomplishments at Vancouver would serve as a model for the self-sufficiency the Whitmans hoped to achieve on the Walla Walla River, Narcissa took great interest in visiting the various facilities. "Every day we have something new to see," she wrote. During a stroll through a "tastefully arranged" garden with "fine walks, lined on

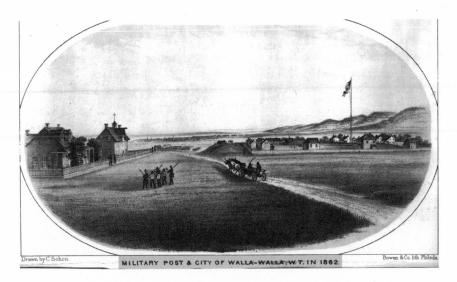

Drawn by C. Sohon   MILITARY POST & CITY OF WALLA-WALLA, W.T. IN 1862.   Bowen &Co. lith. Phileda.

CITY AND FORT OF WALLA WALLA, 1862. The Whitman mission was located seven miles west of present-day Walla Walla, Washington. *Courtesy Library of Congress*

each side with strawberry vines," she saw orderly rows of peas, beans, beets, cabbage, and tomatoes. Beyond were orchards of peach, pear, plum, apple, and fig trees and a "summer house covered with grape vines." The fort also had a school, rooms set aside for church services, a sawmill, a grain mill, and its own shipyard, which at the time was occupied by a man-of-war. "The first ship I ever saw," Narcissa wrote, "we went on board."[37]

Her tour also included a two-story warehouse filled with cargo from two ships, "every article for comfort and durability that we need, but many articles for convenience and all fancy articles are not here." Then there was a horseback ride to the company farm located a few miles outside the fort. At the upcoming harvest, the acres under cultivation were expected to yield 8,000 bushels of wheat and peas and 30,000 bushels of oats and barley.

There were also fields of turnips and potatoes, well-stocked barns for cattle, pigs, sheep, goats, chickens, turkeys, and pigeons, and a dairy whose sixty cows provided an abundance of cheese and butter. And the best part of the entire inspection was knowing all of these bountiful stores Narcissa was viewing were to be shared with the Whitmans for their mission. "Dr. McLoughlin," she inscribed in the journal she was preparing to mail to her family, "promises to loan us enough to make a beginning and all the return he asks is that we supply other settlers in the same way." It would be McLoughlin's terms for repayment of his loan–that is housing, feeding, and clothing destitute immigrants–that would ultimately bring the Whitmans and the Sagers together.[38]

During her stay at Vancouver, the former schoolmistress made herself useful to her host by tutoring his daughter and by conducting a singing class for the school's fifty-one students, all children of the fort's French Canadian laborers and their native wives. Within the limits set by the remoteness of the location, life at the Vancouver fur-trading headquarters was gracious, with weekly horseback rides for exercise and daily five-course dinners which so impressed Narcissa that she described them in full detail. "First we are always treated to a dish of soup." The soup, which was "very good," consisted of a variety of chopped vegetables, diced tomatoes, slivers of roast fowl, and a little rice. This savory concoction was artfully "spiced to taste." "After our soup dishes are removed, then comes a variety of meats to prove our tastes." The meat course included roast duck, boiled pork, pickled pigs' feet, and fresh salmon and sturgeon. "After selecting and changing, we change plates and try another if we choose, and so at every new dish have a clean plate." Next came dessert, "a nice pudding or an apple pie," followed by a fruit course of watermelon and a cantaloupe. "And last of all cheese, bread or biscuit and butter are produced to complete the whole. But there is one article on the table I have not yet mentioned, and of which I never partake. That is wine." Instead of joining the toasts being offered round the table, Narcissa sipped her cup of "good tea" with "plenty of milk and sugar."[39]

Despite the warm hospitality and camaraderie at the fort, Narcissa was anxious to get to Wailatpu, which she planned to conduct in a style more appropriate to a Spartan missionary life. In November she departed for Fort Walla Walla, where Marcus arrived on December 9 to escort her to the mission that was destined to be not only the couple's first home, but also their final one.

"It is indeed a lovely situation," she wrote of the mission's landscape, "we are on a beautiful level–a peninsula formed by the branches of the Walla Walla river, . . . barely skirted with timber." Beyond the trees, "as far as the eye can reach, plains and mountains appear." And to the east, only "a few rods from the house, is a range of small hills covered with bunchgrass." Narcissa's house–built by Marcus, two Indians, and a hired laborer–was a windowless log cabin with a blanket hung over the gaping door hole. Though she had no table, bedstead, nor mattress, her heart "truly leaped for joy" as she seated herself before the fire burning on the hearth.

Gradually, however, Narcissa's initial joy began to diminish. Since the Indians had invited them to come, the missionaries had not expected the labor to be so difficult, but it proved to be demanding, discouraging, and dangerous. "We feel," Narcissa wrote her mother, "that we cannot do our work too fast to save the Indian–the hunted, despised and unprotected Indian–from entire extinction."[40]

As the Whitmans discovered, their charges–the Cayuse Indians who had requested that missionaries be sent West to instruct and edify them–were slow to accept new ideas of religion, education, and agriculture, but quick to demand prompt cures from the doctor for any ills that beset them. When one chief's ailing wife failed to make rapid progress during recovery, he flew into a rage, threatening that if she should die, he would kill the doctor, as was the practice in their society. Marcus, Narcissa wrote home, "was nearly sick with the excitement and care" of the Cayuse people.

Though Narcissa faithfully recorded each event of the 1836 trek West and the many travails at the mission during the first half of 1837, neither her journal nor her letters mentioned a matter of the greatest import to her personally. In true Victorian fashion, she did not reveal her condition in any of her correspondence. But in the latter days of June–just before arriving at the fur-trading rendezvous–Narcissa had conceived a child. Though she had not enjoyed particularly robust health in the East, during the first eight months of her pregnancy she experienced no serious health problems. The second week of March, however, she suffered both inflammation and bleeding. A concerned Marcus prescribed bed rest for his wife, while he assumed the duties of cooking, cleaning, and washing clothes. In informing her family of her illness, Narcissa wrote, "No mother, no sister, to relieve me of a single care–only an affectionate husband, who, as a physician and nurse, exceeds all I ever knew."[41]

On Narcissa's own birthday, March 14, Marcus delivered their daughter. The parents named the infant Alice Clarissa, after her two grandmothers. Only then did the new mother notify relatives of the history-making birth: Alice Clarissa was the first white child born to United States citizens living in the Pacific Northwest. "On the evening of my birthday," she wrote, "we received the gift of a little daughter–a treasure invaluable. . . . Her hair is a light brown. . . . She is plump and large, holds her head up finely, and looks about considerably."

Despite the hardships and dangers of the environment, Alice was able to thrive in the "heathen land" and also to provide much "comfort" to her parents. She not only accompanied them on their visits to heal sick tribe members, but also on a journey to the Spaldings' Lapwai Mission on the Clearwater River, where, in Narcissa's words, both missionary couples had "the unspeakable satisfaction of giving away our dear babes to God in baptism."[42]

Under her parents' gentle tutorship, little Alice displayed great talent and exceptional intellect. By the celebration of their joint birthday in 1839 (Narcissa turning thirty and Alice two), the toddler could speak both English and Nez Perce fluently, sing hymns in both languages, and read from a lesson book. It is doubtful that any parent has ever taken a greater delight in her "most precious and only child" than did Narcissa Whitman. Whether awake or sleeping, Narcissa and Alice were inseparable. "I fear," the doting mother confessed, "I love her too much," for "O! On what a tender thread hang these mortal frames." Her words would prove to be prophetic.

The Whitmans had warned their tiny prodigy of the danger of the nearby river, but because of her cheerful obedience to all of their requests and her precocious sense of responsibility, they were confident she would

avoid the water. Therefore, they were "horror-stricken" one June afternoon to find the child on the river bank, industriously scrubbing dirt from
a radish pulled from the garden. Not wanting to "inflict any punishment
upon her," the anxious parents decided to instead discuss the matter with
her. Later that evening, they reinforced their prior admonition by remind-
ing the child that "if she should fall in the water she would die, and then
father and mother would have no little Alice." She did not respond immediately, but "appeared to be in deep thought" and then with "an inquiring
look," said to Narcissa, "Alice fall in water, . . . she die, . . . mamma have no
Alice." Judging from this cogent response, the parents concluded she had
indeed absorbed the intended lesson.[43]

Early on 23 June 1839–the Sabbath morning that would be Alice Clarissa
Whitman's last day of a life that had lasted only two years, three months,
and nine days–Narcissa related how she awakened her sleeping daughter
with a kiss. Alice stirred, "stretched up her arms and put them around my
neck and hugged and kissed me for a long time."

Later her parents let Alice select the hymn for morning worship, and
she chose "Rock of Ages." Listening to her small daughter sing, "When
my eyelids close in death, when I rise to worlds unknown," Narcissa thrilled
at how the sweet, high-pitched little voice "soared above ours."

That afternoon, Alice climbed onto her father's lap and read to him
from her lesson book, then slid from his knee and went outside to play.
While Margaret, the hired girl, prepared Sunday dinner, Marcus and
Narcissa settled into their own books and soon became engrossed in study.
Since Alice had no playmates, she was accustomed to entertaining herself,
often singing quietly as she played or holding hushed conversations with
an imaginary companion. Any time the small voice fell silent, Narcissa
would interrupt her reading to check her daughter's safety. She had always felt uneasy when Alice was out of her sight, but on this particular
day, she was experiencing an added nervousness. For the past week, the
child had insisted on sleeping on a cot next to her parents, rather than in
her usual spot on the bed, next to her mother. Though she could lay her
hand upon the sleeping child, Narcissa did not rest well, being possessed
by "a very strange and singular feeling." Before, the anxious mother reasoned, "I never could persuade her to lie away from me, not even in her
father's arms, . . . and I could not divest myself of the feeling that she was
laid away for the grave."[44]

So Narcissa's studies that Sabbath afternoon did not lessen her watch-
fulness over a child whose behavior had taken a puzzling turn. After Margaret had set the table, Alice entered the room, approaching the place set-
tings and commenting to herself, "Ha, supper is most ready, let Alice get
some water." Lifting two cups from the table, she walked out the door and
disappeared from sight. After a few moments of not hearing the child's
voice, Narcissa called for Margaret to fetch Alice. While she was waiting
for the hired girl to return, an Indian boy entered the house and reported

he'd seen two cups floating in the river.

"We ran down on the brink of the river," Narcissa later related in a letter, "crossed a bend, . . . and then back again, and then in another direction . . . while others waded to find her." The frantic search continued, but precious minutes were ticking away. "You cannot tell what our feelings were," Narcissa continued, "Neither can I describe them to give you an adequate idea. By this time all hopes of her life were given up for she had been in the water too long now to think of saving her."

An elderly Indian then returned to the point where the cups had first been sighted, waded into the river, dived below the surface, and commenced swimming downstream. As Narcissa breathlessly watched from the bank, the Indian's head suddenly appeared above water. When he stood up, she could see he was holding a limp form in his arms. "I ran to grasp her to my breast," she wrote, "but husband outran me and took her up from the river, and in taking her into his arms and pulling her dress from her face we thought she struggled for breath."

Desperately the rescue party began attempts to revive her. "We tried every means that could be used to bring her to life, for a long time," Narcissa wrote, "but to no effect. Her spirit had been called to rise to worlds before unknown."[45]

Attempting to bear her indescribable pain by communing with a higher power, Narcissa silently prayed, "Lord, it is right; it is right; she is not mine, but thine; she has only been lent to me for a little season. . . . I cannot wish her back in this world of sin and pain." Bravely, the mother bathed the small, lifeless body for the final time, dressed it, and laid it out for burial.

"I cannot describe what our feelings were when night came and our dear child a corpse in another room," she wrote her own mother. "We went to bed, but not to sleep. . . . The morning came, we arose; but our child slept on." Narcissa busied herself in sewing a shroud, but in spite of her fervor to accept God's will, she had "loved too ardently" the precious gift received on her twenty-eight birthday; she was now unable to tear herself from the child she had previously given in baptism to God.

While sitting next to the body of her deceased daughter, Narcissa wrote, "She did not begin to change in her appearance much for the three first days. This proved to be a great comfort to me, for so long as she looked natural and was so sweet and I could caress her, I could not bear to have her out of my sight." Finally, on the fourth day, when her beauty "began to melt away like wax," the missionaries laid their only child in a grave Narcissa could see from the front door of the house.

A month after the burial, Narcissa wrote that she could not seem to shake the impression Alice was still alive: "I seemed to hear her voice–her footsteps near me all day long."[46]

Alice had died in the summer of 1839, and it was the fall of 1844 when Dr. Degen and Captain Shaw delivered a brood of trail-worn, weeping orphans at Wailatpu. Despite a passage of time, both the Sager and Whitman tragedies were still painful realities. The Whitmans were parents grieved by the loss of a child, while the Sagers were children still mourning their parents' deaths on the plains. Though a union of the two broken families might appear to be a miraculous godsend, both sides still clung to bitter memories and fierce loyalties that made the acceptance of a new relationship seem almost traitorous. Preserved records of the thoughts and feelings that emerged as the two separate groups attempted to unite into one family provide rare insight into the problem of child abuse.

Narcissa Whitman was deeply moved by her first glimpse of the ragged, frightened children deposited at her doorstep. Even in adulthood, Catherine Sager well remembered the scene: "Foremost stood the little cart with the tired oxen lying near. Sitting in the front end of the cart was John weeping bitterly. On the opposite side stood Francis with his arms resting on the wheels and his head resting on them, sobbing aloud. On the near side the little girls stood huddled together, bareheaded and bare footed, looking first at the boys and then at the house, dreading we knew not what. . . . Thus Mrs. Whitman found us."

Catherine remembered that Narcissa spoke kindly to the children, but they ran behind the cart and hid there, "peeping shyly" around the corner at her. She then asked the boys why they wept, but quickly answered her own question: "Poor boys!" she said. "No wonder you weep."

"Seeing my lameness," Catherine wrote, "Mrs. Whitman kindly took me by the hand to assist me in, and took my little sister with the other hand, and thus led us in. As we reached the steps, Captain Shaw asked her if she had any children of her own. Pointing to a grave at the foot of a hill not far off, she said, 'All the child I ever had sleeps yonder,' and remarked that it was a great pleasure to her that she could see the grave from the door."[47]

Though it had been Naomi Sager's wish the children remain together, Narcissa considered keeping the girls, but letting John and Francis continue on to the Willamette valley with the wagon train, as they wished. Marcus, however, pondered the wisdom of even attempting to take the girls. The mission was already overcrowded with needy travelers, and since Narcissa was in poor health, he doubted she had the strength to rear the five-month-old baby, an emaciated "little object" no larger than an infant of three weeks. But Narcissa told him if she were to take any of the children, she wanted the baby also, "as a charm" to bind the older siblings to her as their new mother.

"If you are going to have the girls," Marcus answered, "I must have the boys." And so the homeless had found a second home.[48]

The Whitmans, though rather reserved and formal, attempted to welcome the newcomers and lift their spirits, but despite the missionaries' combined efforts, the Sager children felt extremely uncomfortable at the mission. "I thought I could never be happy there where everything was so strange," Catherine recalled, "and shed many tears in solitude. I became so timid as to cry whenever addressed by the Doctor or anyone."

Apparently Catherine's siblings were undergoing a similar agony, for one of their first actions as members of a new family was to pay tribute to the memory of the old. With Narcissa's permission, the older Sagers gave baby Rosanna a new name, calling her Henrietta Naomi, in honor of the two deceased parents.[49]

Since the Sagers harbored doubts the two busy missionaries had a genuine concern for their welfare, convincing them otherwise was a slow process that did not occur with the children jointly, but instead was a matter of the Whitmans' winning them over one by one.

Eventually, Elizabeth came to know her recently acquired father as "a philanthropist in the strictest sense of the word. Never did anyone in need apply to him in vain." He was a "very genial, kindly man" who was "fond of romping with us children." In the evenings, he would often gather the family about him and tell stories or make shadow-pictures on the wall by shaping rabbits or human faces with his hands. And during his numerous trips, he always remembered to obtain some small gift to bring home to the children. But since "Father," as the Sagers now called him, had to spend so much time instructing the Indians, healing the sick of both races, and supervising work in the mission's fields and mills, the burden of child care and discipline fell to Narcissa.[50]

Under "Mother's" firm hand, the children settled into an orderly routine. Daily they arose early, greeted their adopted parents with a kiss, as they had been taught to do, memorized a scripture, attended family worship, and then with any visitors at the mission gathered around the long table to share a simple meal, often consisting of nothing more than cornmeal mush (even for supper). On week days, each child weeded his or her assigned section of a large garden intended to supply enough vegetables for the various families residing at the mission and for passing immigrants as well. During the remainder of the day, the boys performed field labor, while the girls washed and wiped dishes, swept and mopped floors, and sewed. In summer the children spent one hour a day attending the mission school, and in winter several hours. Though Narcissa strictly held the family to this schedule, she rarely nagged or scolded. Instead, Matilda explained, "she would point to one of us, then point to the dishes, or the broom, and we would jump and get busy with our assigned task. . . . We dreaded that accusing finger pointed at us."[51]

Despite the rigidity of their daily existence, the children managed to find some playtime, such as swimming in the river or making boats from watermelon rinds, stringing them together in a line, and floating the green-striped flotilla downstream. And occasionally, Mother would fry doughnuts, make rag dolls, or take the family on a picnic. Her goal was to keep her new charges busy all day; after all, an idle mind was the devil's workshop. And it was mainly the children's minds and souls that concerned Narcissa. Since she placed little value on "worldly matters," she explained, she dedicated herself to "unfolding" the children's intellect and invigorating their "immortal part."

To her great disappointment, she found all of them "uninstructed, especially in the great truths of Christianity," and to develop their aesthetic sense and their appreciation for God's world, she took them for walks to collect botanical specimens, which later were pressed, and also supervised the children in planting a flower garden each. In addition, she enlisted the aid of the mission school teacher, Alanson Hinman, whom she regarded as a pious young man whose instruction was as strong in religion as in academic subjects.

It was at their first winter school term that the Sager children's abuse began. Catherine believed the teacher whom Narcissa held in such high esteem was in reality a man with "a black, licentious heart, ... one of these small-souled tyrants that could take delight in torturing helpless children." Under what Catherine considered "the cloak of religion," Hinman bombarded his students with harsh punishments, reserving the most severe for John and Frank Sager. In Catherine's opinion, her two brothers "were not considered bad boys" by anyone else who knew them, yet the teacher inflicted upon them "some of the most cruel whippings it was ever the lot of boys to receive."[52]

Knowing that Mother was an ardent proponent of obedience at school, the children were afraid to broach the subject of the whippings. And had they been privy to Narcissa's letters, they would have discovered that in avoiding the subject their instincts had served them well. Though it is possible Narcissa failed to realize the severity of Hinman's punishments, she did support his strict discipline. In fact, she explained in a letter, upon the Sagers arrival, they had been "very bad children," mainly because sympathetic fellow travelers such as Dr. Degen and Captain Shaw had failed to administer any discipline. And since at the time Narcissa was too "weak and feeble" to perform the needed corrective measures, she had enlisted Hinman as her "associate in instructing and laboring with the children." The young schoolmaster's acceptance of this responsibility for training the Sagers, Narcissa continued, had relieved her of the "hard task of breaking them into habits of obedience and order." She felt "thankful for the mercies of the Lord" in having placed "dear Brother Hinman" in the family.

Since their first day at Wailatpu, John and Frank Sager had been the most resistant to becoming part of a second family. They resented Narcissa's reproval and held themselves aloof from the unity gradually emerging between their sisters and the Whitmans. For instance, the girls accepted baptism at the Whitmans' hands, while the boys refused, clinging instead to Henry and Naomi's religion. And Frank had been so reluctant to refer to Mrs. Whitman as "Mother," that when he finally acquiesced, his siblings teased him. With some embarrassment, Frank casually responded that he guessed "Mother" was as good a name as any. John, who experienced a similar inner struggle in replacing his original parents, felt obligated to keep Henry and Naomi's memory alive. At any opportunity, he would lift his sisters onto his knee and relate stories about their original family.[53]

Because the two brothers' bonds to the mission family were tenuous, it is not surprising that Hinman's whippings, combined with Narcissa's high opinion of the abusive teacher, drove Frank to run away from home in the summer of 1845. Narcissa spent a sleepless night worrying about the missing twelve-year-old and praying that the Lord would soon "restore the wanderer to our arms again." And Frank, after receiving a horse which his brother had sent in order to encourage return, eventually rejoined the family circle. Not long after, the Whitmans replaced Hinman with Andrew Rogers, a good-natured young violinist who spent more time sharing the joys of music with his students than wielding the rod.[54]

Despite the appearance of restored calm at Wailatpu, during Frank's absence, he had stirred up a hornets' nest that would continue to buzz long after the Whitman Massacre of 1847. The distressed runaway had made a complaint against Narcissa to his former companions of the wagon train, a charge that fellow missionaries found serious enough to report to Narcissa. In turn, Narcissa took the matter seriously enough to respond with a letter defending her actions: "I endeavor in all things to act toward the children as if they were my own," she wrote. "My sincere, ardent and abiding wish is to train them for god and eternity, and not for transient existence in this life. . . . I do not think them difficult children to manage, neither do I have occasion often to use the rod."[55]

Narcissa's defense is substantiated by Catherine, who insisted that, "From morning till night did our adopted parents labor to promote our happiness," and Mother "was particularly adapted to the raising of children, having the happy art of combining instruction with pleasure. . . . Being refined and accomplished herself, she exercised over our rude natures that influence which refines and beautifies a home."[56]

Like Catherine, both Elizabeth and Matilda Sager staunchly defended Mrs. Whitman throughout their lives, yet Narcissa's letter defending herself contains some troubling passages in regard to the two younger children, Louise and baby Henrietta. The baby, Narcissa stated, "manifested a stubborn disposition" which "required subduing." But since the subduing process, she "obeys promptly when spoken to." Four-year-old Louise, Narcissa continued, "I have not been able to subdue so completely."

Without specifically mentioning what disciplinary measures had been so successful in subduing the energetic and mischievous baby, Narcissa sought to silence further criticism by stating that in light of Henrietta's naturally obstinate disposition, there could be no regret over the course pursued. In the same letter of explanation, however, Narcissa did admit that since the disciplinary incidents with Henrietta had occurred about the same time Frank fled the mission, they had undoubtedly been the cause of his charges against her.[57]

Narcissa's response to her critics temporarily stayed the rumors of her unnecessary harshness with the children, and life at the mission once more settled into its established routine of work and worship. And when the boys again got the wanderlust, Marcus persuaded them to remain at home by allowing each to start stocking his own herd of cattle. The following year, 1846, was apparently a period of rare domestic bliss. "We have as happy a family as the world affords," Narcissa wrote her younger sister. "We sleep out of doors in the summer a good deal–the boys all summer. . . . Every one of my girls go to the river all summer long for bathing every day before dinner, and they love it." Narcissa concluded the description of their family life with, "I do not wish to be in a better situation than this."

And Catherine concurred: "Whether riding, walking, or playing, Mrs. Whitman was with us partaking of our pleasure. . . . Thus did our time flow on in an uninterrupted stream of pleasure, our minds drinking daily at the fountain of knowledge."[58]

Though Catherine was perhaps recalling a past made somewhat rosier by its tragic loss and also by a passage of time, it is nevertheless true that in the three years the Sagers and Whitmans lived together as a family, a mutual love and respect did develop. Narcissa took great pride in the children's improved health and in their intellectual and spiritual growth, commenting that is was a satisfaction to labor for them.

Undoubtedly she was a dedicated mother, as well as a devoted missionary whose compassionate care of the sick and needy of both races caused her peers to regard her as "an angel of mercy." How then, even after her death as a martyr to the cause of Christianity, could rumors regarding her abuse of the Sager children continue to swirl? Or, how could a compassionate woman have allowed schoolmaster Hinman's brutal excesses? It is a mystifying puzzle which Narcissa's personal letters help to unravel. As her own words make obvious, she did not take the same delight in her two separate families. Of the Sagers, she wrote, "Although they are not mine by birth, yet I am interested in them."[59]

She was "interested" in the Sagers, as opposed to having loved Alice Clarissa "too well," and this difference in her feelings for the two sets of children extended itself to her methods of discipline. For example, when Narcissa and Marcus had discovered Alice washing a radish in the river, their concern was not that she had disobeyed, but that they might lose their "precious child." In their initial panic, they considered placing her into the water to demonstrate the alarming tug of the current, but after consideration, "feared the effect upon her reason, it being so easy to frighten her."

They agreed not to "inflict any punishment upon their child," but instead to reason with her about the "consequence" of going too near the water. This philosophy of discipline presented a marked contrast to the undisclosed punishment meted out to baby Henrietta for her disobedience, a punishment that prompted a lively toddler to thereafter hasten to obey when addressed.

But in analyzing the difference between the Whitmans' first and second families, it is not necessary to painstakingly dissect and attempt to interpret the material in all of Narcissa's letters. Because her Puritan conscience dictated a merciless self-scrutiny, she herself clearly stated the reason a caring individual, such as she was, could harshly discipline a child who had already suffered the trauma of losing both parents. Narcissa Whitman's candid confession, made in one of the last letters she would ever write, provides one key to opening the carefully kept secrets of domestic violence: "Henrietta, my baby, is a sweet, interesting child, and loves me as my own Alice used to, and I love her dearly." Then comes a startling admission: "But that tender anxiety, so peculiar to mothers for their own offspring, is not for me to feel toward her, because it is impossible."[60]

Unfortunately, in the years following the massacre at Wailatpu, the four surviving Sager children would encounter foster parents who had far less tenderness for them and much less anxiety for their welfare than did Narcissa Whitman during her time as their mother.

On 29 November 1847, during a measles and dysentery epidemic that threatened to decimate the Cayuse Indians, they rose up against the missionaries they had welcomed to their country, killing thirteen inhabitants of Wailatpu. Following the initial slaughter, three of the mission children died from lack of medical care, girls and women suffered sexual abuse, and forty-seven persons remained slaves of their Indian captors.

Among the dead were Marcus and Narcissa Whitman and John, Frank, and Louise Sager; while Catherine, Elizabeth, Matilda, and Henrietta were among the abused captives.

In late December, a Hudson's Bay employee negotiated the release of the captives in exchange for a supply of blankets, clothing, guns, and tobacco. After being ransomed, the captives hastened to the safety of McLoughlin's Fort Vancouver and from there to Portland. And in early 1848, Reverend Spalding, out of his regard for the Whitmans, personally took charge of finding pious families to take in the four surviving Sagers, who had once more become orphans. Though the eldest and the youngest–Catherine and Henrietta–were placed with the superintendent of the Methodists' Pacific coast mission with the understanding the two sisters would remain together, the superintendent soon sent Henrietta to a new home.[61]

Separated and assigned to unfamiliar homes where they were expected to earn their keep, the Sager sisters struggled to perform their daily chores by repressing memories of the horrors they had witnessed. But their attempts were in vain; throughout the rest of their lives they were pained by recurring images of 29 November 1847: Mother dragging their wounded Father into the room, kneeling over him, and trying to stop the flow of blood from a gaping wound in his neck; their former, violin-playing teacher, Mr. Rogers, staggering into the house, "shot through the waist and tomahawked behind the ear"; their current teacher being beaten until his head was "mashed to pieces"; a hired hand being slit open and disemboweled; and then Mother suddenly clapping her hand to the hole where a shotgun ball had entered and crying out, "Lord, save these little ones!"

While still in a state of shock from witnessing these atrocities, the Sager sisters had discovered the body of John, lying on the kitchen floor with the blood-splattered wall behind him and in front of him, "a stream of dark, congealed crimson" that had flowed from the gash in his throat. The following day, the Indians shot Frank; his sisters found him lying dead in the doorway to the house.

Then came the plundering of the mission. Meanwhile, Elizabeth Sager stated, "the bodies laid out in the yard 3 days." At last, survivors were permitted to stitch winding sheets around the corpses–some so mutilated as to be scarcely recognizable. One of the Indians who had not participated in the uprising then "dug a pit not over three feet deep, and wide enough for them all to lay side and side." Soon after the mass burial, six-year-old Louise Sager succumbed to an untreated illness and was buried beside the other graves.[62]

Throughout the carnage and the subsequent burials, the Indians would not allow the survivors to show any signs of grief. Fearing for their own lives, the terrified captives limited their silent weeping to the darkness of each night. During the anxious weeks of serving as the Indians' slaves and expecting death at any moment, the captives endured another form of abuse they did not care to discuss.

Though Catherine was only twelve, she was in constant danger from an Indian man who, as she put it, wished to "woo" her. One night he forced her to climb into a bed where other children were already sleeping and then crawled in behind her. Wisely, she had not removed her shoes, which she "applied to his shins till he cried out lustily." A few nights later, the same man returned while she was sleeping, "flung" one of the smaller children out of the bed, and grasped Catherine by the arm, saying he was going to "take her off." In her "desperation," she attacked him with "nails, teeth, and feet," thus managing to evade his intentions. However, other girls and women were not so fortunate in escaping their molesters, and these instances Catherine refused to discuss. As Reverend Spalding expressed it, "The young women were dragged from the house by night and beastly treated."[63]

The four Sager girls departed the ravaged mission with a severe, long-lingering paranoia. For example, when soldiers fired salutes to welcome the boat that was transporting the ransomed captives to Portland, the panicky children feared they were being fired upon and hid in the bottom of the boat. And when Dr. McLoughlin–who graciously welcomed the Sagers to his Vancouver home for a visit and tour–attempted to lighten their somber mood by playing a practical joke, they became "frightened almost to death" that the doctor intended to hold them as prisoners.

Yet the traumatized sisters received little sympathy or understanding in their temporary, regularly-changing homes. Instead, the girls were chided for "the change in their tempers." Catherine admitted they were irritable and had a tendency to bicker and quarrel, but blamed it on the "ill treatment" during captivity. "I think it never before appeared upon the annals of American history," she wrote as an adult, "where female captives were treated with like brutality."[64]

Gradually, the foster children being bounced from household to household came to realize their "ill treatment" had not ended with their departure from Wailatpu. Of her second foster home, Elizabeth wrote, "I lived there a year, but they were so unkind to me that I would not stay there." A third foster mother put her out of the house for going to visit Matilda, whom she had not seen for four years. Not until her older sister Catherine married, did Elizabeth find a suitable home. Her new brother-in-law was kind enough to take Henrietta also; but it was Matilda, eight years old at the time of the massacre, who suffered the most constant and severe abuse, an abuse which, as mentioned earlier, she did not reveal till decades later.[65]

In fact each time Matilda attempted to discuss her secret, her listeners did not want to hear. She was instructed to "forgive and forget," but she could not. She was never able to free herself of the "bitter" memories of her third temporary home. The first two times her third foster father (William Geiger, who had once been a teacher at the mission) appeared on horseback to collect Matilda and her meager possessions, she became hysterical. But the third time he came, she recalled, "I had to go and all my belongings were tied up in a little bundle.... I rode behind him." This scene of forced intimacy with a powerful male she feared–the pair of them locked together on the moving horse, her arms clutching the man's waist, the side of her face pressed against his back–was a recurring image in Matilda's memories. On more than one occasion, this scene had presaged some unknown but ominous event.

Geiger had recently married a preacher's daughter, and the couple lived in a small log cabin on a farm whose nearest neighbor was a mile distant. In this isolated setting, the twice-orphaned girl who was unaccustomed to being separated from her sisters fell into a routine of perpetual work. Though she was only eight, her chores included milking the cow, churning butter, carrying water from the stream, building the fire, sweeping, ironing, sewing, and when she was so careless as to let the coals on the hearth burn out, walking a mile to borrow embers from the neighbor's fire. A final duty that her foster parents gave her was to "pull the wool off the dead sheep and wash it and get it ready" for spinning.[66]

When the Geigers' first child was born, Matilda was expected to "take care of it and a good deal of the time be nurse." As she viewed her situation, "the supposedly pious people who claimed" they had taken her "out of charity" were working her to the limit "to get their money's worth" out of the cost of her board and room. During her years with the Geigers, Matilda was rarely allowed to attend school, a deprivation made more painful not only by her loneliness for other children her own age, but also by the love for learning the Whitmans had instilled in her.

Her "intensely religious" foster father served as the County Clerk and had an estimable reputation among the settlers. During his months at Wailatpu, Narcissa Whitman had described Geiger as "an excellent young man and superior teacher" whose students were "all happy and learning fast." And in 1844, he had been hired to teach the first school at Forest Grove. Despite his record at the mission, at the Forest Grove school, at the courthouse, and in church, there is no doubt that in the privacy of his own home, this esteemed man committed the crime of child abuse.[67]

"From the time I was eight until I was 15," Matilda at last told a newspaper interviewer who was open-minded enough to listen, "I was whipped. . . . I was never without welts or black and blue marks from constant beatings." For their extreme severity, certain punishments stood out in her memory, such as a beating prompted because she attended a program at the Congregational Church. Geiger said his punishment would teach her not "to desire worldly amusements, . . . the gateway to hell and damnation." And when he learned Matilda had spent time in the company of Mary Allen, a girl from a neighboring farm, he concluded another severe whipping was in order. For Mary, it was rumored, had been "born out of wedlock."

Other beatings were administered with even less provocation. Once while Geiger was preparing for a trip, he ordered Matilda to bring him a switch. As she delivered it, he grasped her by the shoulder and commenced lashing her. When she begged for an explanation, he answered, "You haven't done anything. I am going away. The chances are you will do something to deserve a beating while I am gone, and I won't be here to give it to you, so I'll see to my duty before leaving." After having done "his duty" to her, Geiger mounted his horse to depart and added, "I will whip you as soon as I return, but if you do anything to deserve a beating I will give you one you won't forget in a hurry."[68]

Geiger's repeated abuse, or religious training as he considered it, was psychological as well as physical. On one occasion, he rode up to the cabin on his saddle horse, called for Matilda to put on her sunbonnet and come out, and then pulled her up behind him. Since Matilda realized she was "to be seen, not heard," she merely clung to him in silence as they galloped away from the farm, not daring to inquire where they were going.

Eventually, they arrived at the community of Hillsboro, where Geiger guided their horse toward an assembled crowd. Soon police officers, who were gripping a prisoner between them, appeared and pushed their way through the crowd to a small gallows. Then before Matilda's "horrified" eyes, the officials carried out the execution.

"I brought you to see the hanging," Geiger advised her, "to impress on your mind what happens to people who do not mind their elders and do exactly what they are told."

In Geiger's defense, it should be stated that he was not the only adult who believed that watching a hanging was an appropriate "lesson" for children. The same practice was carried out by some parents in Bannack (then in Idaho Territory, now in Montana) during the outburst of lynchings there in 1864. But in Matilda's special case, the lesson was exceptionally ill-advised. During her waking hours, she was already haunted by mental pictures of the wolf-desecrated graves at Wailatpu, the scattered and gnawed bones of her loved ones, and the loose strands of Narcissa's "beautiful, long, golden hair" strewn to the winds. And after witnessing the execution at Hillsboro, she spent many troubled nights at the isolated farmhouse. "For weeks I woke up," she related, "covered with the sweat of terror at seeing the man hanged in my dreams. I could see him twitch and his tongue hang out and his protruding eyes."[69]

Though Matilda could not get the picture of the hanged man out of her head, she did have a period of respite from the beatings while Geiger was gone for a few months. Her foster father was not so pious as to place no value upon money, and on hearing of the gold discoveries in California, he deposited his family of four (his wife Elizabeth and their small son and infant daughter, plus Matilda) at his father-in-law's farm and traveled south. The hiatus was brief, however, for Geiger had no luck at the mines and soon returned to Oregon, collected his family, and resumed the corporal punishment.

Over the years, word of Geiger's cruelty to Matilda leaked into the community, and at last responsible citizens initiated a court case against him. When challenged about his harsh discipline, Geiger argued to the judge that he could discipline his foster child "more effectively" if the court would grant him legal custody of her. Perhaps because of Geiger's status as a county official, the judge agreed to grant the request. While the court was waiting for proof of the foster child's age, however, Matilda found a means of escape from her plight. A California miner who visited the Geiger home was in need of a wife and noticed the single teenager. Though he was in his thirties and she was only fifteen, the miner promptly proposed to Matilda, married her, and took her with him to live at the gold mines in Shasta County.

In the wilds of California, and later in Oregon again, Matilda bore eight children, was twice widowed, built a house to shelter her fatherless children, and took in washing to earn money to feed and clothe them. In return, her children cared for their dedicated mother in her old age.

During a 1921 interview for the *Oregon Journal*, given at one of her children's homes when she was eighty-two, she not only revealed for the first time the details of her early abuse, but also confessed that the experience had left her "bitter and vindictive." Looking back over the past, Matilda summed up her frontier childhood as "a time of terror."[70]

Afterword To Sager Story

It must be remembered that the physical punishments described in previous pages are usually presented from the viewpoint of the child, and that the adults involved might not have considered themselves abusive. Nevertheless the frequent and severe beatings of frontier orphan Matilda Sager in a household presumed to be respectable and charitable does not appear to be an isolated instance in the annals of the West. Though Matilda's sister Elizabeth did not provide details of her experiences in foster homes, she may have suffered abuse similar to that of her younger sister. It was while Elizabeth was living in the home of Mr. W. H. Willson–a citizen of sufficient prominence to have a square in Salem named for him–that she endured a year of "unkindnesses" so severe they eventually drove her from the home.[71]

As Narcissa Whitman made clear in her letters, the usual reason for accepting an orphan into a frontier home was to obtain free domestic help. Unable to find "permanent help" upon their arrival at Wailatpu, the Whitmans had written to Vancouver "for an orphan girl," and Dr. McLoughlin had promptly sent them one. Later, the Whitmans received several letters of application from other children but, Narcissa explained, we "refuse all except one or two who are willing to labor."

Like the Whitmans, Captain John Sutter had needed labor to carry out enterprises conducted at the fort he had established prior to the California gold rush. Among Sutter's work force, one visitor noted, were "Indian boys who were being trained to work." The visitor found it "peculiar" that Sutter fed the boys not at a table, but in a "trough," where "with their fingers" they would "scrape up" barley gruel and suck it into their mouths. The boys' punishment for breaking any of Sutter's rules was to "be strapped, face downward" to a log and then "flogged on the back with a five-tailed rawhide."[72]

As another example of the plight of children who found themselves parentless on the frontier, an Oregon immigrant named Allan Sanders purchased a twelve-year-old Indian boy, cut his long, black locks, and dressed him in suitable clothing. But when the ungrateful child had the audacity to appear "very unhappy" in his new situation, Sanders gave him a "sound thrashing." Witnesses to the whipping did not interfere, but instead concluded the punishment seemed to make the boy more "contented."[73]

And in one final illustration of abuse suffered by an orphan, when Oregonian J. W. Blakely's parents died in 1854, authorities placed the boy in the home of foster parent John Downing, considered both "reputable and responsible."

"Although I was only seven," Blakely recalled, Downing "expected me to do a man's work. I had to feed the stock, clean the barn, . . . and if I did not do everything just as he expected or just as quickly as he thought I should, he would whip me unmercifully. . . . I would have liked to have killed myself, but I didn't know how." After one particularly brutal beating, Downing left his ward, by then eight years old, lying on the ground. "From my shoulders to the calves of my legs," Blakely stated, "my flesh was torn and bleeding. . . . I crawled out of his sight, and as soon as I could travel I ran away."[74]

In a society where labor was an orphan's main justification for existence, where a willow switch or five-tailed rawhide whip was an accepted implement for enforcing discipline, and where a sound thrashing was a remedy for rendering a homesick child content, it seems possible that Matilda Sager's foster-home "terrors" were representative of the life of many a frontier orphan.

Abuse Of Stepchildren on the Frontier

It was not only the parentless child who was defenseless under the roof of an abusive adult. A child living with one caring birth parent could be as vulnerable as an orphan. As Thomas C. Watts–who was transplanted from Missouri to the Far West at an early age—learned in his remote wilderness home, the cruel stepmother of fairy tales could become a reality. Though his father was a reasonable man, Watts believed, "My second stepmother was a woman of sudden and violent temper, and she clubbed me with whatever was handy when she was out of humor, so I have scars all over my body to remind me of her." At age eighty, Watts could still back up his claim of abuse by pulling up a shirt sleeve and displaying noticeably visible scars on one arm.[75]

After the arrival of this second stepmother, the Watts home had fallen short of the ideal set out for youngsters in an early reader entitled *The Gospel Primer*. One section of this lesson book dealt with the appropriate topic "The Happy Home." "My father and mother are God's children," early students read. "They love him, and he loves them. Our home is a happy home. Our father and mother love their children, and love each other. Their children love them. . . . Love makes us happy. . . . No home can be happy without love. In heaven, all is love."[76]

Though in the Watts case it was the stepmother who displayed a lack of love in the home, a stepfather–though not so vilified in folklore–could also destroy the "heavenly" atmosphere which the primer said God had intended for a family. Ed Carr, an Ohio emigrant who as a child arrived in California aboard the steamer *Central America* (and as an adult became the captain of a Columbia River steamer), found himself in a new frontier home with a new father who showed him little of the love present in "The Happy Home." Shortly after his mother's marriage to the unloving doctor, Carr ran away. Like many abuse victims, Carr did not list the specifics of his mistreatment at home, nor in the foster home from which he also ran away. Later, however, when a committee of concerned citizens ordered the youth to return to his family, Carr responded that he could not because his stepfather "made home a hell-on-earth."[77]

Unfortunately, some children who fled an abusive stepparent and then attempted to make their own way in the developing Western society did not become such productive adults as Captain Carr. One notorious example is gold-rush desperado Charles Reeves, a young gambler who twice escaped San Quentin prison in the 1850s, fled Washington Territory with a lynch mob at his heels in 1862, and in 1863 accepted banishment from the mining camp of Bannack, Idaho Territory just in time to avoid the vigilantes' 1864 hanging spree.

Reeves had first fled danger at age nine, when he ran away from his home in Mercer County, Pennsylvania in order to escape his stepmother's beatings. He ended up in Texas, thus acquiring the nickname "Texas Charley," and then joined the gold rush to California, where he was imprisoned for committing a theft. The beatings the youth received during his incarceration in the California state prison followed the pattern of his childhood, and it is not surprising that during his brief marriage in Bannack, he continued this cycle of abuse by beating his Indian bride until she at last returned to her own people.[78]

Like Narcissa Whitman, Reeves's stepmother might have protested that it was "impossible" for her to feel "tender anxiety" for young Charles because he was not hers by birth. Yet many abusive parents lacked even this excuse, since the children for whom they could muster no feelings of tenderness were their own offspring.

Abuse by Frontier Birth Parents

A list of frontiersmen who left their childhood homes at an early age because of repeated harsh punishments by birth parents would include the leader of the Montana Vigilantes, Captain James Williams. Captain Williams was described by one of his contemporaries as an individual who "has done more hanging than any other man in the West." During a thirty-day period in the winter of 1864, Williams directed more than twenty-one lynchings, his band of heavily armed riders leaving in their wake a trail of frozen victims dangling from a cottonwood limb, barn rafter, corral rail, log cabin eaves, or butcher scaffold.[79]

Story of Stock Detective Hanged for Murdering Teenager: Tom Horn

The roster of frontier children who escaped abusive birth parents would also include Tom Horn, the noted military scout, Pinkerton agent, and stock detective who was hanged in Wyoming in 1903 for murdering a teenage boy. Tom Horn's own boyhood had been marked by violence, namely an extended series of whippings alternately delivered by his teachers, his mother, and the father for whom he had been named.

Thomas Horn Senior and his wife, both natives of Ohio, had in the

1850s followed the Westward migration as far as Scotland County, Missouri, and there taken up a farm. Of their nine children–eight of whom survived–Thomas Junior was the fourth. His great love for rambling the woods and hunting played continual havoc with his education and religious training. "I had nothing particular against going to church and Sunday school," he wrote in his autobiography, "if it had not been for the 'coon, turkey, quail, rabbits, prairie chickens, 'possums, skunks, and other game."[80]

The boy's love of the outdoors was too great to be deterred by his school teachers' "lickings," his father's "regular thumpings," or his mother's scoldings and whippings. "My mother was a tall, powerful woman," he wrote, "and she would whip me and cry, and tell me how much good she was trying to do me by breaking me of my Indian ways." But despite the "many hundred times" she tried to civilize him, all it took to revive her son's temporarily suppressed tracking instinct was the sight of a rabbit trail left in fresh snow beside the path to the schoolhouse. "Then," Horn wrote, "the stuff for school was all off." He would sneak back to the house to retrieve his dog Shed and the hunt would begin. "I could see far more advantage," he stated, "in having a good string of pelts than in learning to read, write, and cipher."

Tom Junior and Shed were on constant call to prove both their prowess as hunters and their ability to whip any other boy and his dog in the countryside. The pair had come by this compulsion for proving manhood honestly enough, for Tom Senior was known in the community as "the hardest man to whip in Northwest Missouri." It was not unusual for him to vent his violent temper upon his incorrigible son, as well as upon the boy's loyal dog when Shed accompanied Tom Senior on trips to town. "Sometimes," Horn stated in his book, Shed "came home looking pretty badly used up" and "would not leave me for days."[81]

When Tom was a teenager, a neighbor boy shot Shed for protecting his young master during an unfair fist fight. In Tom's final days before the hanging, he recalled Shed's death as "the first and only real sorrow of my life." Soon after the loss of his beloved dog, the juvenile had a disagreement with his father, who subdued his rebellious son with a harness strap. "Dad had done his work well," Horn wrote of what would be the last flogging received from his father, "next morning mother and the girls carried me to the house and put me in bed where I lay for a week." On recovery, Tom Junior kissed his mother farewell, made a final visit to Shed's grave, and left home, never to return.[82]

The year of his departure from the Missouri farm was 1874, and Tom Junior was only fourteen years old. His following years would prove to be every bit as tempestuous as his boyhood years had been, for he would serve as an army interpreter and scout during the Apache wars, track and shoot suspects during his Pinkerton days, become a stock detective, and eventually face murder charges in Wyoming.

Though on 22 July 1993, the Supreme Court of Wyoming granted a posthumous retrial for Tom Horn, and on 16 September 1993, defense attorney Joseph William Moch succeeded in obtaining an acquittal from this second panel of jurors, at the original trial, the jury found Horn guilty.

On 20 November 1903, Horn was hanged on the Cheyenne gallows. The jury believed he was guilty of shooting Willie Nickell while the boy was herding sheep on his father's ranch near Iron Mountain. Ironically, at the time of Willie's murder, the boy was fourteen, the same age Tom had been when his father's whipping drove him away from home. And there is one final irony: Horn's schoolteacher sweetheart, Glendolene Kimmell, had steadfastly contended Horn was innocent. She claimed that Willie Nickell's actual murderer had confessed his guilt to her, but she could not bring herself to report the confession to authorities because the confessed killer was himself a teenager![83]

Afterword to Horn Story

In the nineteenth century, parents such as Tom Horn's were usually described–even by the recipients of their punishments–as strict disciplinarians rather than child abusers. The following statement by J. B. Hoss, an 1870s resident of Pendleton, Oregon, illustrates the century's typically tolerant attitude toward severe parental discipline: "My father believed in discipline with a capital D, and when he wanted to whip me he grabbed the first thing handy. . . . He probably meant well but he had a heavy hand and a quick-trigger temper, so when I was 14 I lit out. I took one of Father's saddle horses, leaving a note that I would send the money for it later."[84]

Hoss's willingness to excuse his father's beatings is understandable in light of the pervasiveness of violence in the Western environment. And before attempting to assess the effects of the harsh punishment supervising adults administered to frontier children, it is necessary to first consider the other forces of violence that impinged upon the children's lives. As an example, apart from her foster father's abuse, Matilda Sager undoubtedly suffered great emotional damage from witnessing the killings and mutilations during the mission massacre and the hanging. And the sexual abuse Catherine Sager and other girls suffered during their captivity at Wailatpu also had lasting effects, partly because of the shame assigned to the victims.

Sexual Abuse of Frontier Children

Though sexual matters were considered too delicate to discuss openly, frontier communities expected strict adherence to sexual mores, and those who dared to violate them were treated as pariahs. As evidenced by the case of Mary Allen (the girl born before her parents wed), the stigma associated with illicit sex also fell upon the victim. Therefore, Catherine Sager would not reveal all she knew about the sexual attacks at Wailatpu. "In giving a history," she wrote, "I had had to touch upon a delicate subject–one that I have always avoided in conversation, namely the treatment of the young women by the Indians. I have endeavored to present them in such a manner as to spare the feelings of those concerned. For this reason I have not related many things that would be interesting."[85]

Catherine Sager is not the only early storyteller to withhold information that would have been not only "interesting," but also valuable to succeeding generations. James F. Meline, who in 1866 traveled throughout the Great Plains, the Rocky Mountains, and the Southwest, wrote that it was "invariable" that Indians sexually abused their white female captives, and just as invariable that the female captives denied "anything beyond mere hardships. . . . They are scarcely ever known to admit anything more."[86]

Since shame which should have been reserved for the perpetrator also fell upon the innocent victim of sexual abuse, it is only natural pioneer girls and women concealed the sexual mistreatment they suffered while in captivity or in their own homes. It is quite likely that like her sister Catherine, Matilda Sager also withheld details of her abuse which would have been too painful or too shameful to divulge. Why should she subject herself to the treatment Mary Allen experienced? In addition, Matilda's interview was conducted in a home where her grandchildren were present and might overhear, and also, she had to relate only those incidents reporter Fred Lockley would be able to print in an early-twentieth-century newspaper. Never in her monologue did she state that she was revealing all the "truths" she would have liked to include in her previous book. Her memoirs do contain passages in which she seems on the point of charging her foster father with a crime beyond battery and emotional abuse. But corporal punishment is in itself an intimate experience between punisher and recipient, in Matilda's case an intimacy that lasted until she was fifteen (long past the age of becoming "a young woman in society"). And Geiger, who had duties in the community as well as on the farm, dedicated an inordinate amount of time to disciplining Matilda, in fact seemed to display an obsession with her.

Yet throughout the lengthy session with interviewer Lockley, Matilda not only withheld the name of her abuser (which had to be ascertained through independent research in other sources), but went so far as to mask any information that might enable a later reader to track down Geiger's identity from her memoirs. And it was not she, but neighbors who at last charged her foster father with a crime. Thus during her interview, Matilda was not only protecting herself or other victims, such as Catherine, was, but also protecting the abuser who had created her lifelong bitterness.

Though such walls were erected to guard the secrets of sexual abuse in frontier households, evidence does exist of children being abused in residences which they were forced to inhabit temporarily. Some teenage girls were held prisoners in Western brothels, and from the 1850s through the 1870s, wayward teenage boys were sentenced to prisons where older inmates sodomized them. These cases became a matter of public record when reformers urged legislators to take preventive action, but the sexual abuse practiced in homes remained what it has always been, a crime of silence.

Seepage of Frontier Violence into the Home

Present-day adults rightfully register concern about young people being exposed to simulated violence on television. In the previous century, however, parents themselves exposed their children to violence that was real. It was a society, remember, who viewed hangings not only as a valuable lesson for the young, but also as a form of entertainment to which the audience might carry a picnic lunch. Other popular entertainments were dogfights, dog and badger fights, bull and bear fights, cock fights, domestic fowl shoots, or the sport of placing hundreds of rats in a pen, then introducing a dog, and taking bets on how many of the rodents the dog would kill before tiring of the slaughter.

In addition to such recreational bloodletting which children sometimes attended with their elders, the daily lives of frontier children were frequently steeped in forms of bloodletting that had nothing to do with mere amusement.

Story of a Most-wanted Outlaw: John Wesley Hardin

The life of Texas outlaw John Wesley Hardin presents a classic example of a violence-steeped childhood. Hardin became a fugitive from justice at age fifteen and by age twenty-five was one of the most wanted criminals of his day. Yet his decade of crime, extending from 1868 to 1878, did not appear to stem from any violence suffered at the hands of his parents. "My father," Hardin wrote in his autobiography, "was a Methodist preacher and circuit rider. My mother, Elizabeth Hardin, was a blonde, highly cultured, and charity predominated in her disposition. She made my father a model wife and helpmate."[87]

Judging from his autobiography, Hardin received continuing support and love from his entire family throughout his life, even during his years as a fugitive from justice. He recorded only one instance in which his father "thrashed" him, and that was for, at age nine, concocting a plan to run away, join in the Civil War, and "fight Yankees." In fact the Hardin household apparently bore a striking resemblance to the happy home outlined in The Gospel Primer. As Hardin viewed his family, the parents loved God; they loved each other; they loved their children; and their children loved each other and their parents.

Reverend Hardin was a community leader who not only preached for

J.D. BORTHWICK, DEL.   M A H HARRART LITH

BULL & BEAR FIGHT.

"BULL & BEAR FIGHT," by John David Borthwick, gold-rush artist and correspondent. Frontier audiences enjoyed bloodletting spectacles. *Courtesy History West Publishing Company*

remote congregations who had no other spiritual leader, but also organized an academy and practiced law. "Our parents," John Wesley Hardin wrote, "had taught us from our infancy to be honest, truthful, and brave." In spite of the mutual love and the emphasis upon morality within the home, the Hardins lived in a hostile wilderness environment during times which were fraught with social violence.

Five children, Joseph, John Wesley, Elizabeth, Martha, and Benjamin, were all born in the wilds of Texas. At the outbreak of the Civil War, the Reverend, who had initially opposed secession and did not himself participate in the fighting, did serve the cause by organizing a military company on behalf of the South. But Lee's eventual surrender did not put an end to strife in Texas, for during the bitter Reconstruction period, bloodshed was common. Intense hatreds festering in Texas communities often erupted into clashes between freed slaves and defeated slave holders, feuds between Mexicans and Texans, exchanged barbarities between settlers and native Americans, altercations between Texans and travelers from other regions of the United States, and a life-and-death struggle between vigilance organizations and the established justice system. Gradually, this social warfare weakened the barrier of morality the Hardin parents had tried to erect around their family.[88]

In addition to inroads into the home made by racial, regional, and judicial conflicts, the difficulty of surviving in the unsettled land demanded a certain brutality of its inhabitants. Upon those inhabitants who demonstrated sufficient skill and courage to kill either man or beast, rather than be killed or starve, frontier society bestowed great respect and highest honors. And the stories Hardin related of his childhood days and youth reflect this criterion for evaluating human worth. Hardin was capable of demonstrating a complete lack of respect for all forms of life, and he took fierce pride in the bloodletting exploits he considered to be proof of his manhood.

Like Tom Horn, Hardin's greatest boyhood pleasure was the "sport" of killing deer, bobcats, raccoons, and opossums. At age eight, he happened across four raccoons huddled near the top of a large oak tree. The boy felt certain his older brother Joe would "laud him to the skies" if he could provide his father's hired hands with a coon stew for supper that night. By standing on his horse's back and lassoing a limb with a rope, the boy managed to climb to the top of the tree. "The coons," he reported, "decided to charge me. They began to form in line, one behind the other, to growl and show fight."

Nevertheless he refused to be cowed. He tied himself to a limb and engaged in combat with bare fists. "I fought hard and long, and one by one I knocked those coons out of that tree top . . . and they no sooner hit the ground than the dogs made short work of them." In capturing his "trophies," he had — like the protagonist in the Stephen Crane novel — received "a red badge of courage." "I was covered with blood from head to foot; my hands, face, and breast were torn and lacerated, being badly bitten and scratched." On examining his wounds, the Reverend's work crew marveled that after such an experience, young Wesley "was not lying a dead boy in that swamp." He responded, "It was pluck that both saved me and captured the coons." It was the same "pluck" that would later make him a wanted man.[89]

By age eight, Hardin had not only demonstrated his manhood through the coon hunt, but also seen a man killed. While visiting a town in Trinity County, he watched a man slit an antagonist's jugular vein with a Bowie knife. And throughout the Civil War, Hardin wrote, "I had seen Abraham Lincoln burned and shot to pieces in effigy so often that I looked upon him as a very demon incarnate."

At age fourteen, Hardin committed his first stabbing, an incident which occurred in the unlikely setting of a school room. During recess, he and a classmate had argued over the authorship of a verse of poetry inscribed on the schoolhouse wall: "I love Sal, and Sal loves mutton, etc." Later, the classmate continued the argument inside the building. "He came over to my seat in the school room," Hardin wrote, "struck me and drew his knife. I stabbed him twice almost fatally in the breast and back." But since it was the stabbing victim who had first drawn a weapon, Hardin continued, "the courts acquitted me."

The following year, Hardin claimed, he committed his first murder, shooting "a Negro . . . who had belonged to . . . a brother to my Uncle Barnett Hardin's wife." Though Hardin maintained that the ex-slave had threatened his life and therefore he was forced to shoot in self-defense, he doubted he could receive a fair trial under the "misrule" of the Union military and a Reconstruction police force composed mainly of freed slaves. So he became a fugitive, not from justice, he insisted, but from "injustice."

Hardin boasted that in succeeding years, he killed an assortment of Mexicans, Indians, and whites, becoming so inured to taking lives that on one occasion he bet his cousin a bottle of whiskey he could shoot out a man's eye. By the time Hardin composed his life story, he could no longer be certain, but "supposed" he had won the bet.[90]

Wesley Hardin's solution to most of the problems he encountered during his outlaw years was an immediate application of violence. For instance, while he was on a cattle drive to Abilene, Kansas, a neighbor's white ox caused "considerable trouble" by attempting to join the herd. "I pulled my .45," Hardin wrote, "and shot him, aiming to shoot him in the nose, but instead hit him in the eye. That ox gave me no more trouble."

Hardin also bragged of his trail crew's visit to a Mexican camp to play monte. When they returned to their own camp after the gambling spree, he related, they were still chuckling over the "total casualties," which—if we are to believe the boastful outlaw—amounted to "a Mexican with his arm broken, another shot through the lungs, and another with a very sore head." Neither did those particular Mexicans give Hardin any more "trouble." Though it appears that the outlaw's memoirs are not always accurate, they are consistent in one aspect, and that is showing his pride in committing acts of violence.

In 1878 John Wesley Hardin was finally captured and sentenced to prison, where he spent much of his time studying law books and the Bible. After his release from prison, he passed the bar examination in Texas and attempted to start a new life on the right side of the law. However the young man who had lived by the gun was destined in middle age to die by the gun. In 1895–while he was in El Paso to serve as prosecutor in a court case–he entered a saloon and was standing at the bar when one of his enemies approached from behind and shot him in the back of the head. Sadly enough, two decades before Wesley's death, Reverend Hardin had lost his eldest and most peaceful son to the violence that plagued early Texas. On a June night in 1874, Joseph Hardin–who had followed in his revered father's footsteps and become a teacher and lawyer–was lynched by a vigilante mob.[91]

Afterword to the Hardin Story

Though Hardin's parents apparently resorted to little violence in the home and spent their lives struggling to bring civilization to the Texas wilderness, they can be held responsible for instilling a strong regional hatred in their offspring. The North, the elder Hardins believed, was "waging a relentless and cruel war on the South to rob her of her most sacred rights." As their son Wesley admitted, "The justice of the Southern cause was taught me in my youth," and "I grew up a rebel."[92]

In addition to fostering an attitude that prompted violence, Hardin's parents were also responsible for selecting the frontier as their children's home. Their outlaw son's reminiscences of Texas in the 1860s and 1870s underscore the violence inherent in the struggle to survive in a hostile physical environment, coupled with a society embroiled in life-and-death feuds. In some manner, this environmental violence usually invaded the individual's daily existence and could make an especially strong impression upon formative young minds.

Story of Child Witness to Lynchings: Mollie Sheehan

The problem of environmental violence infiltrating the home was not peculiar to Texas, but instead existed in nearly every region of the West. In Idaho Territory, a devout Catholic named James Sheehan opposed summary executions being carried out in his community and did his utmost to protect his eleven-year-old daughter Mollie from exposure to such atrocities. Yet in spite of Sheehan's precautions, within a period of only three months, Mollie would be a witness to seven lynchings.

Mollie, who had not only a caring and protective father, but also a stepmother whom she described as "gay and gentle," had gloried in the overland trek West: "I recall so vividly the feeling of wonderment and perplexity at the bigness of the world," she wrote, "a dim road winding out of sight on a wide prairie that undulates endlessly toward a vast shadowy background of looming mountains." When her father halted the wagon each night, Mollie would continue walking for a few minutes, peer ahead into the vast expanse, and try to imagine the exciting adventures awaiting her. It was not in Mollie's nature to imagine that some of those adventures might be terrifying.[93]

In 1863 her father became the first freighter to bring a wagon filled with supplies into the newly discovered mines at Alder Gulch, now in Montana. When an English gentleman named Thomas Dimsdale opened a school in Virginia City that winter, James Sheehan enrolled his daughter, and on the afternoon of 14 January 1864, Mollie was returning home after class. As she approached Wallace Street, where her parents' log-cabin boardinghouse stood, Mollie noticed that though the day was quite cold, a huge crowd was gathered in front of an unfinished building. "The air was charged with excitement," she recalled. "I looked. The bodies of five men with ropes around their necks hung limp from a roof beam. I trembled so that I could scarcely run toward home."

With the horrific picture frozen in her memory, she fled toward the security of their boardinghouse, only to be overwhelmed en route by an equally horrible realization: one of the limp forms still visible to her mind's eye belonged to Deputy Jack Gallagher, "a tall and dark and striking-looking" young man who sometimes ate with her family. "To us," Mollie stated, "he was always courteous and soft-spoken," and in addition, one of his special kindnesses to her had resulted in a treasured memory. Gallagher had traveled to the mines in the same wagon train as the Sheehans, and during night camps, he would sometimes sit and listen to Mollie read the Bible stories her father had provided her. She recalled how after she had read each story aloud, Jack Gallagher always "spoke in a pleasant, quiet voice and praised me for reading so well. I would sit by the campfire in the dim light, one or the other books on my lap, . . . say the words by heart, and enjoy the adulation."

A few weeks after viewing the corpses dangling from a beam on Wallace Street, Mollie experienced a second shock. "One frosty morning," she related, "I opened the back door of our cabin. I saw in the gulch below a crowd of men gathered around a scaffold. High above other men and directly beneath the scaffold stood a young man with a rope around his neck." As the young man drew a black hood over his head, Mollie suddenly remembered that the face of one the five lynch victims on Wallace Street had also had his face covered with a black scarf and "knew the portent." Quickly retreating inside the house, she slammed the door to extinguish the sight. Still, she said, "I could not shut out from my memory, then or ever, that awful creaking sound of the hangman's rope."[94]

And on a springlike day in March of that same year, Professor Dimsdale detained his students at the school longer than usual because a mob was assembled at the Wallace Street corral. Looking down from the hill above, Mollie "recognized Joseph Alfred Slade, dressed in fringed buckskin, hatless, with a man on either side of him, who forced him to walk under the corral gate." She could see that Slade's arms were pinioned, his elbows bent, and his hands at his chest. "He kept moving his hands back and forth, palms upward, and opening and closing them as he cried, 'for God's sake, let me see my dear, beloved wife!' I distinctly heard him say this three times in a piercing, anguished voice." On an approaching trail, Mollie saw Slade's wife furiously galloping toward town on her thoroughbred horse, Billy Boy.

Again, Mollie turned away from the scene and hurried toward the refuge of home. Meanwhile, James Williams (the abused child who had grown up to become a vigilante captain and was now in charge of Slade's lynching) ordered his men "to do their duty quickly" before Mrs. Slade arrived and attempted to soften their hearts with her pleas. Though Mollie was safely inside her home when Captain Williams's men did what he considered "their duty," she was not spared the details of the execution. Unable to shut out the excited conversations of neighbors who had watched, she was forced to listen as they reported how the vigilante executioner had

HANGMAN'S BUILDING, VIRGINIA CITY, MONTANA. On her way home from school, Mollie Sheehan saw five corpses dangling from a beam inside the then-unfinished building. *Photo by F. E. Boswell*

"hastily adjusted the rope, had kicked the box from under Slade so that he swung with a broken neck from the crosspiece atop the corral gate."[95]

Her heart "aching" for Slade's wife, Mollie later slipped away from the house and went to find the newly made widow. Vigilantes, after cutting the rope and removing the deceased victim from the corral-gate bar–ordinarily used for suspending butchered beefs–had delivered the corpse to Mrs. Slade at the Virginia Hotel. "I found her sobbing and moaning," Mollie said, "bowed over a stark form shrouded in a blanket. I stood beside her for a moment, trembling and choking." Though Mollie had searched out Mrs. Slade for the express purpose of telling her "how sorry I was for her," the distraught girl left without being able to speak. She could find no words sufficient to express her feelings.[96]

There is a special irony in Mollie's girlhood stress at Alder Gulch. Her schoolteacher Thomas Dimsdale was a consumptive Englishman whom she still could remember distinctly in her final years. The Professor, as Mollie called him, was "small, delicate-looking and gentle. It seemed to me that he knew everything and I liked him. In his school all was harmonious and pleasant." While Mollie and the other pupils were supposed to be studying, Professor Dimsdale sat at a makeshift desk stationed near a window of the log schoolhouse. He needed the light for the writing that so

VIGILANTE CAPTAIN JAMES WILLIAMS. A contemporary claimed Captain Williams had "done more hanging than any other man in the West." *Courtesy Montana Historical Society.*

occupied him, he took no notice when his pupils "buzzed and whispered over their readers, arithmetic and copybooks."

Not until the publication of Dimsdale's book praising the lynchings etched in Mollie's memory, did she come to realize the contents of the writing that "had so engrossed" her teacher. At his window desk, she later surmised, Dimsdale had been composing the Montana Vigilantes' defense

THOMAS DIMSDALE, author of *The Vigilantes of Montana*. Mollie Sheehan described her schoolteacher as a "gentle man who seemed to know everything." *Courtesey Montana Historical Society.*

of the executions of Jack Gallagher, Joseph Slade, and numerous other victims.

Her admired teacher, as Mollie correctly guessed, was approvingly recording for posterity the very executions which had jolted her from her naive world of frontier pleasures, such as viewing beyond the heaps of mining slag, an untrammeled hillside of waving buttercups; inhaling the fragrance of a patch of moss-flowers; or listening as a meadowlark's song trembled through an otherwise silent gulch. But Mollie would never come to realize that the teacher who had dedicated himself to molding children's minds and character was in all probability a member of the violent vigilante organization himself. Thus in expressing her childish faith that Dimsdale "knew everything," Mollie had unwittingly uttered a well-turned phrase. The treatise that the "gentle professor" was preparing while Mollie and her classmates whispered instead of studying was intended to convince future generations that the lynchings directed by Captain James Williams were a "protest of society on behalf of social order and the rights of man."[97]

Institutional Violence Sanctioned by Parents

Though the physical and psychological abuse children experienced at school and church cannot be considered domestic violence, both institutions were not only sanctioned, but in most cases, required by parents. Yet it was in a classroom setting that a court determined a teenager had assaulted Wesley Hardin with a knife, and where he in return had stabbed his first victim. And instances of teachers having abused students, (as well as the older male students having abused teachers), are rife in pioneer memoirs.

A major qualification for a frontier teacher was being able to control unwilling and unruly students, especially the older boys. As J. C. Cooper learned during his days in early Montana and Oregon, sometimes the ability to discipline was the sole yardstick which a school board applied. As a young man, Cooper was splitting wood on his father's farm when a former neighbor from Missouri passed by and halted to watch him wielding the axe.

"Cal, you're good and husky," the observer finally remarked, "I want you to come to our neighborhood and teach school." Cooper replied that he did not feel qualified to teach because he had little education. "You don't have to know much to be a school teacher," the former neighbor informed him, "the principal thing you have to be is strong enough to lick the big boys."[98]

Another young teacher, Robert G. Smith–who weighed only ninety-five pounds, but believed himself qualified because he had passed the teachers' examination–reported in the fall of 1882 to the Klamath Falls, Oregon school that had hired him through the mail. When the judge, steamer captain, and doctor who directed the school "looked me over," Smith said, they "shook their heads" and suggested such a frail young man should "surrender the contract." They even offered an added incentive for the resignation: they would pay his way back to where he had come from. When Smith appeared reluctant to give up the teaching position, the doctor advised him he would make no more than "a mouthful" for the "big boys" who had "put out the last two teachers through the window." But Smith held the directors to the contract and succeeded in establishing himself master of the school by giving "a good licking" to a boy who "insisted on tearing up his books."[99]

There is another instance of the older students of a frontier school not only throwing their teacher out the window, but also "running him off." But despite such occasional outbursts by reluctant students, or perhaps because of them, most of the violence in early schools appears to have been inflicted by the teachers, and receiving severe whippings, warranted or not, are standard memories of male pioneers. The example of the punishments received by the Sager boys at the mission school has already been given, but more relevant to this section are the memories of J. D. Matlock. In the spring of 1853, he had walked barefoot every step of the way from Missouri to Oregon. Though he had never seen the inside of a school, at age fifteen he put on his first pair of shoes so he could enter a classroom to learn his A, B, C's. On being turned out for his first recess, he immediately removed the uncomfortable shoes to relieve his aching feet. As punishment for this breach of school etiquette, the teacher seated Matlock on a bench. When he complained that the bench was hard and asked to borrow the master's coat as a cushion, his teacher flew into a rage. "He jerked me off the bench and whaled me till he was nearly worn out," Matlock recalled. Not until Matlock became a teacher himself did he make the amazing discovery that "you do not have to use a club to control children."[100]

The club often employed at religious services was a psychological weapon, an attempt to "put the fear of God into you," as George Turner's boyhood minister used to put it. Turner,

a pioneer of Wyoming and Oregon, recounted how his mother forced him to go to Sunday school and church to listen to a preacher who "was an artist at describing hell. I used to wake up at night covered with goose-flesh, I was so sure I was going to hell." The boy thought he was man enough to endure being "burned up" once, but "what got me," he added, "was to think of burning in hell for ever and ever." Thus in addition to the actual savagery present in the environment, some children were tormented by an imagined violence awaiting them in the afterlife.[101]

A third institution that influenced young people has already been mentioned briefly, that is the fraternity of manhood with its initiation rites and mystique involving such activities as fistfighting, wrestling, bearing arms, hunting, and warring. One young gold seeker, who believed that in California he would find either "wealth or an untimely death among strangers," explained that his goal in joining the 1849 rush was to demonstrate he was worthy of belonging to the fraternity. At the outset of his overland excursion, he inscribed in his journal, "Who can tell which or how many will fall by disease, an Indian arrow or the several dangers that will beset our path, but to the West we have set our faces, and to the West we go." In that same 7 April 1849 entry, the initiate formulated his version of the life awaiting him at the goldfields: "All is work and excitement and proving ourselves men."[102]

When carried to its furthest extreme, the brotherhood of the strong and courageous evolved into the nineteenth-century phenomenon of desperadoism, the cult which enticed Charles Reeves and a host of other young men of the gold-rush era into a life of crime. Isabella Bird, during her stay in Colorado, befriended a noted fugitive and through him became familiar with the following articles of the desperado creed: "To resent insult with your revolver, to revenge yourself on those who have injured you, to be true to a comrade, . . . to be chivalrous to good women, to be generous and hospitable, and at the last to die game."[103]

That this creed had a strong attraction for the younger generation is made plain by a Nevada newspaper editor, who in the 1860s described "the desire to be a desperado" as "a curse" that had taken hold of the youth of the Far West. And an early history of Montana stated that desperadoes were treated not as "criminals," but "more like heroes." Mark Twain agreed that "the desperado stalked the streets with a swagger graded according to the number of his homicides, and a nod of recognition from him was sufficient to make a humble admirer happy for the rest of the day."

The ends to which a youth might go in quest of this deference afforded desperadoes is shown by an incident Isabella Bird included in one of her books. While staying at a hotel in a remote section of Colorado, she spent an evening listening to other guests spin bloodcurdling tales of "violence, vigilance committees, Lynch law, and 'stringing'" that had occurred in the vicinity.

Then came an account related by two women who ran a boardinghouse in the South Park mining country. One of their boarders, the women said, was a boy of only fifteen years, who believed that "he could not be anything till he had shot somebody." Armed with a revolver–and if following desperado protocol, also wearing a long-tailed coat, shiny boots, and slouch hat–the boy stalked town streets, searching for a man whom he could provoke into a duel. But at each opportunity, he discovered he did not have the courage to complete his mission. Giving up the search of the streets, where he would have to meet his opponent face to face, he decided to hide himself in the town stable. While concealed, he then "shot the first Chinaman who entered." Though not under the valorous conditions he would have preferred, the youth had at least "killed his man" and could — to borrow Mark Twain terminology–join the coterie of the "long-tailed heroes of the revolver."[104]

CHURCH AT BANNACK STATE PARK, MONTANA. Some frontier preachers were "artists" at describing hell. *Photo by F. E. Boswell.*

Effects of Violence on Frontier Children

In the cases of children such as the South Park teenager just mentioned, desperado Charles Reeves, vigilante captain James Williams, outlaw Wesley Hardin, and cattle detective Tom Horn, violence appeared to have bred violence. Yet many children seemed to come through the frontier experience without having been brutalized. Jesse Applegate, for example, suffered the shock of watching his brother and cousin drown, killed wildlife in order to survive, and experienced his share of skirmishes with the local Indians. And like Tom Horn, Applegate was whipped at school; and like Matilda Sager and George Turner, he was psychologically abused in the name of religion.

"When I was about four years old," Applegate wrote, a schoolteacher "struck me with a switch because I could not distinguish between the letters 'B,' 'P,' 'Q,' and 'D.'" Four years later, another teacher terrified him by reading the following religious lesson to the class:

"There was a little boy whom his parents had never taught to pray

CEMETERY AT NOW-VANISHED MINING CAMP OF FLORENCE, IDAHO. As this grave marker indicates, some gold seekers subscribed to the desperado creed: " To resent insult with your revolver." *Photo by F. E. Boswell.*

to the Lord before retiring to rest at night. He did not know how to ask the Lord to forgive his sins and protect him from the evil one whilst he slept. One night he went to bed and fell asleep. He never awoke and was lost."

When eight-year-old Jesse retired that night, he lay in bed pondering the lesson of "the lost boy." "It seemed plain," he thought, "that I was in as much danger as he. The chances would surely be against me should I fall asleep." To keep himself awake, he got out of bed, went to the fireplace, and stirred up the live coals. While he sat gazing at the glowing embers and searching for a solution to his dilemma, his mother awoke, watched him for a few moments, and then questioned him. After hearing his problem, she assured him he was a good boy and had no reason to be frightened of falling asleep.

"I went to bed and to sleep immediately," Applegate wrote, "I had confidence in my mother." He had confidence in her because, he explained, "I had never known mother to cause a child to suffer pain."[105]

Unlike Matilda Sager, who had no one to turn to after witnessing the hanging at Hillsboro, Jesse Applegate had a supportive adult who counteracted the potential damage of his childhood terrors. It is not surprising that Matilda and Jesse, two children of the frontier, developed opposing outlooks on life. "Notwithstanding our privations and many hardships," Applegate wrote, "we children found much pleasure in life. . . . We had that greatest of life's possessions, youth, with its hopes and dreams."[106]

On the other hand, Matilda had been stripped of all hope, "for nothing could be done." Her ordeal was "inevitable." "They say I am hard and bitter," she stated in her final years, but "if some of the people who have life made easy for them had been through what I have, maybe they would feel bitter and vindictive, too." Justifying her attitude with the argument that the Holy Bible required one to forgive but not to forget, she insisted, "As long as I live I shall never forget the injustice, the indignities, and cruelty I had to suffer when I was a helpless little child."[107]

Though the effect of violence upon the frontier child varied with the individual and the circumstances, a shutting off of compassion appears to have been common. Matilda Sager described herself as "hard." Like her adopted mother Narcissa Whitman, suffering had caused her to lose her former feelings of tenderness. According to Reverend Walter Smith South– a Methodist minister who migrated to Texas in the 1840s and whose various experiences included once being reduced to dining on the flesh of a "half grown panther"–the loss of sympathy expressed by both Narcissa Whitman and Matilda Sager was a common experience. After Reverend South learned his neighbors had captured and shot a lone Indian traveling near their farm, he wrote in his diary that in the wilderness setting, where the mind becomes "so long familiarized with savage deeds of blood and carnage," even "the most tender-hearted naturally become relentless and cruel." South's commentary on the hardening of the settlers was, "God of Heaven pity this people!"[108]

In their memoirs, pioneers often revealed a nostalgia for the days before their hardening, that is before their initiation into the brutalities of the environment. "When I was a boy," George Turner related, "I was very tenderhearted . . . and I loved horses and dogs devotedly." Likewise, Captain Ed Carr admitted that as a boy he used to "sneak out into a back alley and . . . pet and fondle some homeless cur." These two quotations bring to mind the transformation of Tom Horn, who during his boyhood reserved his most benign emotions for his dog Shed and who, after Shed's death, felt no other "real sorrow" for the rest of his life, apparently even as he waited to be hanged.[109]

In addition to losing their capacity to feel sorrow or compassion, the abused children retained a resentment which could be turned inward, or else might erupt in some form of violent behavior to others. The extent to which an abused child could eventually be driven in an effort to alleviate a pent-up resentment is illustrated by the case of J. W. Blakely, the seven-year-old orphan who for a year endured savage beatings from foster father John Downing. Initially the boy had been suicidal, but after his escape from Downing, Blakely eventually became obsessed with turning his anger back on the abuser. "When I was 17," he said, "I put an ad in the paper, trying to locate Downing. . . . For more than eight years I had worked toward one end, and that was to go back and beat Downing within an inch of his life." To Blakely's disappointment, he received a response to the advertisement informing him his foster parent was dead. His abuser had been killed during a fight with another man.[110]

Another recipient of an abused child's hostility, (besides self or the abuser), was quite naturally the second-generation family, as in the case of Charles Reeves. "Texas Charley" continued the cycle initiated in his Pennsylvania home to his wickiup in Bannack, where he beat the Indian bride he had purchased for two blankets. But since spousal battery was common on the Western frontier, the topic will be reserved for a separate section of this book.

Status of Children on the Frontier

As the preceding examples make clear, frontier children were often regarded as their guardians' property. They were kept if useful and disposed of when no longer of use, like the blind boy mentioned earlier. When a doctor later restored the boy's sight, he was elated at his newfound value. "I was some good once more, and you don't know what that means." To many children, being "some good" meant nothing more than a life of unadulterated toil. En route to the California mines, wagon master J. Goldsborough Bruff observed a stalwart ex-army officer using his two daughters, ages ten and twelve, as "pack-horses." With each step, the poorly clad, heavily laden girls sank through the crust and into the snow covering the trail over the Sierra Nevada. Meanwhile, their oblivious father walked ahead, carrying only his rifle and saber. Though Bruff was powerless to intervene, he did manage to find stockings and gloves for the half-frozen girls and also to patch a hole in one girl's shoe so her toes would no longer protrude.[111]

Unfortunately, some children suffered a fate worse than being used as beasts of burden by their parents. The bondage of teenage girls in houses of prostitution eventually became such a problem in gold-rush California that citizens urged state legislators to pass a law prohibiting such treatment of any girl under fourteen! And the California legislature was eventually forced to open a detention facility for male teenagers being held in San Quentin. Before the construction of the San Quentin facility, teenage boys had been confined on a prison ship with criminals the gold rush had drawn from all over the world. This practice of housing young offenders in adult facilities was not unique to California. For example, the prison where John Wesley Hardin served his term in Huntsville, Texas, accepted inmates as young as ten years old.[112]

Though in their advanced years many pioneers retained a sense of their childhood suffering, they also took pride in recalling their adversities: the

SAN QUENTIN PRISON, 1871. Like other frontier prisons, San Quentin housed teenage inmates. *Courtesy California State Library.*

hard labor and rigid moral training. But those who bore the scars of abuse were often deprived of the counterbalancing feelings of pride. Matilda Sager summed up the status of frontier children by stating, "When I was young, children had no rights." It was this lack of rights that made them so susceptible to abuse.[113]

II

Spousal Battery on the Frontier

Status of Women on the Frontier

Though children commanded little respect on the frontier, nearly all accounts of life in the early West agree that women were accorded great deference. Gold-rush veteran Charles Ferguson wrote that in the mining
camps, women were treated "with higher consideration" than they would
have received in any Eastern city; while John David Borthwick observed
that in California, "A woman, like the king, can do no wrong." Isabella
Bird, who often ventured alone in the Rocky Mountain wilderness, agreed
that "the law of universal respect to women" was "in full force" wherever
she traveled. And as Bird pointed out, even the desperadoes took special
care to give good women their due respect. In his book about the Montana
vigilantes, Dimsdale carried the point a step further, claiming that at the
Western mines, "Anything like an insult offered to a lady" would probably
prove "fatal" to the insulter.[1]

Despite these four early writers' consensus on women's high status on
the frontier, a lady pioneer of both Idaho and Oregon protested in an interview that "the history as it really happens, and as you read about it, isn't at
all alike." Early records and accounts seem to bear out the contention that
the highly touted respect paid to women was somewhat superficial. The
issue of women's status in the developing West brings to mind the Stephen
Crane poem about the man who said to the universe, "Sir, I exist!" And the
universe, while acknowledging the man's existence, responded, "The fact
has not created in me a sense of obligation."

To paraphrase Crane, a frontier woman might have protested to the
oppressions of the male-dominated society, "Sirs, I am highly respected!"
But regardless of how much respect the brotherhood professed—and may
actually have had—for women, it was not the sort of respect that engen-
dered an obligation to grant women equal rights.[2]

During the trek West, women were allowed little voice in decisions
that affected the entire wagon train. When a small company moving from
Sutter's Fort to Oregon in 1846 discovered an Indian child who had been
abandoned beside the trail, it was only the men who voted on her fate.
Benjamin Franklin Bonney, a member of the party, reported that "this little
girl was perfectly nude, her long black hair was matted solidly, and she
could make only a pitiful moaning sound." Bonney's uncle, a medical
doctor, examined the girl and stated that in addition to being covered from
head to feet with open sores caused by biting flies, she was suffering from
starvation. "A council among the men was held," Bonney said, "to see
what should be done with her." Though Bonney's father voted to take the
child with them, the majority chose to "leave her where we found her."

Bonney's mother and aunt stayed behind to nurse the child as long as
they dared, then, before hurrying to catch up to the train, knelt and uttered

a prayer for her protection. After the distressed women's return to their wagon, Bonney stated, "one of the young men felt so bad about leaving" the Indian girl that he went back and "put a bullet through her head and put her out of her misery." Bonney remembered the reaction of his mother and aunt: "Their eyes were red and swollen from crying and their faces were wet with tears." But despite their grief, neither woman dared to challenge the decision of the all-male council.[3]

Even a woman of such strength and courage as Narcissa Whitman would not think of defying the elders of the church. When they criticized her for praying aloud in the presence of men, asserting the practice was "wrong and unseemly," she responded only that she thought "all the sisters would be willing to pray if their husbands would let them." But the men preferred "the more dignified way," that is with the women remaining silent at religious services, and Marcus put up no argument to their ruling. "My husband," Narcissa stated in his defense, "has no objection to my praying, but if my sisters do not, he thinks it quite as well for me not to." Graciously, Narcissa bowed to the males' preference and thereafter never again marred the dignity of worship sessions by raising her "refined" voice in prayer.[4]

In addition to the church, the male-dominated economic system discriminated against women who attempted to support themselves and their families by entering the professions usually reserved for men. While on the other hand, proper homage was extended to those wives who stuck to managing their own households, or to widows who eked out a living by taking in laundry, sewing, teaching school, operating a boardinghouse, or baking pies for the miners. Such women, Borthwick wrote in an article for *Harper's Weekly* in 1857, "are the real pride and hope of the country, and to their noble presence is due the thousands of comfortable cottages, or humble cabins."[5]

In a similar vein, physician's wife Louise Amelia Clappe spoke admiringly of a widow who was struggling to support nine children in a remote California gold camp in the early 1850s. "She made me think of a long-legged very thin hen scratching for dear life to feed her . . . brood," Clappe wrote in a letter. The admirable widow was "immensely tall, and had a hard, weather-beaten face, surmounted by a dreadful horn comb and a heavy twist of haycolored hair. . . . She had set that stern, wrinkled face of hers against poverty. . . . She used to wash shirts, and iron them on a chair, in the open air." Out of sympathy for her plight, miners often added extra payment to the price the widow charged them for their laundry.[6]

In contrast to the widow laundress, those women who attempted to depart from their traditional roles might encounter caustic social opposition, or even legal barriers. After decades of work in early hospitals, Dr. Berthine Adair, who was revered as "the first woman graduate physician on the Pacific Coast," concluded, "It is the women who are the sufferers from bad laws." Married at age fourteen, Adair soon found herself a single parent with a child to support. She earned their living by taking in washing, but reserved the hours from nine P.M. until midnight for study. Later she became a teacher, though the salary was minimal, and she had to supplement it by rising at four A.M. to milk cows at the home where she and her son boarded. When in the 1870s she announced she wished to become a doctor and attempted to enroll in a Western medical school, college authorities informed her "it wasn't done" and denied her entrance. To embark on her study of medicine, it was necessary for Adair to leave the West.[7]

The Far West gold rushes are credited with liberalizing restrictions previously placed on females. Dimsdale, for example, editorialized in his book that the mountain mines were, for women, a "paradise" of "liberality unknown in other climes." Yet various forms of discrimination coexisted with the new liberties. Montana mining records of the 1860s do indeed show that women owned claims. At Bannack for example, Mrs. Annette Stanley purchased for the sum of twenty dollars Claim Number Seventeen on Geary's Bar. And at Alder Gulch, some seventy miles distant, miner John Grannis noted in his diary that his estranged wife had "Bot a claim to Day for $200 Dust."[8]

But women who obtained claims sometimes discovered the "democratic" miners' associations, who rightfully prided themselves on their fairness and efficiency in settling claim disputes, had little interest in arbitrating a case involving a female. Thus when Annette Stanley sent a desperate message to the miners' court, informing them "toughs" had jumped her claim, no action was taken. Instead, the executive of the association issued the response that the miners had not banded together "to make a general fight against bad citizens." [9]

Some miners were wary of women who donned men's clothing in order to work their claims. An 1854 town ordinance of the mining town of Nevada City, California decreed that "any female who shall dress and appear in the streets in men's clothing ... shall be fined." The following year, neighboring Grass Valley incorporated and passed sixteen ordinances. On the first day of enforcing these ordinances, the new marshal arrested four violators. Two of those arrested were women who were guilty of "parading the streets in male attire."[10]

And at the Montana mines, an educated woman desperate for some means of supporting her family hired on as a dancer in a Virginia City hurdy-gurdy house. On her first night at work, an acquaintance explained, the woman did not realize her new job was considered demeaning, but "the rough men soon convinced her and she left the room in tears." After suffering humiliation at the hands of her male clients, the mother of two acquiesced to adopting a less lucrative occupation which was considered suitable for a gentlewoman: taking in washing. Her mistreatment by miners who were themselves frequenting the dance hall is an example of the "double standard of morals" which Dr. Adair encountered throughout her

GRASS VALLEY, CALIFORNIA, 1852. In 1855 Grass Valley had an ordinance against women "parading the streets in male attire." *Courtesey Sacramento State Library*

career. And the improved treatment which the hurdy-gurdy who turned washerwoman undoubtedly received from now-approving miners—known for their generosity to their laundresses–completes a typical vignette of a working woman on the frontier.[11]

But many women who appeared to be fortunate because they did not have to become the breadwinner for a family, led miserable, degrading lives under the rule of the men upon whom they were dependent. A man might bestow the greatest respect upon women in general, yet in his own home it became quite a different matter when he was dealing with the wife who bore and reared his children, baked bread and pies, served his meals, cleaned the house, washed and ironed the clothes, dipped candles, dyed muslin and then sewed his shirts, braided him an oat-straw hat, spun yarn from sheep wool (or even wolf hair if necessary), knitted his stockings, milked the cows, fed the pigs and chickens, gathered the eggs, salted down the meat, grew a vegetable garden, picked and dried wild fruit, chopped wood, and nursed family ailments.

When Elvina Apperson, another Oregon Trail child, summed up the status of the frontier woman, she did not include the word "respect." "Back in 1851," she told an interviewer, "we had slavery of Negroes in the South, and we had slavery of wives all over the United States." Elvina's story, along with similar accounts, will be told in detail in a following section. First, however, it is necessary to discuss the reverse side of the coin, the instances in which wives became abusive to their husbands or their husbands' guests.[12]

Abusive Frontier Wives

With sufficient searching, it is possible to find instances of frontier women committing acts of violence against men within the home setting, but they are few and far between. There is the case of an unidentified woman who during the 1847 crossing of the overland trail became angry at her husband and refused to climb into their wagon so they could commence the day's march. Another female traveler recorded in her diary that the frustrated husband "had his cattle hitched on for three hours" and was coaxing his wife to go, "but she would not stir." Finally the exasperated husband drove on without his wife, but she took a shortcut and intercepted his wagon. When he asked her if she had seen their son, she replied: "Yes, and I picked up a stone and knocked out his brains." While the husband hurried to find the boy, who was in reality safe, his wife set fire to the wagon. After the husband had extinguished the flames, wrote the approving female diary keeper, he "mustered spunk enough" to give his wife "a good flogging."[13]

As a second example of violent females, in April of 1860, the justice of the peace of Grass Valley, California heard an assault-and-battery case against a housewife. Her husband had invited male guests to their home for a drink and when the group became rowdy, the wife picked up a chair and attempted to drive an inebriated man outside, striking him with the chair in the process. Justice S. C. Richardson, known for his fairness on the bench, reluctantly passed judgment against the woman.[14]

As a final example, in June 1862, native American Mrs. Jack Dempsey attacked one of her husband's guests at their cattle ranch in the Deer Lodge valley of Montana. Two witnesses reported that Mrs. Dempsey was chopping her day's supply of wood when guest Charles Allen approached her and "begun to issue orders." During the fight that ensued, Mrs. Dempsey "landed away with the axe, but missed." Thereupon, Charles Allen "grabbed for the lady's hair. . . . The lady lit in with both hands and in two seconds Charlie's face looked like he had had an encounter with a wildcat. . . . She had blacked both eyes, knocked out a tooth and scratched his face." Upon hearing of the affray, Granville Stuart, who at the time was also a resident of the valley, wrote in his diary that Mrs. Dempsey was "a lady of uncertain temper," but added, "Who could put up with the gang of drunken loafers that hang around Dempsey's without losing their tempers."[15]

Abusive Frontier Husbands

Far more numerous in records of life on the frontier are the cases in which the victim of domestic violence was the wife. The major culprits according to Dr. Berthine Adair were "liquor and lust." However some progress had been made in the national thinking since the days when it was legal for a husband to beat his wife as long as he adhered to "the rule of thumb"

HAMILTON HALL, GRASS VALLEY, CALIFORNIA, about 1860, the same year a Grass Valley justice of the peace found a housewife guilty of assault-and-battery. *Courtesy Califonia State Library*

regarding girth of the weapon. Nevertheless, the offense of wife beating appears to have been widespread throughout the Old West. Widespread enough that when soldiers at Fort Riley, Kansas heard about the racket caused by Libby Custer and her husband "Autie" while they were joyously romping about their quarters, some of Custer's men were willing to believe that "the commanding officer was beating his wife."[16]

Despite an under-reporting of domestic violence, the following list is offered as a sampling of the many cases that can be gleaned from early newspapers, divorce court records, trial testimony, diaries, autobiographies, and memoirs:

At the South Park mines of Kansas Territory in 1860, Sarah Grannis fled the camp of her abusive husband, John, but later returned to him. Three years later, John, who had given up mining and was now a cattle herder, quarreled with Sarah and struck her on the mouth. When Sarah again fled, John pursued her through five states.

In the Hotel de Paris on the main street of Nevada City, California in September of 1857, the town marshal and his deputy intervened to deter gambler John Vedder from further battering his wife Lucinda. When Lucinda tried to file for divorce, the lawyer advised her to remain in the marriage and "get along if possible with her husband."

In Grass Valley, California on the night of 20 June 1906, Mrs. H. Lewis fled to a neighbor's home. Her husband, a violin teacher, had threatened to kill her. Since police judged that Mrs. Lewis "was too badly frightened to know just what she did want to do," they charged her husband with "disturbing the peace of his wife."

In Oroville, California on 3 August 1906, Lulu Russell filed for a divorce from her husband, James T. Russell, on grounds of "extreme cruelty." Lulu explained she could "no longer endure" her husband's "abusive conduct and constant threats to injure her or take her life." James warned her that "he would kill her if she carried out her plans" to leave him. When Lulu proceeded with the divorce anyway, her husband followed her to the lawyer's office, begging her to return to him. The lawyer reported that "the young woman was in great fear all the time he was in her presence and timidly turned down his offers."[17]

In Salt Lake City, Utah in 1864, James D. Lee struck his pregnant wife Ann Eliza, knocking her unconscious. During her second pregnancy, James attempted to strangle his wife and would not release his grip on her throat until Ann Eliza's father came to her rescue. Prophet and seer Brigham Young recommended Ann Eliza obtain a divorce from the Probate Court, which she did on 23 December 1865. Later, Ann Eliza became Brigham Young's "Wife No. 19."

At Bannack, Idaho Territory during the winter of 1863, native American Mrs. Charles Reeves returned to her father's wickiup in order to escape her husband's abuse. After becoming drunk, Charles enlisted the help of a friend and fired into the Indian's camp, killing two natives and one French bystander.

On 28 February 1864 at the Alder Gulch mines of what would become Montana Territory, a miners' court found in favor of Mrs. McCarty in a case brought against her abusive husband. McCarty's punishment was banishment to a camp one mile distant.[18]

In Laramie County, Wyoming in January 1892, Mrs. Frederick Powell brought a suit against her husband, testifying he had threatened to shoot her and had also pursued her with a knife in hand.

In a narrow valley of Idaho Territory's Owyhee Mountains, concerned neighbors went to check on the welfare of a woman whose husband had made an unexplained exit from the area. Inside the couple's log cabin, neighbors reported finding that "the table was set, with old food on it." Later they discovered "a shallow grave near the house" that held "the wife's skeleton . . . with a bullet hole in the center of her forehead." Further search uncovered "a gun buried near the house of the same caliber as the bullet fired into the woman's skull." Since the husband did not return to the area, no charges were brought against him.[19]

The list, which could go on and on, concludes with two examples of wife abuse that would have fitted equally well in the section dealing with child abuse:

In Portland, Oregon in 1851, Oregon Trail child Elvina Apperson wed Julius Thomas, age forty-four. Thomas not only beat his fourteen-year-old wife sporadically, but also told her he wished to kill her.

The following year in Polk County, Oregon, Mary Allen (the girl supposedly "born out of wedlock") married Adam Wimple, age thirty-five, who promptly began to inflict violence upon his thirteen-year-old bride.[20]

Crimes such as those mentioned above were often considered "family matters" and if brought to court, might be treated lightly. Some judges felt that since the wife was a man's property, he had a right to punish her as he deemed necessary to obtain the desired obedience. A typical punishment for a husband whose discipline did not seem justified was that dispensed in an 1866 case reported by a Nevada City, California newspaper: a man was tried for beating his wife and found guilty; the judge levied a fine of fifteen dollars.[21]

As at the present time, a more rigorous judicial intervention might have saved the lives of some battery victims. But since authorities hesitated to get involved, timid and immature wives— such as the two Oregon teenagers who conclude the preceding list—had little hope of extricating themselves from their perilous situations alive.

Story of Abusive Husband Who Pursued His Wife Through Five States: John and Sarah Grannis

NEVADA CITY, CALIFORNIA, 1852. In 1866 a Nevada City newspaper warned that one resident had been fined fifteen dollars for beating his wife. *Courtesy California State Library*

In spite of the difficulty in freeing oneself from an abusive marriage, Sarah Grannis, the first woman mentioned on the list, was strong-willed enough to make the attempt.   Since most accounts of wife abuse are reported by the battered wife, the husband involved often appears to be a cruel, half-insane monster. But Sarah's narrative is unusual because events unfold not from her lips, but from the pen of her husband, who regarded himself as a God-fearing man and whose acquaintances considered him an upright citizen.

In examining the couple's troubles, it is important to remember that Sarah's emotions and burdens can be surmised only from the actions John Grannis so tersely reported in his diary. Since most of this diary covers the period after John struck his wife and she fled their home, there is little description of battery. Instead, the entries describe only the blow that caused Sarah to flee their home and then John's pursuit of his wife to each new site where she located, a pattern which continued even after she had divorced him and married another man. John's comments, especially those revealing his obsession with a wife whom he was regularly maligning in the pages of his notebook, provide insight into the psyche of an abuser.

On 7 February 1863, when her husband struck her on the mouth, Sarah decided she had suffered enough punishment and left their small ranch house. It was not the first time she had attempted to disentangle herself from the situation.[22]

Sarah was born on 24 March 1826 in the state of Indiana, which had entered the union ten years earlier. Sarah was approaching twenty-six years of age and must have been considered an "old maid" when Jonathan W. Grannis, age twenty-three, proposed they marry. The ceremony took place on Christmas day of 1851. It would appear Sarah had made a wise, safe choice. The Grannis family, who resided in a farming community south of Lake Michigan, was respected and fairly prosperous; the patriarch of the family, John's father, was known as a generous man who had taken in a needy child of the community and reared her with his own offspring.

As for John, he was an experienced, hard-working farmer with a deep love for the land. But from the first, there were sorrows in the marriage. Only one of the couple's children survived, a son whom they named Walter. The boy was six when his father heard inflated rumors of the gold strikes in Pike's Peak country and developed a severe case of mining fever. Grannis decided to abandon the farm; his new goal was to make a fortune while he was still a young man.

Leaving Walter with relatives until they could return with their fortune, John and Sarah set out on the Platte route to that portion of Kansas Territory that is now Colorado and at the South Park mines, (the setting of the fifteen-year-old boy's debut as a desperado), staked a claim in Iowa Gulch. The rush of gold seekers–who had come from the East as well as from earlier mining sites in the West–created a population of more than 34,000 in the area where Grannis was mining. Another 4,000 were clustered to the north around Boulder, and hundreds more, called "go backs," had become discouraged by high prices, snow storms, and unavailability of claims and thus returned home.[23]

Like the "go backs," Grannis soon became discouraged. He was making no fortune in Iowa Gulch, and evidently the resulting stress brought on a quarrel with his wife. Far from friends and relatives, Sarah sought refuge from her husband's fit of temper with a party of nearby miners, who agreed to let her stay if she would perform their housekeeping chores.

Later, however, Grannis persuaded Sarah to return for another try at the marriage. The couple then abandoned their unprofitable claim, but wished to remain in the new country. In an attempt to return to the profession he had loved and thus reestablish a home so they could send for Walter, Grannis hired on as a cattle herder at the Clark and Griswold ranch near Canon City.[24]

By New Years day of 1863, the area where the couple resided had already been Colorado Territory for nearly two years, but Grannis still had not established himself sufficiently to send for their son. "Bought this Book of Woolworth & Moffat in Denver City Col Territory," John inscribed on the first page of his 1863 diary. On the first Saturday of the next month, he jotted down a rather revealing entry, raising questions as to whether or not he regarded the day's two main events with equal casualness: "Herded the cattle as usual. Had some words with Mrs. Grannis & spatted her on the mouth." Perhaps Grannis should have added that the "mouth spatting" was as usual as the cattle herding, for on February 8, when Sarah left, she informed her husband that this time it was "for ever."

Just as at the South Park mines, she went to the closest neighbor, pleading not just for shelter, but for employment as well. The scarcity of females on the frontier was in Sarah's favor, and the two ranchers who had employed John (Mr. Clark, a white-haired, fatherly man and Mr. Griswold, a young widower) happened to be in need of a housekeeper. Though she had left her own home under stressful circumstances, the swiftly made arrangement turned out to be fortuitous for all involved. Sarah was a mother without her child, and Griswold, a native of Vermont, had a two-year-old son without a mother. Thus one of Sarah's major duties as housekeeper at the ranch was the care of little George Griswold.[25]

But the new arrangement was not fortuitous for the abandoned cattle herder. On a Sunday morning, he found himself home alone in a small dwelling in the wilderness. Grannis was a man of limited education, yet well versed in the Bible and fond of quoting scripture to shed light on each situation that arose. The appropriate passage for this Sunday was found in Chapter 20 of Exodus: "Six days shalt thou labour, and do all they work: But the seventh day is the sabbath of the Lord thy God: in it thou shalt not do any work. . . ."

These were commandments Grannis faithfully obeyed; for six days he labored diligently and on the seventh day he always rested. But on this particular Sunday, it was not *his* obedience to the commandments that was in question; the problem was a lack of obedience on the part of both his wife and his neighbor. Grannis–whose entries reveal a jealous, suspicious nature—felt certain young Mr. Griswold was guilty of coveting his neighbor's wife, who of course was Sarah. And Sarah, who at their Christmas Day wedding had promised to obey Grannis and remain with him until death, had now broken her vow and deserted him. Though he had no way of knowing what Sarah and Griswold, the two commandment-breakers, were doing at that moment, in Grannis's judgment, they were violating another commandment, the one that read, "Thou shalt not commit adultery."

So on that 8 February 1863, Grannis vented his distress in his diary, recording the alleged sin of the couple who in his opinion had determined to take their chances in life together "on the free love Principal." In spite of Grannis's harsh judgment of his wife, he still considered her his possession. Furthermore, he held out hope Sarah would return eventually. After all, she had in the past.

JOHN GRANNIS, Indiana farmer who joined gold rushes to both Colorado and Montana in order to "make his fortune." *Courtesy Montana Historical Society*

After three weeks of futile waiting, Grannis could no longer bear the uncertainty and loneliness. To jar Sarah to her senses, that is to the realization she could lose him "for ever" if she did not return quickly, he resigned his position with the two ranchers. Even this drastic measure of giving up his means of livelihood failed to bring a response from Sarah. Still hopeful for a reconciliation, yet nagged by a foreboding he might have to attempt life without his companion of eleven years, Grannis spent much of his time loitering about the nearest town, Canon City. "Got on a Big Drunk for the first time in my life,"he wrote in the diary, "Came Home, was carried in and Put to bed."[26]

Little is known about the woman who had driven Grannis to drink, except that she married later than most females of her day, chose to hold the ceremony on the biggest holiday of the year, did not strike back when her husband hit her, and convinced at least two men she would make a desirable mate. Both of these men whom Sarah attracted were younger than she, and it may have been this discrepancy, or perhaps simple vanity, that caused her to misrepresent her age in two consecutive census records. For example, while she and Grannis were at the South Park mines in 1860, he reported his true age of thirty-one, but Sarah, who was actually thirty-four, told the census taker she was one year younger than her husband.[27]

Despite her one evident character flaw–telling a falsehood in order to appear more youthful than her mate in the eyes of the national census takers–her actions, as reported in her estranged husband's diary, show Sarah had a strong love for her son; she was resourceful enough to find means of supporting herself; and she was confident enough of her own worth to leave a husband who had violated her sense of dignity, not only by striking her, but also by accusing her of being sexually promiscuous. Though Grannis had described his abusive physical action as a mere "spat," Sarah might have described it quite differently. But leaving aside the probably disputed amount of force behind the impact of his hand upon her mouth, the act was also a form of psychological abuse. During an argument, Grannis had punished his disobedient wife on the offending part, her mouth. It was a restriction of her freedom to freely express her emotions or ideas, a warning not to talk back to someone possessing greater status and power than she.

But Sarah had been unwilling to submit to his control, and so Grannis was temporarily alone. Though during their eleven years together he may have forgotten Sarah's birthday, now she was gone it was the only thought he considered important enough to record in the diary on 24 March 1863: "My wifes Birth Day. She is 37 years of Age." And when in April he learned Clark and Griswold were preparing to leave for gold diggings in Idaho Territory (created just one month earlier) and that Sarah planned to accompany their train, Grannis quickly made his own plans to join the mule train of George Berhinger and Xavier Beidler.[28]

Grannis had no way of knowing that the train master, X. Beidler, who was described as "a diminutive, short, young man" whose shotgun muzzle "stood up a few inches above his head," was destined to become one of Captain James Williams's most notorious lieutenants in the Montana vigilance organization that was to become so powerful in 1864. Nor could Grannis have guessed that Beidler's involvement would also draw him into the controversial movement. At the time, the abandoned husband's thoughts were focused on migrating to the same area as his escaping wife. In preparation for the scheduled trip, he sold their former home for twenty-five dollars and purchased food supplies, a wagon, and two oxen whom he named Old Brin and Old Buck. But on April 29, the day set for their departure, Beidler failed to make an appearance at Canon City. The unexplained delay made Grannis impatient. "I want to be on the Road," he grumbled to his diary.[29]

Not until the evening of the next day did Beidler arrive at Canon City. The alibi of the diminutive packer, who at the drop of a hat would abandon his labors to play amateur stock detective, was that he "had found some Stolen Stock . . . and got 3 thieves." Finally on the second of May, the Beidler party got underway for Bannack, on the banks of Grasshopper Creek, the site of the fabulously rich gold strike that was summoning prospectors from all parts of the world. Other gold seekers en route to Bannack were "high with gold fever," that is they were inflated with a boundless exuberance and limitless confidence; rumors were that the gold at Bannack was not only easily panned, but also the purest in the world.

The journey would take the former Indiana farmer through a marvelous landscape he had never before viewed–up the Laramie plains, between the Medicine Bow and Laramie ranges, to the North Platte River, over the Continental Divide, to a stopover at Fort Bridger, past Soda and Steamboat Springs, across the sinuous Snake River, alongside the trappers' rendezvous point called Market Lake, over the pass, and then north to Bannack on the Grasshopper. Despite the motivation of quick and easy riches waiting on the creek and the anticipation of magnificent scenery along the trail, a pall of morbidity veiled Grannis's vision. For unlike the other travelers, he was not following a gold rush; he was in a quite possibly futile "pursuit" of Sarah, "his flown happiness."[30]

Thus in the pages of the Grannis diary, wonders–such as valleys boxed in by towering mountains, deep-gorged rivers, curious rock formations, bubbling hot springs, a community of lodges occupied by French traders and their native wives, a long column of soldiers bound for battle with Indian warriors, and a dance held by a colony of polygamous Mormons–are all overshadowed by a premonition of impending doom. In passing these many wonders, Grannis was treading the very path on which, somewhere ahead, Sarah was traveling with another man, a younger man in need of a permanent mother for his small son. And every awe-inspiring sight Grannis viewed alone, Sarah and Griswold had already viewed together. He lived with a growing conviction these were the preliminary days to the fulfillment of his most profound fear: that Sarah really would abandon him "for ever" as she had threatened. And if she should, he seriously doubted he could survive the loss.

Beidler moved his train at a lively clip, sometimes covering as much as thirty miles a day. The surefooted little mules set the pace, while Grannis's wagon, drawn by Old Brin and Old Buck, lumbered along behind. In entry after entry of the diary, the writer's mood of gloom and hopelessness transforms the landscape to a hostile, eerie wasteland:

> "Moon light, no wood; Killed a Rattle Snake the first Snake of the Season; Went fishing but caught nothing; Wood scarce; Went to hunt some lost Stock; Very cold & windy this morning; Commenced Raining; It Rained and snowed; No wood; A cold storm; No wood; Country destitute of wood & grass; A barren country covered with Sage; The country is a wide Barren waste, no wood but Sage & no water that is fit to Drink; A Rain Storm; Lost our animals; Very windy and Dusty; A cold windy Day; The most Barren Desolate waste that I ever saw; Bad water, it will act as a Purgative; The Donkeys Stampeded & Run off."[31]

As they traveled, Grannis became fascinated by the grave markers lining the trail and carefully recorded each inscription in his diary. On June 4, the sight of four graves moved him to comment on his own condition: "I am the creature of fortune," he wrote, "Cast abandoned on the world wide Stage And doomed in Scanty Poverty to Roam. At no Distant Day some traveler may see my name written upon a lone Board By the way side." Though marked by pessimism and self-pity, his entries do reflect a genuine love for Sarah. One particularly poignant line reads, "Never again can I lay my head Beside my wife and enjoy happiness."[32]

At Soda Springs, the fast-moving Beidler mule train overtook the Clark-Griswold party, and Grannis at last caught a glimpse of his wife. Two days later, while both trains were halted to feast on wild strawberries, he had the opportunity to speak with her. Then in another two days, he went to talk to her during night camp, but after that visit, did not see her again for the rest of the trip.

On June 11, after forty-one days on the trail, Beidler guided his party into Bannack City, later to become the first capital of Montana Territory. In spite of the international influx of miners, the town nestled in a narrow valley between barren hills was no more than a single main street lined with log stores and a plethora of scattered residences, ranging from hillside caves and brush wickiups to mud-chinked log cabins. Only a few days previous, the mule-drawn wagon of Mollie Sheehan's father had rolled down the steep grade and into town, and James Sheehan had pitched a tent for his family on the banks of Grasshopper Creek, "richly mantled with tender green watercress." But during Mollie's brief stay, a rich dis-

covery seventy miles east had created a stampede to Alder Gulch. Therefore upon Grannis's arrival, he found the mining camp smaller than its
peak population.[33]

It took him three days to locate Sarah. By some means, he managed to
find her when she was alone, doing laundry in the creek. She was making
preparations, she informed him, for the Clark-Griswold party to leave
Bannack. Her employers had decided to continue on to the newly discovered mines.

BANNACK STATE PARK, WITH GRASSHOPPER CREEK IN BACKGROUND.
When John Grannis located his wife at Bannack, she was washing laundry in the
creek. *Photo by F. E. Boswell*

After Sarah's departure for Alder Gulch, Grannis suffered another bout
of severe depression. Though he turned to his Bible for consolation, he
could not revive his flagging spirits. "My thoughts are sad," he wrote, "O
happiness though gift of Heaven thou hast forever flown."[34]

The journey to Bannack had consumed Grannis's entire fortune, which
had been minimal to begin with due to his failure to find gold at South
Park mines and his weeks of unemployment after leaving the Clark-
Griswold ranch in Colorado. From necessity, he took work as a laborer at
Bannack, but hearing daily of the success of the miners, he again felt the
impulse to search for gold and therefore commenced prospecting. At the

first attempt, he panned out two dollars; the following day, "Did not make much," and on the third day, after investing his previous wages in a wheelbarrow so he could work with a rocker, "Made 85 cts." Then came Sunday, not only his usual day of rest, but also the traditional day-off at the mines, so he "Done nothing." When he returned to rocking the following week, his highest daily profit amounted to one dollar and fifty-five cents.[35]

Though the hard work and small returns were discouraging, his main complaint to his diary was his loneliness. On June 28, he wrote, "Was lonesome to Day," and on June 29, "Concluded to go to the new mines." Of course Sarah was at the new mines, and in spite of his pessimistic remarks to the diary, Grannis still had hopes of recovering his wife; though in another man's possession at the time, she was property that rightfully belonged to him.

On July 1, he rode all night through barren countryside which Mollie Sheehan–who had traveled during the daytime–had described as tobacco-brown ground dotted with parched sagebrush, over which hovered a cloud of alkali dust. By daylight, Grannis had reached Beaverhead Rock, the landmark at which the Sheehans had marveled the previous week and which more than half a century earlier Sacajawea had pointed out to the Lewis and Clark expedition during their passage through the area. It was midmorning when Grannis passed through the final miles of a grassy valley cut by the slow-moving, cottonwood-lined Stinking Water River (now called the Ruby River) and at last reached the Alder Gulch metropolis of Virginia City. To locate Sarah amid the beehive of prospectors and traders swarming the gulches for a twelve-mile stretch would be no easy task.[36]

There were "hundreds of tents, brush wickiups, log cabins, even houses of stone quarried from the hills," Mollie had observed on her arrival, and "every foot of earth in the gulches was being turned upside down. . . . Rough-clad men with long hair and flowing beards . . . were digging for bedrock, others were bent over barrow loads of the pay dirt." The streets of Virginia City and the six other boom towns that had sprung up on either side of the largest camp were jammed with cursing bullwhackers and muleteers: "Bull trains of sixteen and twenty-horse teams pulling three and four wagons lashed together, and long strings of packhorses, mules or donkeys." Though the Alder Gulch camps were less than a month old, Mollie had noted that already "loafers lolled at the doors or slouched in and out of saloons and hurdygurdy houses too numerous to mention."[37]

But John Grannis had no time for loafing; with the cutthroat prices charged at the new mines, the sparse funds he had accumulated at Bannack were evaporating rapidly. Also, despite his depressed state, the frantic activity he witnessed about him was beginning to renew the gold fever which had initially driven him to Pike's Peak country. First, he attended a miners' meeting to familiarize himself with local regulations and then staked a claim in the Highland mining district, the second camp south of Virginia City.

By only his second day in the area, he had found Sarah. Even after their fruitless meetings on the trail and at Bannack, he had continued his pursuit of "Mrs. Grannis." Apparently, this meeting on July 3 did not go well either. She may have resented his trailing her, but at any rate when Grannis departed, he and his wife were no longer on speaking terms.[38]

Though there is no proof Sarah and Griswold had actually developed a relationship at this point, after Grannis had visited her in Virginia City, he felt a need to denigrate the character of his estranged spouse. On the day she had left him back in Colorado, he had been taken with this same urge, accusing her in the diary of fleeing his home so she could become a slut. That earlier entry was telling for a variety of reasons: first, Grannis refused to connect his wife's departure with the blow he had delivered to her mouth; second, he made no mention of the necessity of Sarah finding a means to support herself; and third, the essence of the day's entry was an innuendo about the couple's sexual life, an unwarranted judgment regarding his wife's morals, and a fear of abandonment: "This morning Mrs Grannis concluded to make her Bed By her Self & leave me for ever & take her chances in life with Mr Griswold on the free love Principal," he had written back in February.[39]

Now after the disappointing visit of July 3, Grannis returned to his diary and stripped Sarah of the title he had bestowed upon her the Christmas of 1851. No longer did she deserve the honor of being called "Mrs. Grannis." He summed up the day's activities with, "Got me a claim," followed by the sarcastic, "Called on Mrs. Gris," and closing with, "Camped with George and X."[40]

Grannis had little time to brood over the discouraging turn his marital relationship had taken. He and his mining partners found themselves embroiled in a dispute with another miner. "We had started in to clear our ground of brush," Beidler related in his memoirs, "when a big Irishman jumped Grannis's claim." Anxious for justice, Grannis appealed to the miners' court, but after listening to the facts on both sides and deliberating, the court ruled in favor of the Irishman. In his haste to once more commence the process of becoming rich, Grannis had inadvertently jumped the "big Irishman's" claim, rather than the other way around. The same day as the court's ruling, however, Grannis stumbled onto new ground that showed "Big Prospects." It would be necessary to clear away the sagebrush, divert a creek, and then dig a drain ditch before the partners could commence mining their adjoining claims.

Though they were eager to start realizing a profit, they were held back by the drainage excavation, which even under normal conditions would have been a major project, but was made even more difficult by a sudden onset of rain. "I stood it about 10 days in the water," Beidler said of the ditch digging, and then decided "there was lots of work of the kind I did not like. Then I looked after the horses–got supplies, etc., for camp and done chores." Beidler should have added, "and left the ditch digging to Grannis."[41]

While Beidler was riding to town for supplies, visiting other camps, watching the ponies, and occasionally spurting off on a gold stampede to some touted gulch, Grannis doggedly persisted in digging the ditch, even though he was "sick with the Diarheo." He also kept his ears open for news of Mrs. Grannis, as he had resumed calling her in the diary, perhaps because her latest activities indicated she was not seeking a new husband, but instead seeking to support herself. "Mrs. Grannis Bot a claim to Day for $200 in Dust," he wrote in the diary on July 19. Subsequent entries reveal that though Grannis was absorbed in working on the ditch and also preparing to sink a mine shaft, he was also keeping tabs on Sarah's attempt to achieve independence: "Heard Mrs Grannis was making 50 Dolls. Per Day from her claim," and later, "Heard Mrs. Grannis wants to sell her Claim & quit mining."[42]

While both John and the apparently discouraged Sarah were engaged at the mines, the ever-restless Beidler embarked on a business venture. Returning to Bannack with his eight pack mules and a "big sack of gold dust," he purchased sugar, shovels, picks, and mining boots, which he packed back to Virginia City. "I bought sugar for 60 cents per lb.," Beidler reported, "and sold it in Virginia for 1.20 per lb. I bought shovels for $14 each and sold them for an ounce. Picks at the same price. I sold gum boots for an ounce an inch–that is, if the foot of the boot was 8 inches long I got 8 ounces of gold for a pair. . . . But the miners were making money fast and didn't notice it–had to have boots."[43]

Beidler's abandoned mining partner was not among those "making money fast." In fact, work at the John Grannis claim was still bogged down in providing drainage. For a solid week beginning with July 27, Grannis jotted down the same entry in his diary: "Worked on the ditch." This entry continued throughout August, supplemented with brief notations about Beidler's comings and goings: "X got home from a new Gulch this evening," "X found my Poney," and "X went on a Stamped."[44]

Grannis stuck to the mine, but more and more, Grannis's former mining partner, X. Beidler was involving himself in the conflict over the best means of administering justice in the mining districts. Though X. had objected to digging the drain ditch, he did not mind digging in the cemetery on the hill above Virginia City. As he put it, he would work like "a beaver" when building scaffolds or digging graves for condemned men.

Henry Plummer, the former California marshal whom Bannack and Alder Gulch miners had elected as their chief law officer, had appointed deputies at each of the new mining camps. But Beidler, who favored summary executions rather than Plummer's system of jail and miners' courts, concluded the popular sheriff was actually a "notorious road agent," whose deputies "did pretty much as they pleased, murdering and robbing promiscuously throughout the Territory."

This notion of Beidler's was based on a false rumor that Plummer had previously broken out of San Quentin prison, shooting a guard during the escape. Therefore, Beidler was anxiously awaiting the day when the miners' existing judicial system headed by Plummer could be overthrown. And if the propitious moment for the overthrow arrived, he intended to be one of the ringleaders. Of course the movement would also have to rely upon hard-working miners such as Grannis to provide the needed manpower.[45]

While enjoying the miners' day of well-deserved rest near the end of August, Grannis paid a visit to his former employer, the fatherly Mr. Clark, ostensibly for the purpose of getting a haircut, though in reality the barber-sitting turned out to be a conversation "about Mrs. Grannis." Clark's advice during the session is not recorded in the diary, but the following Sunday, Grannis was off to Virginia City, where he found Sarah and "had a long talk with her."

It is interesting to note that throughout the painful weeks of their separation, Grannis had never assumed any blame for their breakup, never confessed in the diary pages to his own shortcomings — as a husband who had struck his wife on the mouth — never expressed an anxiety to send for his son Walter, and never seemed to realize that the separation and indecision about a reconciliation were also ordeals for Sarah, not just for him. While Sarah was attempting to make the painful break with the father of her only child, hoping to establish a home for Walter, struggling to find a means of supporting herself, and perhaps considering a new relationship, she was repeatedly interrupted by the intrusions of her estranged husband. He continued to attempt to persuade her to resume their relationship, though in the same breath, he insulted her by assuming she was committing adultery in order to satisfy her slatternly tendencies. In Grannis's narrow, rigid view of his disintegrating family, maintaining a stable home for his son was not the major consideration; all of the blame for the marital troubles lay with Sarah, and all of the woe was his. His immoral wife had "played him false," and he was suffering.[46]

He spent his thirty-fourth birthday, 14 September 1863, working on the ditch. And though he steadfastly continued with the project, for the rest of the month he was plagued by illness, along with a series of rain and snow storms which made the physical labor at the so-far-unproductive mine even more miserable. One day he became so ill he "came home & went to Bed" at noon. By "home" he meant the tentless camp where he had been sleeping on the ground since the day he took up the Highland claim. As yet he had not had time to build a shelter and after each day of dawn-to-dusk toil was forced to sleep in the open air, no matter how cold and stormy the night. Undoubtedly the exposure — as well as the poor diet, exhaustion, and depression–contributed to his deteriorating health.

During the hours of inactivity dictated by his illness, his thoughts focused on the impending loss of his wife. "Could not Sleep nor lay comfortable," he wrote, "thought of the home I once had. But alas for a false Hearted woman I was betrayed." The next Sunday, he walked to Virginia City to see Sarah and "had a long talk" with her about a "Settlement." The entry would appear to mark the first visit at which the couple had agreed upon a divorce, but a later entry makes clear that what Grannis meant by "Settlement" was the two of them getting back together! Apparently Sarah was not firm in her resolve to end the marriage. Her wavering and the resulting willingness to grant Grannis lengthy audiences furnished him the lifeline of hope he needed to stay afloat.[47]

October was a repeat of the previous month: recurring illness, no "Settlement" with Sarah, occasional snow storms, and backbreaking labor at the mine. "Done the hardest Days Shoveling that I Ever Done," he wrote on October 10, but at least they were now sluicing and daily recovering profits ranging from $21.10 to $129.70. Grannis's share of net profits for the first seven days' work was eighty-five dollars. The same Sunday he drew his money, he went to see Sarah and again "talked about a Settlement," though none was reached.

By November, Grannis had completed his log cabin, except for a door, and was at least sleeping under a roof. Though his living conditions had improved, his mining returns were now diminishing. There was also a rash of other troubles: his wagon broke down and had to be repaired, and both his pony and Old Brin, the ox, were missing. Precious days had to be wasted in scouring the countryside for the livestock: "Hunted old Brin all day," but to no avail. Then four days later, "Went to the Madison Valley & found old Brin." But within two weeks, the oxen had again "Run off." "Walked hard all Day," he wrote of his livestock search, "got home after Dark," but with both oxen in tow. And at last he found his "Poney," who had also strayed. Though the cold weather hikes had left him "Worn out," there was no time for rest; unpleasant chores awaited him, chores Sarah was no longer there to perform: "SUNDAY. Staid at home & Darned my Socks." But the big news of November was not that he was learning to do women's work; it was instead that one Tuesday Sarah sent a note, saying she wished to see him. All days of the week except Sunday were usually reserved for work, but for this special occasion, Grannis hastened to Virginia City on a Wednesday.[48]

During their visit, Grannis made his usual promises and entered his usual pleas for a reconciliation, but when he returned to his cabin that night, he wrote his final, "Could not settle with her." Sarah had at last made up her mind. She would file for a divorce with authorities of Idaho Territory. This long-delayed decision showed a great deal of courage on her part, not only because she was giving up a familiar relationship with a provider who could have offered security in the unfamiliar country, but also because of the prejudice both she and her son would have to endure, even on the liberal frontier. "Back in 1859," Captain Ed Carr (a child of divorced parents) recalled, divorce was considered a "disgrace. . . . Not only divorced couples were looked at askance, but the children of divorced parents were pariahs and were treated as if they themselves were responsible."[49]

TYPICAL MINER'S CABIN WITH MINING EQUIPMENT. *Photo by F. E. Boswell*

As Sarah undoubtedly realized, the end of her months of indecision did not mean an end to her trials. Instead, it meant the need to adapt to new situations under trying circumstances. As for Grannis, the long-dreaded axe had finally fallen, severing him from the woman he felt was essential to his existence. Diary entries following his wife's declaration to sue for divorce suggest he had entered a state of shock. For a period of over seven weeks, the notations regarding his loss, abandonment, betrayal, doom, loneliness, unhappiness, and physical illnesses completely vanish. Until the final day of December, the diary becomes a series of weather reports and a curt summary of a winter spent sluicing, hunting lost oxen, hauling timber, and staying home alone.

Other than this impersonal picture of the loneliness and drudgery involved in working a remote mining claim, the diary contains but one episode of historical significance. While driving Old Brin and Old Buck to a boarding ranch on December 16, Grannis passed through Nevada City (the first camp northwest of Virginia City) and on the main street noticed an agitated crowd surrounding a wagon. Grannis paused to determine what the crowd was gaping at and then after his return to Highland that evening, wrote, "Saw a Dead man that was found Dead on Stink water."[50]

The murder victim discovered near the Stinking Water River was an orphaned youth named Nicholas De Vault. Beidler, who was footloose after his decision that digging a mining ditch was not his sort of work, also saw the raven-pecked corpse on display in the wagon at Nevada City, and, as he explained, the sight set his life on a new course: "The people . . . were at this time in an excited state of mind, and I concluded to quit prospecting for gold and prospect for human fiends."[51]

Though the vigilance movement in which Beidler was eager to participate loomed just on the horizon, for the time being, the democratic association of miners and their elected officers still controlled the Bannack and Alder Gulch mines. Nevertheless, a group of vigilantes arrested several suspects on their own, and on December 21, a miners' court conducted a trial for the suspected murderers of "the Dutchman," as the young German immigrant had been known at the mines. While court convened in

MAIN STREET OF RESTORED NEVADA CITY, MONTANA, where John Grannis viewed corpse of murder victim Nicholas De Vault. *Photo by F. E. Boswell*

the bed of a freight wagon parked on Nevada City's main thoroughfare, Grannis agreed to act as the night guard for the vigilantes' prisoners being held in a log warehouse.

Beidler also volunteered to act as a guard, but unlike Grannis, he insisted on being close to the action at all times. In fact, Beidler impressed prosecutor Wilbur Sanders (who later helped organize the vigilantes and then became Montana's first senator) as one of the most "noticeable" of the guards: "vigilant, supple, observant, now here and now there wherever anything was to be done to secure the orderly conduct of the affair." And when on the following night the jury returned with a verdict, Sanders noted that Beidler, "armed to the teeth" like the rest of the guards, left the audience clustered about the bonfire, crossed main street, and clambered onto the dirt roof of a log cabin, where he squatted to survey "the crowd surrounding the prisoner."[52]

With Beidler observing intently from the cabin roof, the miners' jury announced a split decision as to the guilt of defendant George Ives, the young rancher accused of murdering "the Dutchman." Rather than acknowledging the hung jury, prosecutor Sanders leaped to his feet and made a motion that since the majority of the jurors had voted "Guilty," the entire audience accept that as the verdict so the defendant could be "forthwith hung by the neck until he was dead." The court audience vociferously passed the motion.

Slowly, the chained prisoner rose from his seat near the fire, worked his way over to the prosecutor, and courteously requested the execution be postponed till morning to allow him time to write his mother a final letter. While Sanders was deliberating how to phrase a denial that would not incite the crowd, many of whom were inebriated and might have become sentimental when Ives mentioned the word "mother," a hush fell over the proceedings. But Beidler, who vigorously opposed any delay in an execution, sensed the dilemma and "holloaed" from the roof: "Sanders, ask him how long a time he gave the Dutchman!" Beidler's comment amused the crowd, which "lifted a considerable load" from Sanders's mind. By moonlight, hasty preparations for the execution proceeded. Then before an audience of over a thousand, Grannis reported that "the Prisoner was taken out & hung By the Neck untill he was Dead." (Later, an Oregon newspaper reported that another man had confessed to shooting the orphaned youth.)[53]

After the Ives hanging, Grannis returned to Highland and for the remaining days of the year worked at constructing drifting cars, laying track for the cars, cleaning out the drift (horizontal passageway of a mine), and raising dirt with a "winless." Apparently he was unaware of the vigilance organization being formed in the towns along Alder Gulch. Nor did he seem to know when a party of vigilantes–which Beidler would eventually join–set out from Nevada City on their first foray to round up suspected road agents, including the man who had reportedly confessed to the crime for which George Ives had been hanged. Meanwhile, Grannis wrote in his diary that he "worked to Day," "Staid at home all Day," and "nothing of interest transpired."[54]

On New Years Day of 1864, the solitary miner–completely absorbed in his own small world of work at the claim and therefore oblivious to the fact momentous historical events were underway in the Territory–commenced a new diary. The first entry of the new year reveals that Grannis's emotions–which for weeks appeared to be frozen as solid as the ground he was

SHERIFF HENRY PLUMMER, hanged by X. Beidler and other vigilantes at Bannack on 10 January 1864. *Drawing by Callison Diaz*

GALLOWS AT BANNACK STATE PARK, MONTANA. In Hangman's Gulch on the night of 10 January 1864, about seventy vigilantes, including X. Beidler, hanged Sheriff Plummer and two deputies. *Photo by F. E. Boswell*

attempting to excavate–were at last beginning to thaw: "I commence this year alone in the world without a wife," he wrote.

From the time he had awakened in the predawn darkness of January 1, Sarah had been on his mind. He arose, lit a candle, and flipped through his Bible to locate Chapter nineteen of the Gospel According to St. Matthew. He wanted to reread a passage which was excruciatingly relevant: "For this cause shall a man leave father and mother, and shall cleave to his wife; and they twain shall be one flesh." And, Jesus propounded to the Pharisees, a man and his wife "are no more twain, but one flesh" and what "God hath joined together, let no man put asunder." Griswold had first put the Grannis marriage asunder and next, might marry Sarah himself. As Jesus had warned, "Whoso marryeth her who is put away doth commit adultery." Certainly Jesus would have considered the fortunate man who would next lay his head beside Sarah to enjoy happiness to be a usurper and an adulterer. But that damning judgment was probably small comfort to the companionless miner huddled above a wavering candle.[55]

The first part of January, Grannis spent a good deal of time at home alone, and when weather permitted, worked on a drift at his claim. He was unaware that on the night of January 4, which he described as "severely cold," Beidler and other well-bundled and well-armed vigilantes were collected about a candle lantern whose feeble rays flickered over a sturdy cottonwood limb supporting two dangling, limp forms. The vigilante foray led by Captain James Williams had produced its first two victims: one man had been lynched for writing a note warning a potential victim that vigilantes were after him; the crime of the second man had been delivering the note.

Nor on the following Sunday, January 10, did Grannis know that on the gallows at Bannack, vigilante lieutenant X. Beidler and some seventy other men lynched the man known as "the law of the country," miners' sheriff Henry Plummer, along with two of his deputies. While the vigilance movement that Grannis would eventually join was caught up in their coup to wrest control of the mining districts from the elected officials, Grannis was busy at his mine: a large rock was blocking his drift.[56]

After carrying out five lynchings at Bannack, Beidler and party returned to Virginia City, and Grannis suddenly found himself part of the new regime. "Obeying a notice of the vigilance committee I went to Virginia this morning," he wrote on 14 January 1864. To adequately cover the historic events that occurred that day, he made an entry a few lines longer than usual. Though Grannis did not admit to being a member of the vigilantes, he did record that he was among the more than five-hundred armed men patrolling the streets of Virginia City on January 14: "Some parties Implicated in the Road Agency Business. . . . 5 were found guilty and taken to the gallows & hung untill they were Dead. . . . I was on guard nearly all Day & saw them hung. The five was hung in a Row. All of them maintained their innocence to the Last & cursed the Vigilance Committee."

BOOT HILL, VIRGINIA CITY, MONTANA, contains graves of five men John
Grannis helped to lynch. Though Dimsdale claimed the five men confessed to
belonging to a road agent gang, Grannis wrote in his diary that "All of them
maintained their innocence to the Last." *Photo by F. E. Boswell*

As one of the guards, Grannis was required to remain in position for
an hour after the lynchings, a precaution to be certain that all five victims
were indeed dead. Thus he was still standing as a sentinel when Mollie
Sheehan passed on her way home from school that afternoon and recognized the swinging corpse of her former reading mentor, Deputy Jack
Gallagher. It was after dark when Grannis got back to the cabin, feeling
"very well Satisfied" with his day's participation in the execution of the
five untried men, one of them a deputy. His only complaint was that the
changeable weather, "cloudy & clear By Spells," had not made "a very
good Day" for the spectator sport of hanging.[57]

Neither the changeable weather, which lingered on to the next day, nor
Grannis's new status as a participant in vigilance activities, deterred his
mining operations beyond January 14. His determination to make a fortune while he was still hale enough to enjoy his wealth now became as
strong as it had been when he abandoned his Indiana farm. At Bannack,
his mining efforts had taken place on the surface, but here at the Highland
District, underground operations were a necessity that placed his life in
constant peril. On January 22, he experienced a cave-in, but managed to

escape from the collapsed shaft unharmed.

Some of his fellow miners, however, were not so fortunate. On Claim 29 in his district, a disaster occurred: "The alarm was Given that 2 men were buried in a Drift. . . . They could hear one of them alive and they worked with all speed to get him Before he would Die." Desperate efforts continued for five hours, but when expert excavators at last reached the first body, they found the miner dead, "his head was Broken and he was Badly mangled."

Four hours later, they discovered the second man. He was still breathing and "not Badly Bruised & no Bones were Broken." The survivor had endured "9 hours of intense suffering" underground, but his suffering on the surface was briefer. Shortly after midnight, he died. Grannis recorded in his diary the names of the deceased miners: Don Shields and Jerry O'Leary. Realizing that but for the Grace of God, there lay he, Grannis closed the day with a somber reflection on his own life: "Alas what Dangers will not men encounter for the Sake of Gold."[58]

Though Beidler was more committed to prospecting for "human fiends" than for gold, Grannis's priorities were in the reverse order. Thus when Captain James Williams and Lieutenant Beidler led a heavily armed column toward the Deer Lodge valley to search out suspected road agents, Grannis elected to stay on his claim and search for gold. Yet when he heard of a new strike elsewhere, he was ready to look for greener pastures. "I thought I would go out on the great Stampede to some new mines said to Be 150 miles from here," he wrote, so "Went Down to the ranch for my Pony." To his dismay, he discovered the pony gone, but on being informed of the reason, acknowledged the superior rights of the Cause: "The Vigilance have taken him to Deer Lodge. So I did not get him [the pony]. Came home & let the Stamped go."

Like many of the Montana vigilante leaders, John Grannis was a Mason. And being a civic-minded miner, he also participated in proceedings of the miners' courts, those cases vigilantes considered too minor to merit their attention. Due to Grannis's denial of his own abusiveness to Sarah, he probably failed to recognize the irony of the court deputizing him to carry out the sentence of one particular convict: "There was a miners meeting in the evening to take the case of McCarty into consideration in Regard to his Abusing his family," he noted in the diary. After a decision was rendered, it became Grannis's duty to inform the guilty man of his banishment, allow him two hours preparation time, and then provide the wife and child abuser an escort along the one-mile stretch to the next camp.[59]

Though his participation in a variety of social and civic activities seemed to indicate Grannis was making a speedy adjustment to the loss of his wife, the diary contains a few hints the case was otherwise. In early March, he had his fortune told, but did not record the predictions, and March 24, Sarah's birthday, he felt too sick to work. After the day's entry, he added in parentheses: "Mrs Grannis was 38 years of Age to Day." His illness persisted into the next month, as did the hard work and intermittent snow-falls. Then on April 4, a "Disagreeable" day marred by gusting snow, his partner relayed some disagreeable news: "George told me of Mrs. Grannis' Marriage with Mr. Griswold which took place last night at Nevada." Then with a magnanimity not previously shown in the diary, he added, "Joy to them."[60]

After news of the marriage, Grannis's health went rapidly downhill, as this series of entries shows: "Was sick this morning & could not work; Was in Pain all Day; Was not Well, had a very Bad cold; Was sick all night & worse this morning; Did not go to work; Was sick this morning over Done myself yesterday; My cough is very Bad yet; Took very sick coming home & went to Bed, was in great Distress all Day; Was very bad all night; Very weak; Was not well to Day, lay in Bed most of the day; Was Sick with Neuralgia in the ear all night and all forenoon; My Back is lame & my head aches tonight; My health is poor, have worked to hard."[61]

Though in poor health, Grannis continued sluicing. He had participated in controversial lynchings which were now being quietly criticized, and he had lost his wife, but he still had the dream of becoming rich. On a good day, he sometimes grossed over two hundred dollars. "I feel the need of Rest," he wrote, "a years hard work in the mine has made me feel ten years older." But he took no rest; he was determined to "make his fortune" before he passed "the Meridian of life" and thus could not "Dodge" the hard work needed "to make it Pay" at the mines. His hard-earned profits he quickly reinvested in additional claims, his idle funds he lent out on interest, and he worked, worked, worked. He was homesick for the beautiful, plowed fields of Indiana, but he could not spare the time to write his family. In Grannis's words, his sacrifices were all "for the sake of gold." His existence had degenerated into what Isabella Bird had deplored as an "exclusive pursuit of gain," with a resulting "indifference to all which does not aid in its acquisition." It was the same "hard greed" which Bird blamed for "eating up family love and life throughout the West."[62]

After each day's toil and even on Sundays, Grannis kept busy. He attended miners' meetings, dabbled in camp politics, and at last broke down and "Bought me an outfit to cook for myself." Though he had not changed claims nor residences, he was no longer keeping house and mining in Idaho Territory. On May 26, President Lincoln had signed an act creating Montana Territory, which included both the Bannack and the Alder Gulch mines. Nor was Virginia City a mere mining camp any longer; the past January–the same month Grannis had agonized over the sinfulness of Sarah's divorce and then later stood guard as fellow vigilantes hanged five men–the largest settlement of the Alder Gulch mines had incorporated.[63]

And there were other signs of approaching civilization. On August 27, Virginia City's first newspaper appeared. The *Montana Post*, a six-column sheet printed in a sod-roofed log cabin, promised to provide "the latest telegraphic news" from America, so that Alder Gulch readers would be

PRESENT-DAY VIRGINIA CITY, MONTANA, as viewed from Boot Hill. Montana's first govenor referred to the area as the "Switzerland" of the Americas. *Photo by F. E. Boswell*

aware of "what is passing in the outer world." As for their own booming little world, described by the newly appointed Territorial Governor as the "Switzerland" of the Americas, the *Post* reported that one hundred buildings were under construction along the Gulch; the phenomenal rate of growth was a "work of magic–the vision of a dream. . . . Many persons are taking out $150 per day. . . . Old miners have the preference. . . . All the claims . . . have long since been taken up. These must be purchased, and that too at very high figures. . . . The abundance of gold makes everything high."[64]

Grannis was one of those fortunate "old miners" who already had claims, but he was not fortunate enough to get a copy of the first issue of the *Montana Post*, (whose editorship would soon be turned over to Thomas Dimsdale, Mollie Sheehan's tubercular school teacher). For like many of the overworked miners, Grannis did not go to town on the Saturday when over nine hundred copies of the premier issue sold out at the exorbitant price of fifty cents each. In the work week preceding August 27 (the date of the first newspaper), Grannis had spent six days cranking the windlass on one of the claims which the *Post* said he was so lucky to have. Even with the necessity of paying a hired drifter, Grannis's profits made the arm-wearying cranking of the windlass well worthwhile. His gains were in excess of the *Post's* optimistic figure of $150 per day. "Worked all week at the winless," Grannis recorded in the diary on August 27, "got $1062.45." His entry also included a piece of news that had not reached the *Post*: a miner in the district was killed on his claim and Grannis helped carry the deceased back to camp.[65]

The ill-fated miner had at least died an honorable death, a marked contrast to another of Grannis's acquaintances, one Charles Lindsey, who "got Drunk and Drew his Revolver on a man and got shot." Grannis's advice on the matter was that "if the Shooting was left entirely to the Pimps there would Be very little harm Done." Charles Lindsey, however, had lacked the wisdom to draw on a pimp; instead he had confronted "a real man," that is somebody who knew how to use a weapon, and now the hapless Lindsey lay dead. "Surely the way of the transgressor is hard," Grannis mused to his diary. His own way had also been hard during the past two years, but not because of any transgressions on his part; the root of his sorrows was "Simply because I ever loved a woman, yes, my wife and She Played me false for another man."[66]

But contrary to what Grannis had feared, his life did go on. And in preparation for the approaching cold weather, he spent some of the mining profits to lay in a large supply of his two absolute necessities: "Some Candles & flour for winter." By mid-November, it was often "to cold to Sluce," and even when he was able to eke out a few hours between snow storms, he "got But Little Dirt and Less gold." With this decrease of income weighing on his mind, he could no longer feel justified in paying out good gold dust to board Old Buck and Old Brin, the oxen who had brought him to the mines. Accordingly, he slaughtered the two mild beasts, peddled their meat in town, and then spent an entire day rendering out Buck's and Brin's tallow for more candles, a job that–in addition to cooking, washing dishes, shopping, and darning socks–rightfully belonged to the woman who had played him false. By November 20, the burden of playing two roles had become too much for him; he awoke with "cold chills" and "Suffered Badly" throughout the day. After ten such days in bed, he was forced to call a doctor, who made a diagnosis of lung fever. Even though Grannis recovered sufficiently to be able to dance all night the first part of December, two days later he was again plagued with a cough and "Diarheo."[67]

Weeks of labor at the isolated claims placed him out of touch with the rest of the world, but the diary-keeping created a continual awareness of time. Throughout his marital difficulties, three days had been hard for him to bear: Sarah's birthday, his own birthday, and Christmas, which was their wedding anniversary. These three holidays usually prompted feelings of depression, but Christmas Day of 1864 found the diarist in surprisingly good health and spirits. "Felt well But thought how time had changed Since 13 years ago. 13 years ago this morning I was married, young & Buoyant with hope. I thought not of what awaited me in lifes journey. . . .

Still life Does not look Dark."

For the first time since the separation that had occurred in Colorado, he expressed "hope for the future." But the final lines of the day's entry are puzzling. "It will Soon Be two years Since I left my wife," he wrote. Perhaps the difficult adjustment to his abandonment had been facilitated by rewriting history in his memory. It was no longer the "false hearted" woman who had abandoned him; instead, he had left her. And in a second wave of magnanimity within one year, plus a bit of glossing over past suffering and sorrows, he closed the entry with, "God grant that She has Spent these two years as happy as I have." Within only three days, the high spirits were flagging a little; he was hit with a pang of homesickness for Indiana. "Thought of old times," he wrote, followed by two days' entries reading, "Staid at home all Day" and "Staid at home."[68]

However 1865 opened with a whirlwind of social activities: on January 1, "Plaid Billiards for the first time in my life." The next day, after first loaning out one hundred dollars at 8 percent, he put out more money to watch "the hardest Prise fight on Record," a boxing match "between Con. Orem and Hugh Oniel, the fight lasted for 3 hours & 8 minits, 188 Rounds." And on January 3, he attended a tea and a ball. From that date until the final day of January, he spent eight evenings at a dancing class in Highland, made one social call, made another loan, visited the billiard hall for a second time, "got tight on Wednesday evening," and the following Monday, ate out with friends and "Paid the oyster supper." When he was not fortunate enough to hitch a ride to town in the butcher cart, he had to walk the eight and a half miles to Virginia City. Still, he was determined to take full advantage of his new freedom. He was having a "nice time," undoubtedly a much nicer time than Sarah Griswold, who was burdened with a husband, a small child, and household duties.[69]

Unfavorable mining conditions facilitated Grannis's social fling. High winds, snow squalls, freezing temperatures followed by brief warming spells which converted the upper layer of frozen earth to quagmire, and one avalanche which dumped over twenty feet of snow in a Highland valley made it possible to continue socializing into March. The good times were also facilitated by the continuing development of Virginia City, now the territorial capital. With streets that were "a Perfect mud hole," this cosmopolitan mining and political center–which had offered the Indiana farmer his first billiards game and his first glimpse of "some Chinese"–outdid itself on March 17, when "the Irish had a Grand Exebetion . . . in honor of St. Patrick."[70]

Also, since the previous December, the town had provided a first-rate theater–toured by leading actors, musicians, and lecturers–which Grannis had not yet visited. After the March 23 wedding of a dancing-school crony named Dick McClarren, Grannis "kissed the Bride" and then accompanied the newlyweds to a performance at the theater. Nor was his civic life neglected. Beidler had put in an appearance at Highland, summoning Grannis to jury duty on a case that dragged on until the end of the month.[71]

Throughout this period of relishing his emancipation from both mining toil and marriage vows, he often "danced all night till Day light" and in general was having "a very pleasant time," yet strangely enough, Sarah was still on his mind. It had been two years since he and his wife had separated in Colorado, he noted, and "Do not know where she is now or whether I shall ever see her more." The wedded bliss of the McClarrens was a constant reminder of his lost happiness with Sarah. And in conjunction with returning thoughts of her, came the return of the former health problems: on March 28, "Was Sick with Billious Colic," and the following day, "Did not feel well."

April brought some distractions from personal problems. First, there was a flour famine at the mines: "Flour is worth 130 Dolls Per Sack. . . . A committy of Miners have been Appointed to see that it is Put down." Second, the telegraph brought news of national import: "Heard of the murder of Lincoln & Seward." But most important, the ground had at last thawed sufficiently so mining could be resumed: "Started a New Drift . . . worked all Day; Worked all Day at the winless; Worked on the Ditch all Day; and Worked on the Side Ditch." The monotonous drudgery was a far cry from the exciting adventure he had envisioned in 1860 when he had deserted the lush, green fields of home.[72]

He maintained the rigid work schedule through the end of April and on into May. As he had learned by now, in the Highland mining district, it might snow any day of the year. On May 14 he wrote, "Snowing when I got up and Snowed all Day. Was Snowing when I went to Bed. Snow 2 foot Deep on the level." Alternating with snow storms were rains which brought "a general flooding of the claims." The more wholesome activities of the first part of the year were gradually degenerating into poker games and drinking bouts: July 4, "Got Tight and Run the Hurdy gurdes till Midnight." The following morning he was unable to report to the mine: "Did no work toDay, was all Day getting over the Spree of yesterday." And the last week of the month, he became so ill that, for the second time since he had been at the mines, he had to resort to the dire measure of paying for a doctor's advice.

During the entire year of supposedly savoring the delights of recovered bachelorhood, he had been keeping his ears open for news of Sarah, and in August, he at last picked up a piece of information that explained her mysterious absence: "Heard that Gris and the old woman had got into Nevada City and got my Boy with them." Evidently one of Griswold and Sarah's first priorities after marriage had been to recover her child. Though Grannis had been separated from Walter for five years, he waited four days before traveling the nine and a half miles necessary to see his only child. After a brief visit with the boy, he rode thirty miles to visit a friend, and the next day, traveled fourteen miles to attend a dance. If the absentee father felt any great concerns for the adjustments his child was undergoing with a stepfather, they are not mentioned in the diary. The only concern Grannis expressed during that period was for himself. On September 14 he wrote, "To Day is my 36th Birth Day. Age is Advancing with Rapid Strides. The Meridian of life is passed and my fortune is not made yet."[73]

In fact for the rest of 1865, he would visit Walter on only four other occasions, and the following year, only once in January and once in February. He did take enough interest in the boy to pay his school tuition and to buy him a slate and arithmetic book, but by March, Grannis had a new interest in his life, a young lady named Ellen. The blossoming romance, however, did not prevent him from commemorating Sarah's birthday in the diary: "Mrs. Griswold my former wife was 40 years old to Day," he wrote on 24 March 1866. And in April, the McClarren's gain, the birth of a daughter, was a reminder of his own loss. An added concern was that Sarah would soon be out of visiting range. Griswold was planning to move his bride, his own son, and Walter to the recently discovered mines on Elk Creek.[74]

It is Grannis's actions on hearing of Sarah's departure that reveal the extent of his obsession with her. Despite the cheery diary entries, and despite the endless round of entertaining activities, such as waltzing with one of Brigham Young's many daughters, and the self-improvement undertakings such as studying German and taking "the Degree of a Fellow Crafts in Masonry," Grannis had not recovered from his loss as fully as he would have liked himself to believe. Telling Ellen they "must part awhile" and that their love would "be the fonder after parting," Grannis loaded his wagon, packed a mule train with supplies and blacksmith tools, and set out for Sarah's new home, the Elk Creek mines.

April winds, snow flurries, and icy roads made traveling difficult, but at one hospitable ranch along the route he enjoyed the "rare treat" of supping on "Mush & Milk." Not surprisingly, the diary records a second rare treat: "Saw Mrs Griswold." There is no mention of his son, only his ex-wife, and the terseness of the entry may suggest that since Sarah's marriage, Grannis was no longer a welcome visitor.[75]

A cool reception from Sarah may have discouraged Grannis, but it did not lessen his determination to relocate to the area where she now resided. But first he needed to find a way of making a living. In addition to prospecting, he experimented with operating a blacksmith shop and packing with his mules, but none of the enterprises succeeded. On May 15 he concluded, "Am not going to pack any more." And on June 6, "Prospected all Day. Sunk several Holes to Bedrock But failed to raise a color." By the end of the month, he had decided it was necessary "to leave this part of the country."

He arrived back at the Highland claim on July 3. It was not a triumphant homecoming. In the Elk Creek country, he had seen Sarah firmly entrenched in a new marriage, and he had wasted much of his accumulated gold dust on ill-starred business ventures.

To combat his depression, he went to visit old friends on the Fourth of July, only to learn that Mrs. McClarren had died that very day, leaving her infant daughter motherless. After attending the funeral, Grannis returned to the claim, hunted for lost ponies which he failed to find, and then commenced sinking a new shaft. After nine days of labor, the shaft had to be abandoned because it intersected an impenetrable rock ledge. Days later a second shaft caved in, and on the heels of that mishap, a mule ran away. It took an entire day of searching in a downpour of rain to locate the errant mule. Then came a final, but perhaps predictable misfortune. The health problems returned: "Was taken with severe pain in my left Hand, have had Intense pain all Day."[76]

During his absence from Alder Gulch, Grannis had written letters to Ellen, his "true love," and she to him, but since his return he had not gone to visit her. Some time following his brief reunion with Sarah, he had experienced a change of heart which now made him too busy to visit the young woman who had been waiting for him. Though too occupied to resume the relationship with Ellen, Grannis did find time to visit the town where she resided. The purpose of his visit to Nevada City was to watch a man "Receive 50 lashes on the bear back for Stealing, By the vigilantes." In addition to vigilance activities, he also found time to attend the Virginia City theater to see a performance by actress Julia Dean Hayne, the "star of the West."[77]

For more than five months, Grannis could not find time to call on Ellen. When the inevitable could no longer be postponed, he at last visited his former "true love." After the call at her residence, he returned to his snug little cabin–now fully equipped with door, fireplace, and furniture–sat down, and informed his diary of the conversation just held in Nevada City: he had explained to Ellen that since he had seen her last April, he had endured "considerable Bad Luck" and "various trials" and at the present time, he was not "Situated to keep her."

Though Grannis had once found room to take another miner into this same cabin as a boarder and also had once found room for an audience to hear a traveling preacher's sermon in the cabin, it now did not provide sufficient accommodation for two people. As he advised Ellen, he "must be without her company again for a long time."

Ellen was a woman who had unwisely depended upon a divorced man's promise that his love for her would grow "fonder" during an absence in which he visited his ex-wife. In response to Grannis's remark, evidently intended as a merciful rejection, Ellen quickly began packing her things. On the October morning she was to depart for Salt Lake City, Grannis made the effort of calling to "Bid Ellen goodBye." She is not mentioned again in the diary.[78]

By mid-October, snow storms were raging, and Grannis drove his mules to a boarding ranch. As he passed through Virginia City, he happened upon X. Beidler, who was elaborating on some of his recent laurels. Early in September, X. related, he had galloped into town with a murder suspect in custody. After he turned the prisoner over to the vigilance committee for punishment, the *Montana Post* had run an article praising the vigilantes for their "promptness" and their "thorough investigation" of the murder case. Apparently Beidler's new line of work and its accompanying recognition agreed with him better than packing and mining had because, as Grannis noted, the once-scrawny X. was now "well and fat."[79]

But Grannis was neither fat nor well. In fact he was in a state of deep depression. Though the diary illuminates the stress brought on by his business losses and the disappointing visit with his ex-wife, there may have been an additional factor which he had very good reason not to mention in a record he intended to leave for posterity. Though he was a member of the vigilantes, no diary entry mentions that fact. And no diary entry discloses his feelings about his now-worrisome involvement in the lynchings. Other vigilantes had been more frank in expressing their concerns. As vigilante officer Nathaniel Langford confessed in his book, he and other members of the organization "knew full well that when the Federal courts should be organized, they themselves [the vigilante members] would in turn be held accountable before the law for any unwarrantable exercise of power."

To avoid the possibility of legal prosecution, Captain James Williams wished to maintain the cloak of secrecy over the organization's history and membership. But Dimsdale, for whatever reasons, felt it essential to justify the many lynchings and thus cleanse the reputation of the movement. Over Captain Williams's objections, Editor Dimsdale persisted in writing articles in the *Montana Post*, articles that were later collected into Montana's first book.

When vigilante captain James Williams later committed suicide, the act was attributed to financial worries, but who is to say that a lingering, though unexpressed, fear of retribution for the many lynchings he directed did not also contribute to the morbid depression that drove him to take his own life. Likewise, John Grannis may have lived with secret fears of being punished for assisting with the lynchings, fears he did not dare to express in written form.[80]

In November, the dejected miner–who had not cranked the windlass at his Highland claims for five months–realized he had squandered a thousand dollars on aborted businesses at Elk Creek. And once again he found himself alone in the world. Nevertheless he laid in a supply of flour and potatoes for winter. Then on 31 December 1866, he entered the cabin he had built in spare moments from his more active days at the mines, sat down at the crude table and chair he had fashioned with his own hands, and opened his diary. "This year," Grannis wrote, "has Been Bad luck to me from the first to last." Since this entry is the final page of the notebook, Jonathan W. Grannis concluded the story of his searches for fortune and marital bliss on a discouraging note. His cumulative misfortunes seem to confirm his longstanding anxiety that with Sarah's departure from his home, happiness had, alas, flown forever.[81]

Afterword to Grannis Story

The Grannis diary contains so little description of wife battery that the casual reader might think it unwarranted to label the diarist an abusive husband. But a man who strikes his wife on the mouth, and then expects her to continue to come back for more, is abusive. And a man who libels his wife's character without any proof is abusive. And a man who trails his wife—a wife who is attempting to escape from him—through five states, begging her to return when she does not want to, is obsessed with possessing his wife.

Though the Grannis diary describes little physical abuse, it does present an abusive husband's view of the world around him. But before discussing this view, one pressing question needs to be resolved: if Grannis did not consider himself abusive, why did he record the mouth-spatting incident in a book intended to preserve for posterity an accurate picture of the gold-rush experience? Several answers come to mind, the most obvious being that he did not consider striking his wife on the mouth an abusive act. In addition, he may have wanted to set the record straight. No matter what Sarah told people, he wanted it down in black and white that his blow to her face was nothing more than a "spat."

His world view could be described as tunnel vision, an unawareness of the significance of historical events occurring about him. His relationship with Sarah took place within the same narrow confines. Grannis was self-absorbed, that is keenly aware of his own pain, but unable to sense the pain he inflicted upon Sarah. In fact he was so lacking in insight he did not perceive his behavior toward his wife as abusive.

To extract a full portrait of a wife abuser from brief diary entries is not possible, but one of the diarist's succinct commentaries seems relevant. After visiting a miner who was in jail for shooting his partner, Grannis wrote, "Felt Sad to See that good men will Shoot one another." A study of the Grannis diary might evoke a similar emotion in a reader: "Felt sad to see that a good man will abuse his wife, especially a wife he loved."[82]

And John Grannis was a good man. He was the perfect example of the individual whom vigilante apologists Thomas Dimsdale and Nathaniel Langford referred to in their books as "a solid citizen." Grannis did not steal, he did not knowingly lie, he did not brawl, he did not provoke gunplay. He did love his wife, he did pay school tuition and buy textbooks for his son, he did read the scriptures and honor his God, he did attend the funerals of friends and visit acquaintances who were confined in jail, he did respect the civic authority in power, he did try to expand his meager formal education by studying German and to increase his spirituality by advancing in Masonry, and he did work very hard at the mines. In addition, he did participate in vigilance activities.

Obviously, Grannis was the model citizen of the vigilante lore created by Mollie's teacher, Thomas Dimsdale. And an interesting parallel can be drawn between the vigilante outlook and the problem of spousal abuse. To pass judgment on either a robbery suspect or an estranged wife without first ascertaining all available evidence, including allowing the suspect to speak, entails not only negligence, but also a presumption of omniscience, or at least a presumption of superior intelligence and morality. For example, after the joint lynchings at Virginia City, Grannis felt "very Well Satisfied with the Days work." That work consisted of hanging five untried men, one a miners' deputy. Grannis expressed no pangs of regret over the hastiness of the affair, even when the five men "maintained their innocence to the Last." The individuals he helped to execute were, he wrote, "implicated" in a road agent gang.

As with the lynch victims, Sarah was only "implicated," in subscribing to "the free love Principal." In both instances, the solution to a suspected problem was an application of immediate violence, directed toward a suspect who at the moment happened to be in a position of less power. It is to Sarah's credit that she refused to remain powerless.[83]

In closing Sarah's portion of the story, one additional record is available which suggests that of the hopeful young farm couple who set out for the Far West in 1860, she was the more resilient. The 1870 census of Jefferson County, Montana Territory lists a Griswold family residing in Boulder Valley. There are two sons in the household, Walter Griswold, age fourteen, and George Griswold, age nine. The head of the household, C. Griswold, age thirty-five and a native of Vermont, is a prosperous farmer, while his wife Sarah, who occupies her time by keeping house, is the same age as her husband, thirty-five.

Miraculously, during the ten-year period since the last census, Sarah had aged only five years! True to form, her vanity would not allow her to admit to the census taker that she was actually nine years older than her second husband.[84]

In contrast to the majority of women in the list given at the opening of Part Two, Sarah Grannis Griswold was strong enough to successfully escape an abusive marriage. The burning question, of course, is the quality of her new relationship with a Yankee husband nine years her junior. It is a question the census cannot answer; however, one modern study of frontier women does provide a ray of hope. After an extensive survey of diaries kept by women during the nineteenth-century migrations to the West, Lillian Schlissel concluded that "Yankee husbands enjoyed the highest reputations among the pioneer women, being universally judged the most considerate and gentle."

To prove her point, Schlissel cites several diaries. One woman, in describing the "difficulty and inconvenience" of performing household chores during the overland crossing, stated that her counterparts from Missouri had to milk the cows. But "I am lucky," she continued, "having a Yankee for a husband, so am well waited on." Even more relevant to the question of Sarah's treatment in the second marriage is the diary of Elizabeth Smith Geer, a woman who like Sarah had emigrated from Indiana with her first husband and on the frontier married a New Englander. Of her second mate, Elizabeth Geer wrote, "He is a Yankee. . . . He is as kind to me as I can ask. Indeed, he sometimes provokes me for trying to humor me so much."[85]

If it should be that Sarah Griswold enjoyed a similar kindness from her Yankee husband, and that Walter gained a gentle stepfather, the "Happy Home" of the four Griswolds would be a just reward for Sarah's courage in escaping an abusive marriage and setting up a second family in the wilderness.

As for the other women on the opening list, few were as fortunate as Sarah in their attempts to free themselves from an abusive marriage. In fact several of their stories will be related in Part Three, the section covering abusive relationships that eventually developed into domestic tragedies.

III

Domestic Tragedies on the Frontier

Stories of Two Oregon Trail Children: Elvina Apperson and Mary Allen

It was Elvina Apperson who commented, "Back in 1851 . . . we had slavery of Negroes in the South" and "slavery of wives all over the United States." Born in the slaveholding state of Missouri on 20 May 1837, Elvina was fifth of the nine children in her family who had survived into childhood. She was ten when with two wagons and several teams of oxen, her family left their home in Neosho and embarked on the route to Oregon. Thus she was old enough to remember her father's death and burial during the plains crossing.

Her mother asked the men of the company to dismantle one of the Appersons' two wagons and make a coffin for her husband, which they did. Then, Elvina recalled, the men "dug a grave in the middle of the trail and buried Father and when the grave was filled they corraled the oxen over the grave so the Indians would not find it." Under the circumstances, they did not erect a headboard. "After a few hundred wagons and the long strings of oxen and loose cattle had passed over it," Elvina stated, "I doubt if we could have located the grave."[1]

The widow Apperson was still in her thirties when she and her nine children, the oldest a girl of fourteen, arrived in Portland in the fall of 1847. The town consisted of one frame house and a bevy of log cabins huddled beyond the bank of the Columbia River. Mrs. Apperson had "no money" and no skills except those associated with housekeeping, but she was determined to put her past experience to good use. She "would go to the ships that came and get washing to do," Elvina remembered, "and so we got along."

Before leaving Missouri, the widow had already lost her oldest son, and within three years of arriving in the Far West, she would lose three of her nine surviving children. The baby, named Milton, died and also Julia, the sister just younger than Elvina; and in 1849, sixteen-year-old Sarah accompanied her husband and her brother to the gold rush and died in California. Elvina, the oldest child left at home, had to drop out of school at age eleven to assist her mother. To supplement her laundry income, Mrs. Apperson also took in boarders, but still she was unable to adequately feed and clothe her family. "In 1851 Mother was pretty hard run to earn enough money for us to live on," Elvina related, "so when a man named Julius Thomas, a cook in a restaurant, offered to marry me, Mother thought I had better take him, so I did."[2]

There was no honeymoon period to this marriage between a middle-aged cook and his bride of age fourteen. Thomas was a heavy drinker and when intoxicated not only became violent, but frequently advised his young wife that he "wanted to kill" her. As the following comment suggests, Elvina did not consider the alternative of leaving or divorcing her abusive husband. "He used to beat me until I thought I couldn't stand it," she related, "but what could a girl of 14 do to protect herself from a man of 44, particularly if he drank most of the time, as my husband did?"

After nearly three years of battering his wife, Thomas attempted to fulfill his threat to kill her. It came about during an especially savage beating. Elvina managed to break his grasp, escape the house, and run to her mother's home. When her husband pursued her, she locked the doors of Mrs. Apperson's boarding house. Not to be kept out, Thomas attempted to open a window to gain entrance, but Elvina grasped the frame and held it down. "Enraged" by her defensive action, he drew his pistol and fired at her through the window. The combined noise of pistol shot and shattering glass so frightened Elvina that she collapsed, and Thomas, peering through the broken pane, spotted his wife prostrate on the floor. "Thinking he had killed me," she said, he "put the end of the pistol barrel into his mouth and pulled the trigger."[3]

Some time after her husband's suicide, Elvina gave birth to his son. Like her mother, the seventeen-year-old was now a widow responsible for feeding and clothing her offspring. But she met Edward Fellows, a "fine" young steamboat engineer who rescued the teenage mother from poverty by marrying her and relocating his instant-family to Lin City, Oregon. By coincidence, Elvina's rescuer was also a Yankee. Though she had no children by this second husband, the couple did adopt a family of Oregon Trail orphans. Later, the household grew to include two of Elvina's brothers, who moved into the house next-door to the Fellows residence. Despite the happiness she enjoyed with this extended second family, Elvina could never erase the memory of her earlier years of abuse: "I still shudder," she commented at age eighty-four, "when I think of the years of my girlhood, when I had to live with that husband."[4]

In many ways, Mary Allen's story is similar to Elvina's; both girls were born in 1837 in Missouri, migrated with their families to Oregon in the late 1840s, and while in their teens married older men who abused them. One difference, however, is that throughout her brief life span, Mary suffered the stigma of having been born to unwed parents. Some time after Mary's birth, her father, a thirty-four-year-old farmer born in Tennessee, did marry the mother of his child, a twenty-three-year-old from New York, and the couple then settled down and continued their family.[5]

On arriving in Oregon, the Allens established a farm and a mill in Washington County, not far from the farm of the county clerk, William Geiger, Jr. But somehow the rumor of Mary's "disgraceful" birth followed the family to the West coast. Though Mary lived within walking range of Matilda Sager, who was near her age, Mr. Geiger would not allow the two girls to associate. As related earlier, Matilda once disobeyed by accompanying Mary on an outing, but the "severe beating" she received from Geiger discouraged any further communication between the two girls.

The loneliness resulting from being the community "pariah" may have contributed to Mary's willingness to wed at age thirteen; however, early marriage for girls was more a rule than an exception on the frontier. To illustrate this point, there is the tale (though perhaps embellished, related as an actual occurrence) of a greenhorn circuit rider and his mule who spent an entire day winding their way up a sinuous Rocky Mountain trail that led to a remote mining camp. At dusk they spotted a log dwelling, and the rider dismounted and rapped on the door. An unkempt girl, appearing to be about eight years old, swung open the leather-hinged door, set aside the dried bush she had been using to sweep the dirt floor, and welcomed the traveler into a sparsely furnished cabin that reeked of rancid bear grease. Seeing several mining tools scattered about the single room, but noting no one else was at home, the weary preacher sank onto a rough-hewn stool to await the return of the miner.

After he was seated, the girl stood next to him, closely examining his neatly clipped beard and even testing, between her thumb and forefinger, the texture of his black frock coat and the stiffness of his white collar. Embarrassed under the close scrutiny of his expensive Eastern garb, the Reverend tried to divert the girl's attention to her own neglected appearance. He smoothed her disheveled calico dress, undid the misaligned hooks at the neck and fastened them properly, and finally, brushed tangled locks from her forehead. When she expressed no objections, he lifted her onto his lap and, having no comb with him, began to unknot the snarls from her long hair with his fingertips.

After leaning down, looking into her face, and giving her an encouraging smile for cooperating with the badly needed grooming, the preacher solicitously inquired, "And when will Papa be home, my little lady?"

Though the child made an attempt at returning his smile, the expression on her small face looked more like a grimace. "Careful, Preacher," she warned, "my husband's apt to walk in on us most any minute."[6]

Ignoring the grim side-issue (apparently the girl had learned to tolerate the unwelcome fondling of an adult male), the point of the tale is supposed to be the rude awakening of the cultured newcomer who inadvertently dandled the lady of the frontier household on his knee. The Eastern preacher was shocked into a discovery that a Western man in need of a wife might view a mere child as "a young woman in society."

In such mismatches, there was little to no time wasted on a courtship. Thus to the girl whom the preacher found sweeping the dirt floor of a secluded mining cabin, it was no matter that the caller who entered her home and quickly became so familiar as to rearrange her clothing and hair was a complete stranger. When she had married her husband, in all probability, he also had been a stranger. And–just as in the cases of Elvina Apperson and Mary Allen–the couples gradually became acquainted after their marriage.

What Mary Allen, age thirteen, soon learned about her husband, one of the few persons in the community who had no compunction about associating with her, was that thirty-five-year-old Adam Wimple — like Julius

Thomas—had an inner rage which he directed toward his helpless young wife.[7]

To whom could Mary Wimple turn for help? Certainly not to the community who had shunned her, and certainly not to the court judge who, after neighbors charged Matilda Sager's guardian with child-beating, agreed to grant Geiger legal custody of his foster child. Before Mary and Wimple had been married one year, he fulfilled his compulsion to kill her. Then to escape punishment, he set their house on fire with her corpse inside. When neighbors extinguished the flames, they discovered that Mary's partially charred body also bore the marks of a brutal murder. Wimple was hanged for the crime, but the legal intervention had come too late to help Mary, dead at age fourteen.[8]

Story of a Gold-rush Gambler's Wife: Lucinda Vedder

John Vedder was not a gambler when Lucinda Bohall married him; the large, well-built young man, known for his forceful personality, was working at his father's stockyards in the city which had just become California's permanent capital, Sacramento. John's father, Vulcan Vedder, was a German immigrant who had received an education in his native land, yet his son–who had been born in New York state but reared in the West–had managed to avoid learning to read or write.

Despite this lack of schooling, John Vedder's swaggering, aggressive manner attracted teenaged Lucinda. Like him, she was a former New Yorker and thus was impressed when he demonstrated an acquired frontier savvy by walking around armed at all times. His weapon of choice, he advised his young female admirer, was a knife; not that he lacked skill with a pistol or rifle, of course, it was just that he "went more by a knife."[9]

In 1854 at a ceremony held in Sacramento City, Lucinda and John became Mr. and Mrs. Vedder. The groom was twenty-one and the bride seventeen, but both were venerable in comparison to the four-year-old state they chose as their home. For the first months of their marriage, the couple remained in the capital. The teenage bride faithfully performed all household tasks expected of her, the sewing, cooking, and cleaning, but she received no praise from her husband. John was not only sparing with compliments, but also inclined to become displeased at his new wife's slightest breach with perfection.

Lucinda was pretty, but she was also intelligent and quite articulate and therefore thought she could reason with her husband about his shortcomings. However it soon became apparent he was not a reasonable man. In addition to being rude to his mate, he was also very jealous and unjustifiably suspicious. But since Lucinda was in love, she put up with her husband's flaws. Gradually, more serious faults began to surface. Any time Vedder took the notion, he would stay out all night, and when his wife was ill, he provided her no care. Also, there was physical abuse.

OLD TOWN OF SACRAMENTO. Lucinda Bohall married John Vedder in Sacramento in 1854, the same year the city became the permanent capital of California. *Photo by F. E. Boswell*

"My husband," Lucinda stated later, "mistreated me from the 1ˢᵗ month of my marriage; he used to beat me." During their second month together, he threw her to the floor and "stomped" her. Since during their marital disputes Lucinda always argued her own case rather than submitting to her husband's will, she suspected she was guilty of provoking the abuse. I "am very quick tempered," she confessed to others, and I "allow no one to wrong."[10]

Vedder also placed the blame for their troubles on his high-spirited young wife, describing her as having "the G-d d—edst tongue." Despite his repeated efforts, he seemed unable to teach her she was not allowed to return his insulting remarks. Swearing was a part of his normal speech, but if an oath came from his wife's lips, he would clap his hand over her mouth.

Yet Vedder admitted that even with her many imperfections, Lucinda "was as good a wife as any." Her grittiness offered a constant challenge to him, and he took satisfaction in being powerful enough to subdue her. One measure he frequently used, in addition to the beatings, was to haul out the trunk in which she had brought her possessions after their wedding. Then he would grasp his wife, plunk her down atop the trunk lid, and tell her to repack her things and return to live with her parents in their Sacramento home. Vedder was not actually serious about the order; it was merely

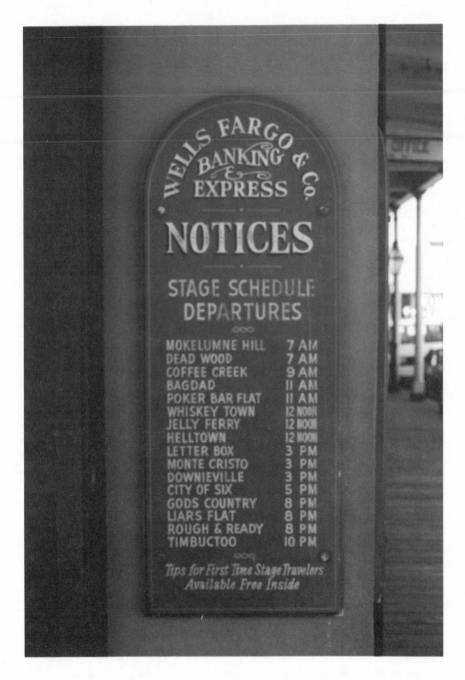

SCHEDULE OF STAGE DEPARTURES FROM EARLY SACRAMENTO. *Photo by F. E. Boswell*

a taunt calculated to remind Lucinda she had no other place to go. As he knew, she had severed relations with her parents when she was fifteen, and they would not allow her to return to their home.[11]

Lucinda's major problem, however, was not that she had no place to seek refuge from her husband's fits of anger; it was instead that she did not wish to leave him. During the months of physical and emotional abuse, she continued to love her husband. In the second year of the stormy union, Vedder took work as a livestock hand and moved his now-pregnant wife to a small house on the Van Young ranch outside Nevada City. The ten miles separating the mining supply center from their ranch home increased tension between the couple by creating an isolation to which both were unaccustomed.

"At the ranch," Lucinda related, "we lived very unhappily. We both had tempers & never agreed."

Vedder boasted to a former acquaintance from Sacramento that during one disagreement at the ranch, he "flogged" Lucinda with a whip, which had made her behave pretty well for a while. He also liked to joke about how he treated his dog better than his wife. "I saw him take beef," another acquaintance recounted, and state that "he was going to feed his dog, but had no meat for the woman."

Though the black humor and the severity of the floggings might have alerted Lucinda that Vedder's hostility toward her was becoming more alarming, she still did not consider leaving him. After all, she argued, he did provide her with food and shelter so that she "never wanted" for anything, . . . well, anything except "care." And in spite of the "bitter days," there were also "some happy days" which in her mind justified her resolution to cling to the relationship.[12]

The birth of their daughter in August of 1856 brought added strain for the teenage wife struggling to hold a difficult marriage together, for from the first of baby Agnes's numbered days, she was described as "feeble." The special care the delicate infant required placed a heavy burden on the new mother's shoulders. Then the following spring, when Agnes was seven months old, came an event that would hasten the impending dissolution of the family of three: Vedder decided to trade ranching for the more exciting profession of dealing monte at a gambling house in Nevada City. It would be a risky venture because their income would depend solely upon Vedder's untried skill as a dealer. Nevertheless, the family packed their few belongings and departed for the county seat and third-largest settlement in California.[13]

Nevada City–a picturesque mining community snuggled among pine-covered foothills of the Sierra Nevada and bordering the meandering course of gold-rich Deer Creek–stretched out for half a mile on either side of the town's hilltop courthouse. Though one year earlier the disastrous fire of 1856 had nearly leveled the town, an array of imposing brick buildings now loomed over the narrow streets that leisurely wound through seven

PRESENT-DAY NEVADA CITY, CALIFORNIA, preserves its graceful Victorian-style architecture. *Photo by F. E. Boswell*

low hills.

The town's level of prosperity was indicated by the presence of eight sawmills and two raucous quartz mills that disturbed the peace by daily pounding out fifteen tons of ore apiece. The level of civilization was indicated by a brick theater where traveling troupes provided entertainment ranging from Shakespeare's *Richard III* to vaudeville acts featuring a dancer,

NEVADA CITY, CALIFORNIA'S NATIONAL HOTEL is still in operation. Lucinda and John Vedder lived only one block from this town landmark. *Photo by F. E. Boswell*

singer, violinist, harpist, whistler, and a mockingbird imitator who had received rave reviews from the local press. And in addition to the town's two newspapers, there were also five churches.

Among Nevada City's more than two hundred businesses were seventy-nine "liquor houses" and twenty-four boardinghouses and hotels. Most impressive of the latter was the three-storied National Hotel, with its ornate balconies and a plushly furnished lobby which was connected by telegraph with Sacramento, Marysville, and even the out-of-the-way mountain camp of Downieville (best known as the town that had hanged a woman named Juanita). From this same lobby—graced with a massive, square piano that had been shipped via Cape Horn—twenty stages arrived and departed daily.[14]

Though John Vedder was anxious to relocate to the city, he had made no prior arrangements for living quarters, and on the spring day the family arrived–accompanied by Vedder's dog and equipped with one crammed steamer trunk, a crib, and a rocking chair–he discovered that a housing shortage existed. Being friendless in the town, Vedder appealed to the city's manager-marshal, and in response, Marshal Henry Plummer vacated his own home on Spring Street and rented it to the newcomers.

LOBBY OF NATIONAL HOTEL still features the massive piano that traveled around Cape Horn. *Photo by F. E. Boswell*

The cloth-roofed house was enclosed within a fence and consisted of a 12' x 12' room divided into kitchen and parlor, and a 10' x 10' bedroom. The large windows of both rooms were covered by curtains, and furnishings included a stove, table, two chairs, bedstead, straw mattress, and mirror. This furniture, in addition to some fishing line, hooks, rifle, etc. that the sporting young marshal had left behind, took up most of the limited space. Fortunately, the Vedders' limited household gear fit in easily, and as a second attraction, their new home was just one block from the heart of town. Thus when Vedder closed his monte table at two A.M., he would have but a short walk home. Grateful to the Marshal for providing him with living quarters, Vedder declared to other town citizens that "Plummer was about as good a friend as he had in the County."[15]

In the bustling mining center they would now call home, Vedder became quite animated by the prospects of a lucrative career. He had heard there were "fewer chances for the bettor" in monte than in any other card game being played in the gambling halls. As dealer, all he would have to do was lay four cards on the table. Bettors would then place their stakes on any of the four cards, and he would continue dealing until a match with one of the original four cards appeared. The winner would double his bet, while Vedder would rake in all bets placed on the three losing cards. His new profession seemed to be a quick, easy way of getting rich.[16]

Pleased with the new turn his life was taking, Vedder commenced treat-

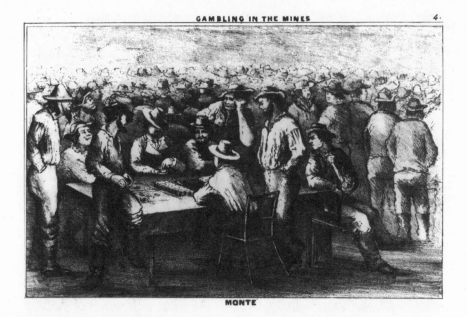

GAMBLING IN THE MINES   4.

MONTE

"MONTE," by John David Borthwick. John Vedder heard there were "fewer chances for the bettor" in monte than in any other card game played in the gambling halls. *Courtesy History West Publishing Company*

ing Lucinda with more kindness than usual. Also, he displayed fatherly concern for little Agnes, who despite her weak constitution was trying to take a few steps. Her increased mobility created the worry she might tumble down the back stairway, a descent of some twenty-four feet in the direction of the creek; and to prevent such an accident, Lucinda blocked the lower part of the back doorway with a board. Vedder not only insisted that Lucinda provide Agnes with constant supervision, but himself took time to play with the child each day. To Lucinda, it seemed that at last the family was getting on "first rate." She had "never lived so happy in her life."

Though it may have appeared they were making a fresh start, it was not long before the Vedders were plagued by the old problems, plus new ones they had not anticipated. The troubles that refused to disappear in the new setting were Agnes's poor health, the eruption of bitter quarrels between Lucinda and John, and John's loss of temper and resulting abuse. Details of these problems would come out in the murder trial following the family tragedy.

While they had moved to escape the monotony, loneliness, and limited economic opportunity in the country, they now missed the financial security it had provided. In Nevada City, Vedder found he was unable to make a consistent profit at his card dealing. His repeated losses left him out of sorts and left the family short of funds. But another problem that cropped up in the more populous setting was even more damaging to the marriage. Lucinda was still an attractive woman, and Vedder's jealousy and suspicion drove him to drastic steps.

He was a controlling person, but Lucinda was not easily controlled. Neighbors confirmed that he now "used violence" to his wife "nearly every day," leaving her covered with "black marks." And using money that was needed for household expenses, he hired a spy to keep an eye on his wife while he was working at the gambling tables. It did not take Lucinda long to discover she was being followed each time she left the house. Angry over his suspicions, she confronted her husband, accusing him of "setting a man to watch" her. The result was predictable: a series of recurring quarrels over the hired spy, each ending with Vedder either beating his wife or dragging out her trunk. Meanwhile the spying continued.

As if the heated arguments over the spy's continual tailing of Lucinda were not causing sufficient problems for the couple, their first Fourth of July in the city brought a serious accident. While Vedder was within one block of reaching home, the local newspaper reported, he "was struck on the forehead by a rocket which had just been lighted. . . . Two splinters were left in his head." The doctor who had treated the wound informed the news reporter that "the splinters went in directly under the eyes and it is feared he will lose the sight of one of them." After receiving the doctor's prognosis, Vedder contacted a lawyer and filed a civil suit against the celebrator who had set off the rocket.[17]

As might be expected, Vedder's physical and mental distress increased his outbursts of temper, but unlike the rural environment, Nevada City offered authorities to whom Lucinda could turn for protection. On one occasion when Vedder pulled out the trunk, flung Lucinda on its lid, and told her to leave town as quickly as she could, she darted out the front door, ran the short block to the city center, turned up the hill to the courthouse, and there reported her husband's violence. The county recorder listened to her account, but in the end, no action was taken. Despondently, Lucinda returned home, while Vedder, encouraged by her failure to arouse any community indignation over his actions, boldly proceeded with the abuse.

At times, pedestrians on the street could hear Lucinda's cries for help, but when one male passerby ran to the door to offer her aid, Vedder shouted, "I'll kill you if you come in." Hastily, the man retreated, leaving Lucinda to her fate.

After such incidents, Vedder often turned to a nearby businessman, a blacksmith, to justify his actions and to enlist support in his complaints against his wife. Though the Vedders had made no close friends, after one quarrel, John dropped in at the blacksmith shop, located only forty rods from the Spring Street house. The smith, whom the couple had previously met in Sacramento, stated that Vedder "called me out & said his wife & him had a fuss, . . . wanted me to call on her & tell her . . . to go to her parents."

When he inquired what the "fuss" was about, Vedder told him the latest quarrel was more serious than usual. "Something had been said on both sides," Vedder went on, "that could not be retracted." At noon of the foregoing day, he had returned home without the coal Lucinda had requested for the cookstove, and as he stepped through the door, he noticed she "had a long face & looked black." Displeased at her show of annoyance, "he called her a God d — —d son of a bitch and she had called him a d — —d whore house pimp."

The blacksmith realized the exchange of insults could cause a split between the couple and therefore returned with Vedder to the house to try to patch things up. First, he scolded both parties for such "disgraceful" conduct before a child. Then after tempers had cooled a bit, he reminded the couple they loved each other and urged them to kiss and make up. They did so, he reported.[18]

But the peacemaker had no means of curbing Vedder's continuing violence. Soon after the first intervention, the blacksmith testified at the trial held several weeks later, he saw Vedder "use violence to his wife, knock her up against side of house, choke her & pinch her nose." When the smith shouted for him to stop before he killed his wife, Vedder replied that "he ought to kill her."

These threats against Lucinda were a regular occurrence. One afternoon in early September, Vedder dragged out the steamer trunk and ordered his wife to return to Sacramento, and as usual, she responded she did not want to leave him. But this time, her submission failed to bring the usual satisfaction. He would not live in the same town with her any longer, Vedder shouted and drawing his knife, held it to Lucinda's throat and threatened to slash her if she did not promise to obey his order to leave. Again she submitted, agreeing she would do anything he wished. Apparently pacified, he left the house to go to work.

As soon as he was out of sight, Lucinda went for help. "I am afraid of my husband," she explained to any acquaintance who would listen, "afraid of my life" and "want protection from my husband."[19]

When several individuals suggested she contact Henry Plummer, Lucinda sent the Marshal a note, asking him to recommend a lawyer so she could obtain "a bill of divorce." Plummer was a compassionate man, and he promptly came to the Spring Street house he had rented the couple, listened to Lucinda describe her fear of her husband, and then advised her to talk with David Belden, one of Nevada City's most respected attorneys. Until the matter could be resolved, Plummer promised, his policemen would keep an eye on Vedder. Though it might have seemed to Lucinda she was at last going to get the help she needed, she was actually entering the most dangerous phase of the violent relationship. For with the Marshal's appearance at her front step, the stage was fully set for the domestic tragedy to follow.

ATTORNEY DAVID BELDEN, of Nevada City, California. Though John Vedder had held a knife to his wife's throat, Belden advised Lucinda "to get along if possible with her husband." *Courtesey California State Library*

Because of Agnes's poor health, the Marshal himself went to Belden's office and asked the attorney to visit Mrs. John Vedder. Belden responded that he did not make house calls. However when Plummer advised him Lucinda was in danger, but had an ailing child whom she should not leave, the attorney agreed to go to the Spring Street residence. Plummer accompanied Belden, made introductions, and then left so attorney and client could talk in private.

At the subsequent court case instigated by the Vedders' problems, Belden described his visit with Lucinda: "She told her grievances, & why she wished to get a divorce. She said . . . John was very cruel–had knocked her down & that he had been in the habit of abandoning & leaving her." Belden found it a "pitiful story," which he believed because Mrs. Vedder referred him to "witnesses who had seen this treatment." But when Belden proceeded to advise the young housewife he could obtain a divorce for her on grounds of cruelty, instead of being pleased she burst into tears. For the first time, Lucinda sensed the coming reality of severing her relationship with a husband whom "she loved better than any other man."[20]

Concerned by her outburst of emotion, Belden questioned Lucinda further, and "she expressed herself as though John loved her" also. "I told her," Belden testified, that "she did not want divorce; matter could be reconciled." Unaware of the explosiveness of the situation (Vedder carrying a knife at all times and his wife now being in added danger because of her attempt to file for divorce) Belden naively advised Lucinda to consider the matter for a few days and in the meantime, "to get along if possible with her husband." With an even greater show of naivete, Lucinda agreed.

It took but a short time for Vedder's spy to bring him the report that while John had been dealing monte, two men had visited his wife. There was no question about the identity of the second visitor; the spy recognized Belden as the counsel Vedder had retained for the eye injury suit, but the identity of the young man who called first and then brought the attorney was unknown. Combining this new piece of information with old suspicions, Vedder concluded Lucinda must have a lover who had visited her, persuaded her to get a divorce, and then summoned Belden.

Like John Grannis, John Vedder could not accept the fact that his mistreatment was driving his wife to seek help. Both men placed the blame on a wife's infidelity and another man's desire to have her for his own. Consumed by rage and jealousy, Vedder began formulating a plan of revenge. His goal, he confided to the blacksmith, was to kill both Lucinda and her supposed lover, but in order to justify his action, he thought it would be necessary that the pair be in the act of making love at the time of their death.[21]

Intent on discovering the identity of the lover, Vedder rushed to Belden's office and demanded the attorney reveal the name of the man who had escorted him to the Spring Street house. When Belden refused to release confidential information, Vedder left the law office and hurried to the blacksmith shop. "He asked me if I went for Belden," the blacksmith later reported, and "I said no; he said he would like to know what son of bitch went for him." Vedder then departed, but later returned in an even more agitated state. So other workers in the shop would not overhear the conversation, the two men left the building and walked the streets as they talked.

Without revealing the cause of his increased agitation, Vedder asked the blacksmith to lend him his pistol. Fearful his neighbor would "get into a fuss," the smith at first refused, but at Vedder's insistence the gun would be used only for protection, he at last handed over his weapon. Then Vedder asked a question that partially revealed the disturbing news he had uncovered during his absence. "He wanted to know," the smith continued, "if Plumer did not go to my house as I went out," and "I said yes."

Even with the blacksmith's confirmation it had been the Marshal who had delivered Belden to the house, Vedder could not believe it. "He said that it could not be possible as Plumer was his best friend." But the blacksmith insisted he had seen Marshal Plummer enter the house. "Vedder . . . said that's all he wanted to know & quicked his pace. I catched him & asked him what he wanted to do." In response, Vedder held out his knife and the borrowed pistol, then stated that "he meant to get under the floor & try to ketch them together" and "he would make a funeral pile of them both." Though the perplexed blacksmith still did not fully understand "what put him in a rage," he attempted to calm Vedder. "I told him not to get into a scrape, as he would have no show," but "he threw me from him."[22]

When the blacksmith returned to the shop, he told "the boys" he thought "there would be a murder committed before morning." But in hopes the threatened double murder would not come off immediately, he also sent a letter to Vulcan Vedder, advising him it would be "better" if his son John and his daughter-in-law Lucinda "never see each other again." Otherwise, John was likely to "get into a big fuss . . . and has no show here where all the Police are watching all his movements."

What neither the blacksmith nor John realized was that Lucinda and Marshal Plummer were barely acquainted. The two had first met when Plummer stopped by the Spring Street house while the Vedders were moving in; later, Plummer returned to get his rifle and some fishing gear. His response to Lucinda's note had initiated their first real conversation.

Nevertheless, Vedder had convinced himself the pair had become intimate, and he was determined to surprise them in a tryst. With the borrowed pistol in his pocket, he slipped away from his monte table at the gambling hall and returned to his home. To his surprise, he found no one in the house except Lucinda and Agnes. However this discovery did not abate his wrath, which he immediately began unleashing upon his wife.

The next day, the worried blacksmith called at the Vedders. No one was at the house except John, who opened the door and in response to questions began to relate the events of the previous night: "It was lucky for them both," he said, "that Plummer was not there." On finding Lucinda had no company, Vedder "had caught his wife by the hair & drew his knife & threatened to kill her." When "she screamed for mercy," Vedder informed her that "he had a good notion to kill her." She replied that she "would promise him all he wanted," and in turn he said that "he would not kill" her.[23]

After obtaining Lucinda's promise to return to Sacramento as soon as a

HOTEL DE PARIS, NEVADA CITY, CALIFORNIA. When her husband
threatened to kill her, Lucinda Vedder took a room at this hotel, but her abusive
mate followed her. *Courtesy Searls Historical Library, Nevada City, California*

divorce was final, Vedder left the house. Later, he told the blacksmith, he
had learned a policeman named Pat Corbett had taken Lucinda and Agnes
to the Hotel de Paris, a small inn on Broad Street, and that Nevada City
police had stationed a guard in the room opposite Lucinda's room.

What Vedder failed to admit during his recounting was that one hour
after Lucinda checked into the Hotel de Paris, he had appeared at her room.
The owner of the hotel noticed that Mrs. Vedder's husband "was vexed"
and heard him say to Lucinda, "Go away from me." Yet instead of dealing
cards that night, John stayed with Lucinda and slept in her room for a short
time. While there, he promised his wife that if she would return to the
house, he would treat her well.

Taking him at his word, Lucinda walked to their home the next day,
performed her housekeeping chores, and cooked a meal for her husband.
She was prepared, she said, "to try & live home," but Vedder was still angry and "he forced me to leave." Returning to the Hotel de Paris, she spent
the night in her previous room, with police stationed across the hall. But
again, her husband came to the hotel and taunted her by threatening to
steal their child. He said that he "wanted to take it to a house of ill fame, &
have it taken care of." Lucinda protested that their daughter should be
raised by "respectable parties," and the usual quarreling began. But in the

end, Vedder spent the first part of the night in the hotel room and again invited his wife to return to the house. When she expressed a fear of returning, he assured her he would remove his things and leave the house to her.

The family fell into a routine that continued for a week. Each morning Vedder would come early to the hotel room, sit on the bed, and play with Agnes; each afternoon Lucinda would walk to Spring Street to clean and cook, but her husband would become angry and force her to leave; and each evening he would again arrive at the hotel to share Lucinda's bed for the first part of the night. Afterwards, he would rise and return to the house (from which he still had not removed his possessions as promised), care for his dog, and retire to his own bed. But since he did not like being in the house alone, he would invite some male acquaintance to sleep with him.[24]

During this hectic week, Vedder had a chat with Plummer, who informed him he had never had any personal involvement with Lucinda. Convinced the Marshal was telling the truth, Vedder returned the blacksmith's pistol and then confided to another acquaintance that "he did not believe his wife had been unfaithful to him with Plummer." And to another person, Vedder stated that "Plummer was not to blame" for the "difficulty between himself and his wife." The person to blame, he continued, was Pat Corbett, the policeman who "made all the fuss" about the recent quarrel and persuaded Lucinda to move into the hotel.

During this same week, Vedder also paid a visit to Belden's office to advise the attorney there would be no divorce after all, because "it was all made up." When Belden brought up the issue of cruelty to his wife, Vedder answered, "I suppose I have slapped her a few times." (Vedder's minimization of his violence to his wife brings to mind John Grannis's use of the word "spat" when he described hitting Sarah on the mouth.)

Though Vedder indicated to the lawyer that a reconciliation between the couple was under consideration, on the morning of September 22, a loud voice issuing from Lucinda Vedder's hotel room wakened Marshal Plummer and Pat Corbett, who were sleeping in the room the police had reserved just across the hall. Hurrying to Lucinda's door, which was standing ajar, the officers observed John preparing to assault his wife. Quickly, Plummer stepped between the couple, asking Vedder if he would not be ashamed to strike a woman. John replied that he would strike his own mother if she treated him as badly as Lucinda did.

But during a brief conversation, Plummer managed to calm John, who agreed to leave the hotel with the Marshal. Though assuming a good-natured air in Plummer's presence, John Vedder was actually seething at the interference in what he considered his private affairs. Later that morning, he made the rounds of town businesses, warning any and all listeners that no man dared to be "intimate" with his wife unless he was married to her and also boasting that he intended to kill the Marshal, in fact, "would kill Plumer if it took him 20 years." Yet to others, Vedder admitted that as much as he would like to kill the Marshal, he had no friends in town and therefore would "have no show."

While the owner of the Hotel de Paris was eating breakfast, he saw Vedder pull up in front of the hotel in a hired carriage, hurry to Lucinda's room, and reappear with "a grimace on his face" and Agnes in his arms. As father and daughter drove away in the carriage, Lucinda burst into the hotel dining room, begging that somebody call the police.[25]

By the time a law officer arrived, there was no trace of Vedder nor the carriage. He had driven to the Van Young ranch, hid his daughter there, and extracted a promise from the rancher not to give Agnes to either Lucinda or the police. When Vedder returned to town, Marshal Plummer informed him he must either return the child to her mother's custody or face prosecution. Vedder then promised he would surrender Agnes to authorities so mother and daughter could depart for Sacramento on the stage.

The promise, however, was merely a ploy, for in reality he had no intentions of reuniting Lucinda and Agnes. He had received a letter from his father (perhaps in response to the blacksmith's warning), asking him to drive a herd of cattle across the plains. John planned not only to make the cattle drive, but also to take Agnes with him.

First on his secret agenda was to obtain a divorce from Lucinda. As soon as Belden's law office opened on Friday morning, which was the fated day of 25 September 1857, Vedder appeared in the doorway. "He wanted papers issued at once," Belden related, and said if there "was not evidence enough, he could make me some." When Belden advised him the cost would be twenty-five dollars, Vedder answered that "he had no money," but would borrow some and return. Shortly after the noon hour, he reappeared with the money, and as though attempting to elicit praise from the lawyer, boasted, "Now didn't I do as I said?"

Since the transaction required the presence of the wife, lawyer and client then walked to the Spring Street house. As they entered, Belden noted that Lucinda "was preparing some cooking." Handing the borrowed money to his wife and ordering her to personally present it to the attorney, Vedder said, "Now by God, I want this thing to go on, want no more fooling." Concerned about this show of hostility, Belden waited until he and Vedder had left the house and then cautioned that "it would not be prudent or pleasant" for the couple "to be living together while this thing was in progress."

Insulted by the well-intended advice, Vedder replied, "Do you think I'm a damned fool? I haven't been with her for some time."

Later the two men visited the courthouse to complete the paperwork, and as they were descending the hill, Vedder sighed, "Now I am a free man." As far as he was concerned, he continued, his ex-wife could "go to hell her own way." He also mentioned the cattle drive and even invited Belden to come along. The lawyer refused the invitation, and the two parted.[26]

Vedder now turned to the next pressing item on his list: raising some needed money by selling the family's possessions. So on a third occasion that day, Belden had an encounter with his client. Vedder was walking down the street, carrying a large rocking chair in his arms. "He stopped me," Belden stated, and "wanted to know if I did not want to buy it." The lawyer explained he was not in the market for the chair, but in the way of conversation commented, "You are getting the traps away are you, John?"

"Yes," Vedder stated, "I've got my child & my dog, & that is all I care a damn about." That same afternoon, Vedder performed the third item of business on the list: he took his dog to the blacksmith for safekeeping. Then he hurried from business to business on Broad Street, pleading at each establishment for the loan of a pistol. When asked why he needed a weapon, he would say, "I want to kill some s– of a b— — in this town." By evening, he had convinced someone to pilfer a gun for him, and this left but one more task to perform before he and Agnes departed town, a final act of vengeance. But worry over the planned shooting had made him extremely tense. Though he was adept with a rifle, he had never before in his life fired a pistol.[27]

Steeling himself for what lay ahead, he entered the dining room of the Hotel de Paris, where he knew Lucinda would be taking her evening meal. With the borrowed pistol concealed in his coat pocket, Vedder seated himself with Lucinda, officer Pat Corbett, and other guests gathered around the long table. The inn was noted for its authentic French cuisine: a five-course meal, highlighted by a main entree the Parisian owner called "goddam rosbif," and topped off with a cup of delicately brewed coffee laced with cognac. But as each vessel of soup, bouillabaisse, roast vegetables, and meat was set before him, Vedder discovered he was unable to eat. The owner asked him if he were ill, but Vedder did not answer.[28]

When Lucinda had finished her meal, she returned to the Spring Street house. There she proceeded to do exactly what her husband had demanded, pack her possessions in her steamer trunk. Since it was a cold evening, she built a fire to take the chill off the house and then began giving the front room a general cleaning. As soon as laundry she had previously done had dried, she intended to do some mending, and lastly, pack her clean, mended belongings.

As she was dismantling the home where the three of them had lived for the past months, she felt "lonely and in trouble" and still had misgivings about the divorce, but there was no turning back. John wanted to be free of her, and she had already paid her fare for the two A.M. stage. She assumed that before that hour, John would surrender their daughter to authorities. Considering police officers' promise to guard her until the moment she and her daughter stepped onto the stage, it appeared she would be able to make the break from John with no further harm to her or her daughter.

When it commenced to grow dark, she lit a candle, placed it on the table, and continued her work. Her first visitor was the blacksmith, who reassured her that her husband had gone to retrieve Agnes and would be back within a few hours. After the blacksmith left, officer Corbett arrived, drew a chair up to the stove, and chatted with Lucinda as she removed the curtains from the windows and patched them. The officer was there to guard her, and in addition, he had promised to help carry her trunk to the stage depot in the National Hotel lobby.

By eleven o'clock, Lucinda was still mending and packing, and Corbett was still waiting. Meanwhile, Vedder had arrived at the Van Young ranch on a hired horse, but rather than coming to collect his daughter, his mission had been to warn Van Young not to release Agnes to anyone except him. Van Young later testified that John "appeared to be afraid that Plummer and Mrs. Vedder would get the child." Vedder also stated that he was going back to Nevada City to sleep at the Spring Street house. "I was fearful of trouble," Van Young said, "and tried to persuade Vedder from going back to Nevada and begged him to stay at my house." But replying that "he had no fear," John mounted the horse and galloped toward town.

After returning the hired animal to the stable, Vedder went immediately to the National Hotel lobby and there verified that Lucinda's name was on the list for the two A.M. stage departure. All was now in readiness for the final phase of his plan, the phase for which he would need a pistol. He proceeded in the direction of his home.[29]

It was nearing midnight when Marshal Plummer dropped by the Spring Street house to help Corbett with the trunk, but he discovered Lucinda still at the house. Sitting in a chair on the opposite side of the stove from Corbett, she was engrossed in her mending. Since Mrs. Vedder was not ready yet, officer Corbett announced, he would leave, take care of some business, and return in a few minutes to help carry the trunk to the depot. Settling into the chair Corbett had vacated, Plummer took up the vigil, but knowing that Vedder still slept at the house, he felt uneasy about the delay.

In light of Lucinda's fear of her husband, the Marshal could not understand why she did not seem anxious to return to the Hotel de Paris. When he attempted to hurry her along by asking if "she had made up her mind to leave the fire," she answered that she "did not like to leave a fire." Plummer then leaned back in the chair, resting his head on one hand and placing the other hand over his eyes, and Lucinda continued sewing.

Apprehensive about the action he was determined to take, John Vedder left the National Hotel on Broad Street and approached Spring Street. His house was lit by a single candle and the front door stood open. Through the uncurtained windows, two occupants were visible: his wife was seated on one side of the stove and Marshal Plummer on the other. Instead of entering by the front door, Vedder skirted the house and walked into the dark alley running along Deer Creek.[30]

Within a few moments, Lucinda and Plummer heard the sound of rapid footsteps on the back stairway. Plummer started, straightened, and turned toward the back door just as John Vedder pushed it open and stepped over the board Lucinda had placed across the doorway to keep Agnes from falling downstairs. Vedder was holding a pistol in his hand, and he aimed it at Plummer. "Your time is come," he said and fired the gun. Rising to his feet as Vedder spoke, Plummer fired back several times, and Vedder, who had been struck twice, hastened back down the stairs. Plummer, who had not been struck by Vedder's shots, then left by the front door and walked to the street, where he commenced blowing the police whistle.

Realizing her husband had been shot, Lucinda grabbed the candle from the table and hastened down the back stairs. She found John lying a few feet from the last step. "He was alive," she later testified, "and his eyes moved." Holding the candle to his face, she knelt beside him, noting that his breathing was very labored. "I laid my hand on his hand & on his forehead," she said, and "I think he knew me before he died."

Spectators who gathered at the scene that midnight reported that the wife of the deceased man was "crazy" with grief. Despite being in a state of shock, Lucinda had been present at the killing and therefore was obligated to be the chief witness at the trial.

When it came time to take the stand, the nineteen-year-old widow made an impressive witness. Though it was obvious she was still in a state of mourning, she handled her grief with restraint and dignity. During cross-examination, her answers showed a forthrightness that could prove disarming to her questioner. Her testimony revealed that even after signing the divorce papers, she had never given up hope of somehow saving the marriage to John. And during their period of separation, when his threats kept her in fear of her life, she was still determined to see that the bed he slept in was made up each day and that he was eating properly.[31]

In fact on the night Vedder was killed, Lucinda's reason for delaying so long at the house may have been that she wanted to be certain of seeing John for one final time before she left town. Her testimony about life with John, as well as her responses during cross-examination, are marked by a decency which contrasts to much of the court proceedings. An ambitious young prosecutor was eager to advance his own career by bringing down Plummer, a local celebrity who was not only the city manager and marshal, but also a prominent political figure who had once been nominated as a candidate for the state legislature. This prosecutor had no compunction about using unreliable witnesses to attempt to portray the Marshal and policemen who had been protecting Lucinda as lustful opportunists desirous of sexual favors.

The wife of the deceased, he portrayed as a "bad woman" who had been unfaithful to her husband and who wanted to be rid of him so she could pursue a man of higher social status. Though testimony of highly respected attorney Belden proved otherwise, the prosecutor called a series of witnesses who insinuated Lucinda had accepted money from Plummer to pay for the divorce, kept in her possession a daguerreotype of the Marshal, and wanted to marry him, all of which she staunchly denied on the stand. But when a witness revealed the secret of her alienation from her parents–that prior to her marriage to John, she had lived with another man–she did not deny the fact.

A twelve-man jury listened as male attorneys, both the prosecution and defense, exchanged wry quips with male witnesses. Even Lucinda's most innocent statements regarding her husband's death, such as expressing relief that John had not "lain and suffered," were distorted so as to make it appear she was glad her husband had died.

And just as Vedder had done when he was alive, the prosecutor trivialized the physical abuse Lucinda had experienced. In addition, her father-in-law, Vulcan Vedder, used the stand to blacken Lucinda's name as much as possible. He accused her of considering the Bible a mere "novel" (which she denied under oath) and not "caring what she did."

Even the blacksmith who had played the peacemaker role for the couple turned against Lucinda, testifying that prior to the trial he had advised Vulcan Vedder that "if the old man could get her to drink, he could get facts from her."

An attorney then asked the blacksmith if he had "ever been in a room naked" with Lucinda.

Though the blacksmith replied, "No," he did go on to add, "but I was always free with my jokes with her." The attorney wanted a sample of the jokes, but the blacksmith could not "remember their exact words."

While this same witness was on the stand, other indignities were aimed at the widow. "I told Vedder that I saw Plumer in the house," the blacksmith stated, and "he wanted to know the positions."

The attorney interrupted with, "And did you tell him that Plumer was setting in her lap?"

The answer repeated the affront, "No, I did not tell him that Plumer was setting in her lap."

But the ultimate insult was the response to the question, "Did you tell old Vedder that Plumer & Corbett murdered Vedder to get her [Lucinda] to a whore house?"

Again the blacksmith answered in the negative, but elaborated with, "Don't think they wanted her at all."[32]

After two trials, Henry Plummer was convicted of second-degree murder. By becoming involved in the attempt to protect Lucinda from her abusive husband, the young marshal earned himself a ten-year sentence in San Quentin.

Like Plummer, Lucinda had been forced to undergo two exhausting trials, but in addition, from the day Vulcan Vedder had arrived in Nevada City to bury his "unfortunate boy," she had been engaged in a struggle for custody of Agnes. Immediately after learning of his son's death, Vulcan Vedder had gone to the Van Young ranch, taken his granddaughter, and placed her in a home in Auburn, a town south of Nevada City. Lucinda obtained a court order instructing her father-in-law to return the child to her, but Vulcan then made an appearance before the judge, who ruled that Lucinda "had the right to keep the child unless Vulcan could prove that she had a bad character."

When Vulcan swore he could prove Lucinda an unfit mother, the judge promptly appointed the grandfather as Agnes's guardian. Using Agnes as a pawn, Vulcan was able to control his daughter-in-law with the threat of canceling her visitation rights. "If she behaved herself," Vulcan told Lucinda, she could see her daughter. But Vulcan's intentions seem far from honorable. He admitted under oath to sleeping at Lucinda's house, being "somewhat intimate with her," and telling her he "would add to her bitterness."

Only a few months after Plummer entered San Quentin, more than one hundred male officials of two counties sent a petition to the governor, proclaiming Plummer's innocence and condemning Lucinda as a temptress who had lured the officers into protecting her on that fateful Friday night in September. "Henry Plumer is a young man having an excellent character, and was elected marshall of the City of Nevada," the petition read, and "the fatal occurrence took place without entrap other than the female." In the eyes of the petitioners, the battered wife was "the cause of the tragedy."[33]

After receiving this petition, the governor pardoned Plummer. But as related previously, X. Beidler and other vigilantes who were not aware of the pardon believed a false rumor that the ex-marshal—whom Bannack miners later chose as their sheriff—had escaped from the California state prison, killing a guard in the process. Therefore, vigilantes reasoned, Sheriff Plummer was a fugitive from justice who needed to be lynched.

Thus the effects of the 1857 domestic tragedy in Nevada City were far-reaching, but Henry Plummer was not the only individual who was unable to overcome its stigma. Neither the widow nor the fatherless child was ever able to resume a normal life. After Lucinda attempted to reestablish a home in Sacramento, her troubles with Vulcan Vedder worsened. Desperate to recover her daughter, Lucinda decided to take matters into her own hands.

A Sacramento newspaper provided details of the ensuing melee: "Mrs. Vedder went to the house of her father-in-law on Sunday evening on a pretense of seeing her child, got possession of it and took it to the residence of a friend." When Vulcan raised the cry that a child had been kidnapped, "a crowd assembled and someone threatened to take the child by force and restore it to its grandfather." Police arrived on the scene, disbanded the crowd, and "both mother and child were taken to the station house where they remained over night."[34]

Though Vulcan and Lucinda eventually worked out an agreement that allowed mother and child to remain together–Vulcan admitting that Lucinda

had been "deeply wronged" and she stating that after their initial difficulty, her father-in-law was "kind" to her–the restored harmony had come
too late to save Agnes. Weakened by the stress of the chaotic days following her parents' separation and the additional trauma created by her father's
death, the frail child contracted scarlatina and succumbed to the disease.
Lucinda buried her daughter at the Sutter's Fort cemetery and tried to re-
build her own life. She did not succeed.

For the past five years, her world had consisted of nothing more than
caring for her husband and child, but now she found herself the sole remaining member of the family she had nourished. Over the course of the
painful months, she had gained a certain amount of insight. Though she
had never ceased to love the husband who had repeatedly inflicted abuse
upon her, after his death, she had gradually come to put their relationship
into a more enlightened perspective. For example, when Vulcan Vedder
testified she had told him she was sorry for alerting police to watch John so
he would not injure her, she insisted on retaking the stand to correct his
testimony. What she had said to her father-in-law, she explained, was not
that she was sorry she had sworn to the facts before the police officers as
she had, but that she "was sorry at the position we occupied."[35]

At Agnes's death, Lucinda became free from Vulcan Vedder's control,
but she was not free from the reputation accumulated during her five experiences with the male-dominated judicial system. The male quorums
who had felt qualified to sit in judgment of Lucinda while they questioned
her as though she were a "loose" woman, were hardly in a position to cast
stones. For example, one witness who testified against her at the trial operated a house of prostitution in Nevada City. There was no shortage of
clientele at his establishment, nor at the various other houses in town; in
fact, California forty-niner Alfred Barstow claimed that many brothels were
"wholly supported by married men."[36]

In addition to keeping houses of prostitution in business, Lucinda's
condemners habitually violated the anti-gambling law they themselves had
enacted. During their leisure hours, they placed bets at the monte and faro
tables or wagered on hour-long dogfights or other savage sports that provided a spectacle of ample "bloodletting." According to a contemporary
newspaper editor, among the citizens gambling and carousing in Nevada
City saloons until dawn were not only jurors and attorneys, but also judges.

As further reminder of the hypocrisy of Lucinda's accusers, these were
the same men who sent wayward boys to San Quentin to be "taught a
lesson," (the problem was their teachers were hardened adult convicts,)
the same men who saw no harm in allowing brothels to employ girls as
long as they were over the age of fourteen.[37]

During the two murder trials, the two custody suits, and the overnight
jailing for trying to recover her daughter, men had branded Lucinda as a
godless woman, an unfaithful wife, an unfit mother, and a kidnapper. In
turn, society treated her as such. And because two years of spousal battery

had already damaged her self-esteem, the damning portrait may have come to seem appropriate even to her, for within a year after Agnes's death, Lucinda became the "bad woman" that society believed she was.

Unlike Sarah Grannis, John Vedder's widow no longer had enough pride to care about the impression she made on census takers. When the 1860 enumerator arrived at the Sacramento residence of the male musician where she and two other women resided, Lucinda Bohall Vedder informed him she was twenty-three years old and her profession was "a lady of the night."[38]

Story of the First Woman Sentenced to Hang by the State of California: Emma LeDoux

Hanging women in early-day California was not unknown; prior to the Emma LeDoux case, popular tribunals in the Golden State had sentenced at least two women to die by the noose. Both of the condemned women admitted to having killed a man, but both considered their actions to have been self-defense. The better known of the two cases is the 1851 execution of a young woman known only as Juanita. One witness to the hanging described the executioners as an "excited mob" and the executed woman as a "friendless and unprotected foreigner," causing the *Sacramento Times & Transcript* to deplore the incident as "a blot upon the history of the state."[39]

Juanita, an attractive woman in her early twenties, resided in Downieville, a mining camp wedged into a small, mountain-lined basin at the junction of two forks of the Yuba River. Miners of the area were noted for their chivalry: when the first female entertainer arrived in camp, they carried both her and her piano up the dusty main street on their shoulders. It would seem that Juanita also would have qualified for gentlemanly treatment since she possessed most of the qualities miners respected. She was known to conduct herself with "a great deal of propriety," in disposition, she was "quiet" and "gentle," and she earned a living by taking in washing. However it was not in her favor that she was a native of Mazatlan, Mexico (the war with Mexico having ended only three years earlier), nor that Jose, her supposed husband, was a "flashy-dressing" gambler.[40]

A Downieville resident who witnessed Juanita's hanging (and later became a newspaper editor) prepared a detailed article on the event. He reported that following an all-day Fourth of July celebration–which included a parade, a band concert, a patriotic speech, and an ample amount of im-bibing–a group of miners in a state of "hilarious intoxication" were carous-ing about the camp's residential section, waking slumbering citizens, and inviting them to have a drink. As the revelers approached the clapboard shanty where Juanita lived, a waggish young Scot named Fred Cannon kicked the door with sufficient force to separate it from its "frail leather hinges." Intimidated by the drunken intruders, the Mexican couple made no complaint about the rude awakening nor the damage to their house.

Instead, they returned to sleep in their now-doorless home.[41]

The following morning, Cannon–a handsome blonde who was more than six feet tall and weighed over two hundred pounds–returned to the damaged home for purposes known only to him. Friends claimed he wished to pay for his reckless destruction, while other citizens believed that for some time he had had designs on the "very comely" lady, but had been repeatedly rejected. At any rate, the "herculean" miner rested both hands on Juanita's empty door frame, leaned inside, and in Spanish called her "a whore." In response, she "sprang out from a place of concealment and with a long sharp Bowie knife, stabbed him through the center of the breast bone and clear into the heart." The stream of blood that issued from the fatally wounded man's chest, the witness continued, flowed for "as much as ten feet."[42]

The trial was held on the same platform where the Fourth of July orator had delivered his patriotic excesses. Whatever respect Juanita had earned for her modesty and industriousness was not sufficient to guarantee her a fair hearing, and those few citizens who became "demonstrative" about the rights of the accused were promptly "driven out of the village in fear of their lives." Though the inflamed crowd bent on a hanging gave full attention to the prosecutor, when the defense attorney attempted to present his case, "he was kicked off the grandstand, driven across the river, and fled up the hill, leaving his hat and mule behind." The jury then rendered a guilty verdict, and a gallows was constructed on the A-frame of a bridge over the Yuba River.

At the appointed hour, "the prisoner and her few terrified friends came down the street in a melancholy little company." After bidding them farewell, Juanita calmly walked onto the prepared plank, smoothed her dress, twisted up her long hair, and then placed the noose around her own neck. At the sound of a pistol shot, men wielding axes chopped the cable supporting the plank, and the condemned woman fell, jolted at the end of the noosed rope, and then swung over the moving current. Later, Jose and friends took Juanita's body back to the shanty and tried to revive her. In his despair, Jose even ripped boards from the wall to increase air circulation, but all efforts were to no avail.[43]

There were opposing opinions about the Downieville execution. Several newspapers of the day condemned it as a lynching. And witness David Pierce Barstow, who later became an attorney, claimed that "no jury in the world, on any principle of self-defense or protection of life and property, would ever have convicted the woman, . . . who was roused from her sleep in the early morning by some ruffian pushing in her door." Barstow deemed the executioners guilty of "showing from first to last the utter irresponsibility of mobs." The hanging of Juanita, he concluded, "was murder." But the majority of Downieville residents disagreed; in their opinion, the execution of a man who had committed such a crime would have been condoned, and the only grounds for condemning the hanging was on the basis of sex.[44]

Thus the Juanita case required gold-camp citizenry to grapple with the controversial issue of equal rights for the sexes, including society's right to mete out equal punishment. A second and lesser-known case of a California miners' court condemning a woman to hang produced the same controversy. Though the woman's identity, the name of the camp, and the date have been purposely withheld by the newspaper correspondent, John David Borthwick, the trial had to occur in a California mining camp some time between 1851 and 1853.

"A woman was convicted of murder in one of the mining towns," the journalist reported in an article published in *Harper's Weekly*, "and though it was rumored that the deed was done in the heat of just provocation, still there was no proof at hand, and she was sentenced to death." On the day appointed for the execution, thousands of miners from surrounding diggings flocked to town to witness the hanging. From the first, proceedings did not unfold smoothly. An unexplained delay made the anxious audience restive, but when the explanation finally came, it was quite disconcerting. The criminal, authorities announced, had fainted.[45]

After her revival, the prisoner and her escorts began the procession toward the gallows, but as spectators noted with alarm, she seemed to be "in a half-conscious state." A "dead silence fell upon the crowd." Observing the men standing about him, Borthwick detected "compressed lips" and a "nervous moving of shoulders," that seemed to warn "that a volcano was working" beneath the apparent calm of the crowd. Authorities leading the convict continued to cut a path through the assembly, edging ever closer to the dangling noose. Gradually, "a murmur" rippled through the crowd, and then "a swarthy Missourian" raised the first voice in protest: "Dern my skin," he said, "but I believe that thar woman oughtn't to be hung."

Other voices insisted she had admitted guilt and the sentence was just. As opposing sides commenced to argue and "the scene began to grow more exciting," a man of prepossessing appearance drew his revolver and addressed the agitated miners in an authoritative tone: "I'll kill the first man that tries to put a rope 'round her neck," he stated.

One Cockney in the crowd remained unimpressed. "Why shouldn't she be 'ung?" he cried. As angry dissidents turned to rebuff him, they heard the report of a pistol and saw the Cockney's hat fly into the air. The ball had just grazed his hair, and the Cockney was unharmed, but he did not wait for further chastisement. Squeezing passageway through the mass of spectators, he quickly departed the scene. Meanwhile, the condemned woman had reached the gallows and stood "staring wildly around her." Sympathetic miners rushed to her, cleared an aisle before her, and shouted, "Run!" But she only "started, faltered, and looked affrighted and hesitatingly into the bearded faces around her." Moved by her pathetic appearance, even those who had formerly favored the hanging joined their voices in urging her to flee on the cleared path. "Taking to her heels," Borthwick reported, "the condemned glided away where none dared follow until she had made good her escape."

A statement by one participant in the affair summed up the feelings of the crowd who had forfeited their expectation of witnessing an execution: "She's a woman," the miner remarked, "and has suffered enough already." Borthwick agreed. "It was enough that she was a woman," he wrote. In the correspondent's opinion, "noble" frontier women daily devoted themselves to the "mission" of gentling a rough society and therefore "should not be executed." Borthwick was a perceptive, reliable reporter and a thoughtful, compassionate individual, and obviously his respect for women was more than superficial, but his assessment of this particular incident denies the legal equality of the sexes.[46]

In addition to Borthwick's unnamed woman freed at the gallows and Downieville's Juanita, Emma LeDoux had predecessors in other parts of the West. In 1863 a Texas jury listened to testimony for two days and then found Chipita Rodriguez guilty of using an axe to murder a horse trader named John Savage. On 13 November 1863, Texas authorities hanged Chipita on a mesquite tree.

But other women hanged in the West were victims of vigilance groups: in the summer of 1873, vigilantes of the Texas counties of Parker and Montague hanged Luduska Hill and her five daughters, the youngest age sixteen. And in the summer of 1889, Wyoming cattlemen hanged Ella Watson in the valley of the Sweetwater River.[47]

Though some of the above-mentioned hangings attracted considerable interest, no gallows decree for a female of the Old West so captivated the public as the death sentence given the fragile, thirty-three-year-old wife of an illiterate farmer from the mountains of Amador County, California. Unlike some of the women mentioned above, Emma LeDoux was granted a courtroom trial, and American and foreign presses' diligent coverage of the mystery-riddled story aroused interest around the globe. With their readers hungering for information, reporters feverishly scrambled to uncloud the mysteries surrounding the murder, to uncover the past secrets of both victim and defendant, and to churn out more and more articles and photographs to splash onto the front pages of a newspaper and continue inside through column after column.

After reading one such article, the district attorney directing the case sarcastically commented that the press appeared to be ahead of him in their investigation. Every day there was a startling new revelation in the newspapers. But because exhaustive investigative efforts only seemed to intensify interest, as well as deepen the mysteries of the murder of which the housewife was accused, the sheer amount of information being pumped out by the press could not satiate a curious public's thirst.[48]

As an example of the amount of press coverage this obscure country woman received after being charged with murdering her husband in a very spectacular manner, one has only to peruse the front page of the 27 March 1906 *San Francisco Chronicle*. At the time, Sarah Bernhardt was touring the Western portion of the United States and making news at each performance, but Emma LeDoux upstaged the celebrated actress. The *Chronicle's* front page contained one item about Bernhardt's performance in a tent in Dallas. "She gave her interpretation of 'Camille' as cleverly and realistically as if she were confronted by an audience of New Yorkers or Parisians," the Texas reporter dispatched, and over eight thousand worshipers (half of them standing) were in attendance at Bernhardt's first-ever tent appearance.

This modestly printed, unillustrated article, titled "Bernhardt In Tent In Texas," occupies only twenty-four lines, while the headlines scream, "Emma LeDoux Is Caught." Two articles–introduced by a two-column blow-up of Emma's face, and bearing larger headings than the Bernhardt article–are titled "Admits Identity When Arrested" and "Admits She Put The Body In A Trunk." These two articles spread across half the sheet and continue on to page two, where they are joined by a third LeDoux article, plus an enlarged snapshot of Emma shortly after arrest. Together, the three LeDoux articles fill the entire second sheet, occupying six columns topped with the headline "Tells Improbable Stories of the Crime."[49]

And this is not the only instance in which editors required "The Divine Sarah" to play a poor second fiddle to the meek mountain housewife, unwillingly propelled into the limelight by a domestic tragedy so bizarre that shock waves echoed round the world. Even the disastrous 1906 earthquake in San Francisco failed to eclipse the Emma LeDoux story for more than a few days.

In the exorbitant amount of publicity generated, this early California trial was the forerunner of the state's 1994 murder case involving O. J. and Nicole Simpson. In fact, the two highly publicized California trials had much in common. In both, the accused was charged with murdering an ex-spouse, a history of previous spousal battery existed, the method of killing was unimaginably horrible, it was difficult to believe the accused capable of committing such a brutal crime, the crime would have been difficult to carry out unaided, the accused claimed to be innocent, the extremely challenging case attracted leading attorneys of the day, defense attorneys professed a belief in the innocence of the accused, a steady stream of leaks flowed from investigators to press, legal questions threatened the admittance of key evidence, the coroner botched the autopsy, and excessive pretrial publicity jeopardized the defendant's chance for a fair trial.

From beginning to end, the murder case involving Emma LeDoux brought a series of shocking discoveries. A standard news headline became "New Sensation in LeDoux Case." First, came the discovery of the corpse of Emma's alleged victim at Stockton, a transportation and agricultural center located at the mouth of the San Joaquin River. At six o'clock in the evening of 24 March 1906, a Saturday, the baggage-master at the Southern Pacific depot entered the baggage room, closed the doors and windows, and built a roaring fire in the stove. It soon became very hot and stuffy in the small, enclosed space, but he was suffering from a cough and sniffles and thought that spending a few hours seated next to the hot stove might "break up the cold."[50]

Later in the evening, he had to move a large, roped trunk that had been left on the scales, and while rolling the heavy object to one side, he later related, he heard "a bumping in there just like a big chunk of meat." Suspecting that "some people going up in the country was taking a trunk load of meat up with them," he said, I "put my nose down to the key-hole . . . and there was a dead smell came out."

Quickly, the baggage-master called Stockton police, notifying them he thought "there was a dead person in the trunk." In response, Chief of Police Edward Baker, the district attorney, and a police captain hurried to the depot. At Chief Baker's order, his captain applied a chisel and hatchet to the trunk's lock and gradually pried it off. With others in the room hovering above him, the baggage-master related, the police captain "lifted the lid," and "I saw a man's leg fly up." The foot at the end of the extended leg was covered with a black stocking, but no shoe.[51]

The bloodstained interior of the trunk measured thirty-two inches long, eighteen inches wide, and nineteen inches high. But into this small space, newsmen were soon reporting, the corpse of a six-foot, two-hundred-pound man had been fitted "as neatly as a chicken fills an egg." The face and torso of the deceased were hidden from view by various articles of bloody clothing, which police removed one by one. "The body was lying on the back," Chief Baker noted, "bent at the hips," knees "cramped up towards the stomach," arms "bent up" at the elbow, and the head wedged into one corner, with the blood-covered face turned upwards. After recovering from his initial shock, Chief Baker searched the body for identification, but found none. Baker then removed the loose articles of clothing for evidence, stuffed them in a barley sack, and as he later testified at the trial, reclosed the trunk and called "the dead wagon."[52]

Stockton's morgue had only three slabs, but fortunately one was unoccupied. With policemen and district attorney looking on, two morgue attendants removed the body from the trunk, placed it on the vacant slab, and by degrees began straightening the limbs, unclenching the fists, and uncurling the cramped fingers. Since rigor mortis had not set in, these tasks were easily accomplished, and they could proceed to undress the dead man, removing the well-tailored vest and trousers, stiff collar, necktie, white shirt, stockings, and lastly the undershirt and drawers. After this, the attendants sponged away the streaks of blood that had issued from the nose and crusted about the forehead, scalp, cheeks, and neck.

Before them, Chief Baker observed, lay a handsome-faced, fine-figured, unclothed, and of more importance, unidentified man who appeared at his death to have been about thirty-two years of age and in excellent physical condition. His eyes were closed, as though he were merely sleeping, and he was a "tall man . . . not stout built, but rather a large man" with "mustache and dark hair." With the blood washed away, it was obvious to the Chief that the only signs of violence to the body were several faint bruises on the forehead. He would have to leave it to the doctors performing the autopsy to discover the cause of death; his responsibility would be to discover who this handsome young man was.[53]

Less than an hour after the discovery of the corpse, the autopsy commenced. Though it was within an hour of midnight, the session lured numerous spectators. Among those gathered about the artificially lit marble slab–and attempting to ignore the unpleasant odor emanating from the cadavers on the other two slabs–were two surgeons equipped with saw, knife, scissors, and a porcelain basin; Chief Baker and two of his officers; the county sheriff; the coroner; the district attorney and his male shorthand reporter; the undertaker and his two assistants; reporters from three Stockton newspapers; and an assortment of other citizens, such as the owner of a laundry, an engineer at the water-pumping station, and a saloon keeper, whose next-door establishment provided a background of music for the grisly operation about to take place. Some of the unofficial observers had gained admission with the flimsy excuse they might be able to identify the body, while others, such as the saloon keeper, had no excuse at all.[54]

With the rapt audience hanging on their every movement, doctors S. E. Latta and J. P. Hull first measured the body and then began an examination of its exterior, noting that the deceased was "a man in perfect physical manhood," his "skin was clear and healthy," and a very distinct vaccination scar marked his left shoulder. Latta raised both of the corpse's eyelids, revealing eyeballs which were "brown, dull, sunken in his head." The forehead and scalp were marked by "five contused wounds," each about "the size of a ten cent piece." An inspection of the teeth revealed that "the two third incisors were decayed, the left one broken off level with the gum." As doctors rolled the body onto its side, "a dark blood clot" dropped out of the left nostril and before they could preserve it, "spattered" onto the floor.[55]

Preliminaries out of the way, Latta and Hull donned their gloves and with a knife, made an incision beginning at the handsome young man's left ear, traversing the top of his head, and ending at his right ear. They then peeled back his scalp, stripping it down in back as far as his neck and over his face in front so they could examine muscles and tissue. Next, they "sawed around the skull just above the ears and removed the skull cap" so they could lift up the brain and probe its various sections. Finding no abnormalities, they severed the "mass" from the spinal cord, and set it aside in a basin.

Throughout this procedure, Chief Baker found he was not able "to pay much attention." The stocky, square-jawed, middle-aged police chief was a brusque professional, but he was viewing his first autopsy. In fact, he admitted, he had never before seen "a naked dead body." Rather than keeping his eyes on the carving which surgeons were performing in their now-bloody gloves, the Chief tried to keep busy with other duties, such as watching who was coming and going in the room or denying entrance to latecomers who had no "business" being present.[56]

As Latta made a swift incision from "the neck to the pubis," the Chief realized the doctors were about to expose "the entrails." Though he would later testify in court that he had attended the autopsy, in reality, he suddenly remembered he needed to get back to the police station and therefore hurried out of the room before the entrails came into view. The dissection proceeded without him, and after his departure, spectators came and went as they pleased.

After cutting out the breastbone, the doctors opened the lungs and heart, but again found both healthy. The lungs, however, did contain a "few pigmented spots" which indicated a previous "inhalation of dust," perhaps from "a quartz mine." As one doctor sliced into the stomach, both men quickly bent over the slit and inhaled deeply, but could detect only "the odor of death." "His body was still warm inside," Latta noted as he inserted his bloody gloves, "pretty nearly the normal heat of a body."[57]

One by one, the stomach, bowels, kidneys, pancreas, and spleen were examined, removed, declared "normal," and placed in the porcelain basin. The doctors found the stomach empty except for four teaspoonfuls of a "thin mucous" which they stored in a small jar. The upper bowel was also empty, but they discovered "a small amount of fecal matter" in the lower bowel. The bladder, however, proved to be "fully distended" with twenty ounces of "a clear straw colored urine," which they drew off with a catheter and retained in a bottle. By two A.M. of what was now Sunday, the autopsy was completed.[58]

When Chief Baker later discussed the autopsy findings with the two doctors, he was disconcerted by the small amount of information obtained from the three-hour examination. Latta and Hull estimated that "the man had been dead . . . eight or ten hours," but they could not "determine the cause of death." They had found no "signs of disease of any kind"; on the contrary, "all the vital organs of this dead man" appeared to be "in a normal, healthy condition."

They believed the blood that had stained the loose clothing, the corpse, and the inside of the trunk "had escaped before death" from a pinpoint hole inside one nostril. Both doctors were also certain the bruises, the "only marks of violence" on the body, had been "inflicted before death," but had not been "sufficient to cause death." The preserved organs and excretions would be sent to a chemist for analysis, of course, but in the meantime, Chief Baker had but three new clues to guide his investigation: the victim may have worked at a gold mine; while he was still alive, someone or something had struck him on the face and head; and he had still been alive when placed inside the trunk.[59]

Despite the police chief's consternation over the coroner's oral report, the press had a heyday with the information. With headlines such as "Victim Is Placed In Trunk Alive" or "Jammed Into A Trunk To Die," followed by lengthy articles describing how the victim "was drugged, then crushed into the trunk and suffocated," reporters informed the world of the outrage. As news of the bloodstained trunk, the corpse concealed within, and the puzzling autopsy findings were released, hundreds of curious Californians flocked to Stockton's main street and lined up on the sidewalk in front of the morgue to wait their turn to view the nameless victim. Though organless and brainless, he was neatly stitched back to his handsome self and once again clad in a tasteful suit.[60]

News stories of the unidentified victim soon brought Chief Baker a host of leads, some from as far away as Colorado and Kansas, and the Chief wasted no time and spared no expense in sending his detectives to pursue them. Even the silver-haired, slightly feeble county sheriff, W. F. Sibley, accompanied by the assistant district attorney, joined the investigation by venturing nearly to the Mexican border in search of a mysterious document in Bisbee, Arizona Territory.

Only two days after the discovery of the body, authorities had identified not only the victim, but also a murder suspect. So had the press. And those who lived too far away to visit the Stockton morgue could view the face of the corpse on the front page of their newspapers, along with a shot of the bloodstained trunk and, of course, a photo of the wanted woman, already being called "The Trunk murderess."

It was early Monday morning, 26 March 1906, when a communication arrived at the small town of Antioch, Contra Costa County, California for the constable to apprehend one Emma LeDoux, believed to be in the area. Since the constable was on a visit to a nearby town, his brother went to make the arrest. He had seen the picture in the paper, he related, and therefore "hunted all over" the little town until at the Arlington Hotel he discovered a stranger registered as Mrs. Jones. As soon as the constable's brother saw a slender, dark-haired woman sitting alone in the hotel parlor, he knew she was the person he wanted. Approaching her chair, he informed her she was under arrest. In a quiet, subdued voice, Emma LeDoux responded, "If you want me, I am here." That is all she said, the constable's brother reported.[61]

The press kept the public informed of every action taken in the ensuing case of The People of the State of California vs. Emma LeDoux, Indictment for Murder. Each time it became necessary to transport the prisoner to a different facility, officers found it nearly impossible to escort her through the mass of humanity that thronged to the site to catch a glimpse of the notorious killer. In the public mind, the small female prisoner had already been proven guilty. Since the day of her arrest, male reporters had depicted "the LeDoux woman" as "brazen in manner and apparently glorying in the attention she has attracted." She had "nerves of steel" and "face of brass," the press claimed, and was "flattered by her notoriety," "enjoyed" being "the whole show."[62]

On the other hand, her victim, who had been "Murdered By Woman He Thought Was His Wife," was a "quiet, industrious fellow" and "not a drinking man," but instead "one of the best workmen" his mine employer had ever seen, a talented individual who "could turn his hand at everything." Not surprisingly, this fine specimen of decent manhood had come from a family of prominent professionals, including one judge.[63]

In a courtroom presided over by a male judge who refused to allow testimony about the abuse and battery suffered by a wife who weighed about half as much as her husband, two male prosecutors bolstered by their male star witness, convinced an all-male jury that the female defendant, described by intimate acquaintances as "a good little woman" and "a lady always" had committed premeditated, cold-blooded murder. After the jury had convicted Emma LeDoux, the judge sentenced her to hang. She was, the press reminded, the first woman the state of California had ever sentenced to the gallows.[64]

The trial testimony, given six days a week from June 9 through June 20 of 1906, filled 1055 pages, but did not really resolve the issue of Emma's guilt or innocence. Though the press, the public, the jury, and subsequent historians have declared her guilty, Emma maintained her innocence up to the day of her death. Her defense counsel, James Fairall (one of the leading attorneys of his day) and Charles Crocker (who had known Emma since she was a child) believed her. Since the judge disallowed testimony about previous spousal battery in her marriage, the defense attorneys chose not to place Emma on the stand, and therefore she did not have the opportunity to tell her own story.

Twelve years after the sensational trial, Crocker wrote a letter stating that "Mrs. LeDoux's story has never been told by her to any one but myself" and summarizing the facts of her life as he knew them. In an attempt to make a fresh assessment of Emma's guilt or innocence and to determine the role spousal abuse played in her alleged crime, the following pages will relate Emma's side of the story, the story her jurors never heard. In the truest sense of the word, the story is a tragedy of the Western frontier.[65]

Emma Cole was born in 1872 on a small farm in the mountains of Amador County, California, only a few miles from the farm where she was living with her new husband at the time of her arrest for murdering her ex-husband. At Emma's birth, her mother was only sixteen years old, while her father was twice her mother's age. Emma was the couple's first child, and though her parents were not happy together, Mary (Emma's mother) was determined to preserve the marriage. After Emma's birth, the Coles had five more daughters and two sons, but following the birth of the eighth child, Cole abandoned Mary and later obtained a divorce.

Though he remained in the county, Cole took no interest in the family, leaving the struggle to support and rear eight children to his ailing young wife. Lines penned by poet Elinor Wylie aptly describe Mary's combat for survival on the limitedly productive farm: "I am, being woman, hard be-set;/ I live by squeezing from a stone/ The little nourishment I get." In Mary's uphill battle to feed and clothe her large family, her eldest child Emma, though scrawny for her age, became her mother's mainstay.[66]

The Coles lived their lives within the bounds of the small frame dwelling and barn, the scrubby, black-trunked trees, and the low, stone-fenced corrals rambling over the velvety-green pastures they claimed as their portion of the earth. Like many residents of the area, the Coles had never been outside the county. Their only contact with urban society was an occasional trip to Jackson, the nearest settlement.

Jackson was the seat of Amador County, a narrow, mountainous strip cutting across the northeastern portion of the state. The county was populated by deeply rooted farmers, impermanent gold miners from all parts of the world, loggers and sawmill workers, inhabitants of ten villages, and small pockets of decimated Indian tribes who had once ranged the area. These surviving natives were listed in the census by the surname "Indian" and first names that showed a contact with a variety of immigrating cultures: Pedro, Mahala,Yellow Jacket, Crying Mother, Tar Face, Old Clothes, Captain Powell, Joe, Mary, Sallie, Muchacha, and–in camp number ten–a seventy-year-old male called simply Old Indian. These natives were the curiosity of the county. And since they held no regular jobs, one census taker listed their occupation as "bummers." During Borthwick's tour of the California's mines, he had been fascinated by these "peaceable" but "degraded" tribal remnants, describing how they wandered listlessly about the outskirts of mining settlements, "begging for bread, meat, or old clothes" and dressing "very fantastically," such as donning a miner's discarded suit coat inside-out, tying a pair of trousers around the waist like a sash, or covering the head with slouch hat stacked upon slouch hat.[67] A second curiosity of Emma Cole's native county were the Chinese immigrants, drawn to America by the Gold rush, but segregated from other gold seekers into either rural camps or village ghettos. Most worked as miners, laborers, cooks, or storekeepers, but one openly admitted to census takers that his profession was "an opium dealer." In order to capture their way of life, Borthwick visited several Chinese camps, finding them "wonderfully clean" and their inhabitants "industrious." As the correspondent's sketches show, the Chinese kept busy at "scratching" abandoned claims for gold missed by previous miners, "getting their heads shaved," "plaiting each other's pigtails," or squatting around "curious little black pots and dishes, from which they helped themselves with their chopsticks."[68]

Of the ten settlements in Amador County (Jackson, Ione, Volcano, Aquaduct, Pine Grove, Amador City, Sutter's Creek, Drayton, Fiddletown, and Plymouth), several had a Chinatown, but even with the addition of the oriental immigrants, there were no towns of more than 800 inhabitants, only supply centers supported mainly by employees of the Mother Lode mines.

CHINESE CAMP IN THE MINES

"CHINESE CAMP IN THE MINES," by John David Borthwick. *Courtesy History West Publshing Company*

Most notable of these gold mines were the huge Argonaut and Kennedy enterprises, whose shafts and drifts honeycombed the gold-rich ground to a depth of over five thousand feet and whose massive heaps of unsightly gray tailings spilled over a once-verdant countryside, marring its pristine beauty. The superintendent of the Kennedy mine lived in an Italianate mansion sprawled across one hillside which the Coles passed on their way to Jackson; it presented a marked contrast to their own humble abode. And even the wage-earning miners–who for a few dollars per day descended into the murky tunnels at the risk of their own lives–had more pocket money to spend on Jackson's narrow, curving main street than did the Coles.

The town offered a variety of services. There were butchers, barbers, shoemakers, saddlers, wheelwrights, blacksmiths, a dentist, doctor, express office, printing shop, brewery, several general stores, four hotels, thirteen saloons manned with professional gamblers, and a brothel which offered "fancy women" as young as seventeen. There were also several churches, a school, county hospital, courthouse, and jail. Beyond Main Street were scattered 154 dwelling houses, and 153 of them, the census reported, were inhabited by families of "whites." The one remaining house was occupied by a family of "free coloreds," the father working as a bootblack and two of his eight children working as servants.

Jackson's Chinatown had no dwelling houses; most of its residents lived in either Chinese-operated hotels or at their own business establishments, consisting of four stores and one barber shop. Of the thirty-eight residents of Chinatown, all were single males except for seven "fancy women," one of whom was only fourteen years old.[69]

The Coles' trips to Jackson, either to renew staples or visit a doctor or lawyer, were brief and infrequent. Earning a living on their mountain farm was a full-time job. The Spartan existence which Mary and her eight children led demanded an intimacy with nature. The family was dependent upon each hen who from her own body produced the eggs they ate for breakfast, each cow who shared the bounty intended for her own calf so growing human offspring could have milk and butter, each fig tree that dropped its sweet fruits for their desserts, each acre of soil that sprouted grass to feed the horses who pulled their plow, and each fallen tree that fueled the cook stove.

Thus Emma–whose life since early childhood had consisted of nurturing animals, plants, children, and a sickly mother–developed a respect for life in all its forms, a respect that caused her to feel tenderness for the farm animals, give them names, and lament the death of even one laying hen. And the loggers who felled timber on nearby hillsides were called "tree butchers." But of course the Coles were butchers as well. In order to sustain the family, it was at times necessary for Emma to sacrifice the life of a plump hen, a tom turkey, or a pet steer.[70]

Whenever the opportunity arose, both Mary and Emma supplemented their inadequate farm income by taking odd jobs away from home. Since both of them were known for their cleanliness, industriousness, and skill at handicrafts, they were frequently called upon to perform housecleaning, sewing, or nursing on neighboring farms. But because Mary was a semi-invalid, most of the burden for earning the living, whether on the farm or at temporary jobs away from home, fell upon Emma.

The undersized girl, however, displayed little discomfort from the load of housework and farm chores placed upon her shoulders. The isolated mountain setting, the partnership with her mother, and the constant contest with the farmland to extract nourishment was the only life she had ever known. And being the eldest child of an unhealthy mother, she was accustomed to assuming responsibility for younger brothers and sisters. In addition, to complain about one's lot was simply not the way of the mountain people, who stoically accepted their allotted fate and took pride in going about their daily labors with quiet dignity. As a city reporter noted, "They are a stolid folk and reticent back there in the mountains. They do not wear their heart on their sleeve, but suffer in silence."[71]

In spite of Emma's duties, Mary permitted her eldest daughter to attend the local school until age fourteen. Because of this limited education, combined with limited contact with the outside world, Emma was naive and unsophisticated. Still, she had such a quick mind that during her brief years in school, she was able to acquire enough learning to impress casual acquaintances in Jackson as being a college graduate; it was not till she resorted to some mountain idiom in her speech that she gave herself away as one of that "queer crowd" who scratched out a living on the hillside farms up beyond the ridge, those mountain folk regarded as the third oddity of the county, surpassed in their queerness only by the ghettos of "heathen Chinese" and the camps of "barbaric natives."[72]

Emma had done what she could to develop her mind, but her body remained small and rather childlike. Still, by the time she was fifteen, she was regarded as the belle of the community. Her rural neighbors considered her a "beauty." She had a delicately formed figure; long, thick, black hair; pale complexion; large, deep-blue eyes; and high cheekbones. (So she could maintain the pale complexion associated with genteel city ladies, she took special pains to protect her face from the sun's rays.) Her wardrobe was limited, but she planned it carefully and tastefully; and being a superior seamstress, she could always appear well dressed. Despite a natural reserve, she displayed cheerfulness and consideration for others, earning in the community a reputation for being "sympathetic" and "willing at all times" to help others.

But it was not just her looks and cheerful, sympathetic nature that enabled Emma to attract the handsomest young men of the area. She also possessed an inexplicable magnetism which drew them to her, and she in turn appeared to feel the same attraction for these good-looking admirers. Her great fondness for dancing–in fact she regretted nothing more than missing a community dance–provided her the opportunity to meet the young men who found her so attractive. When she was sixteen (the same age at which her mother had given birth to her), she fell in love with Charles Barrett, a youth from a neighboring farm, and accepted his proposal of marriage.[73] Since it was necessary for the newlyweds to reside on the Cole farm to assist Mary, in-law problems on both sides quickly developed. Despite Mary's devotion to her own children, she found it difficult to tolerate the faults of those outside the immediate family, and her objections to the marriage soon reached a critical stage. Charles Crocker, the kind lawyer who for years had guided Mary and Emma through legal problems resulting from their farm debts, summed up the situation. The marriage was a "happy union" between "two youngsters," he claimed, until their parents began to "whisper" about the "demerits" of the opposite partner. Though Mary did not approve of the marriage, because she was a devout Catholic neither did she approve of divorce. Nevertheless, Crocker continued, constant interference from in-laws made life so unbearable that the young people were eventually driven to conclude their relationship in "the divorce court."[74]

Following her divorce, Emma had a series of new admirers. Apparently she was the type of young woman who needed to be in love and had the habit of immediately replacing any lost suitor with some eager young man waiting in the wings. For several years she made no attempt to remarry, but instead dedicated herself exclusively to rearing her mother's

EMMA LEDOUX, the first woman sentenced to hang by the state of California, upstaged actress Sarah Bernhardt in 1906 newspapers. *Courtesy California State Library*

children. To help support them, she traveled to Jackson and obtained orders to sew dresses for the town ladies. But when the dressmaking income proved inadequate to rescue the farm from overdue debts, it became necessary for Mary, in order to keep a roof over their heads, to wed neighbor James Head, a widower with three sons of his own.

Mary's second marriage turned out to be nearly as disastrous as her first. Her new mate had one unadmirable trait in common with her ex-husband: both men expected Mary to earn the living. Community members regarded Head as "a ne'er-do-well," who would only add to Mary's "burden." But her religious beliefs, combined with her financial distress, left no choice but to accept the less-than-ideal relationship and move to the Head farm. Mary's own children, as well as the three Head boys, were now old enough to do the field work, and thus to her it seemed that the fifty acres of hay land and the small fig orchard perched on the slopes below Pine Ridge would provide an economic security her family had never before enjoyed.[75]

Management of the Head property fell to Mary and Emma, and gradually the eight Cole children came to accept the hillside farm as their home and the three Head brothers as their own siblings. In succeeding years, the Cole children formed a close friendship with the LeDoux children, who resided on the adjoining farm, often referring to the LeDouxs also as their "brothers and sisters." When Emma's younger sister Liddie reached her teens and became engaged to Louis LeDoux, it appeared the two families would soon be joined. In addition, Louis LeDoux's younger brother, named Peter Eugene but called Jean, frequently escorted Emma to community dances. It soon became common knowledge that Jean was completely "infatuated" with Emma, who was three years his senior. But for a variety of reasons, including Mary's disapproval, it was not certain that Emma returned Jean's feelings.[76]

Worry and toil were beginning to take their toll on the face of the former "beauty." Her look of innocent serenity was gradually being replaced by hardness, yet despite her fading beauty, men still found Emma attractive. And she was well aware of this continuing admiration; as one male observer expressed it, "She felt confident of her power over men." Due to the financial security offered by the Head farm, Mary concluded she should now allow her eldest daughter to have a life of her own, though certainly not with a man so unpromising as Jean LeDoux.

Mary respected her French-Canadian neighbors. Even though the father of the family could not read or write, he was a hard worker and a good provider. But for their third son, Jean, Mary felt a strong prejudice. As a child, he had suffered an illness which destroyed his hearing, so his parents had not sent him to school. Therefore Jean was not only deaf—and consequently unfairly regarded as uncommunicative and "not very bright"—but also completely illiterate. Other than his siblings, Emma seemed to be the only person in the community who recognized Jean's good traits. She was his "true friend," she assured him, and in response to her warmth and acceptance, he turned to her as the sole individual capable of rescuing him from the isolation of his world of silence. He begged her to marry him, and though she gave his proposal serious consideration, she realized the futility of entering into another marriage which Mary opposed.[77]

Mary already had a prospective husband in mind for Emma, a match based on economics rather than romance. A middle-aged gold miner, who had accumulated considerable savings but was suffering from a lung disease and therefore needed someone to care for him, had approached Mary to ask for her eldest daughter's hand in marriage. Mary was in favor of his proposal, and Emma was accustomed to obeying her mother's wishes, especially when they had a bearing on the entire family's future well-being. Thus when Mary urged the consumptive miner upon her as a husband, Emma agreed to marry William Williams.

In order to prolong his life, Williams took his doctor's advice to relocate to the warmer and drier climate of Arizona Territory. Near the town of Globe, he bought a small chicken farm for Emma to operate. The relocation to Arizona was Emma's first trip away from California and her first separation from her family, but apparently Mary's judgment in selecting Williams had not been bad, for during the months the couple spent together, they proved compatible. They made no friends and formed few acquaintances, but Emma was accustomed to an isolated setting and to days occupied from dawn till dusk with farm chores and nursing the sick. Though she undoubtedly missed the mother and siblings whose care had been her entire life for more than twenty years, the family's situation was less of a worry to her than ever before. One by one, the older girls were marrying, leaving Mary with fewer responsibilities.[78]

Evidently it was not difficult for Emma to transfer the concern she had always lavished upon her semi-invalid mother to a dying man who had preferred her, despite her faded beauty, to any other woman in Amador County. Nor would it be difficult for her to apply the value she had always placed upon each milk cow and laying hen to the flock of prize poultry now under her care. Since Williams's time was short, there were to be no children in the marriage, so Emma spent her time, she reported, "ministering" to her consumptive husband's "wants" and striving to improve egg production at the farm.

In gratitude for his wife's selflessness and efficiency, Williams kept up premiums on a $2,000 life insurance policy and also made out a will, naming her as the sole heir to the chicken farm. By the time he succumbed to his disease in 1901, Emma had developed sufficient feeling for her husband to enter a period of mourning. Alone and friendless in a strange territory, she fell into a state of depression, and it was at this time, her mentor Charles Crocker related, that an attractive young man named Albert Newton McVicar came into her life. He was the man who would abuse her, the man whose body Chief Baker would discover in the trunk, the man whose death would motivate a judge to sentence Emma to hang by the neck until dead.[79]

Albert McVicar had first appeared at Emma's door, she said, to offer her "words of comfort and sympathy" following her husband's death. And since she had not only a poultry farm to manage, but also $2,000 from the life insurance policy to invest, he later returned to offer financial advice. On his recommendation she purchased several mining claims, and during the counseling sessions McVicar developed a romantic interest in the young widow whom so many other men before him had considered magnetic.

Like Emma's other suitors, Albert McVicar was a handsome man, described as an example of "perfect physical manhood." He was 6' 1" tall and weighed over 180 pounds; his frame was "lean and muscular"; he had dark hair and eyes and sported a full, drooping moustache; and he was a spiffy dresser. But in addition to his good looks, he was what none of the men before him had been, or could ever hope to be. While the other men in her life had known "little of the ways of the world," Albert McVicar was, or so Emma believed, from "the city." His suaveness was obvious: the reserved manner; the expensive, dark suit with white collar and tie and the well-shined shoes; and his familiarity with city ways, such as sleeping at the best hotels and dining at elegant restaurants.[80]

During a courtship that lasted several months, Emma bared the secrets of her past life, including the teenage marriage and shameful divorce, a subject that apparently held a strange fascination for McVicar. And though he was known as a man who did not "do much talking," McVicar in turn told her about himself. He was the sixth child of a "well-to-do and highly respected" family and had been born in Canada in 1869 to parents who, though of Scotch descent, were like him, natives of Canada. He could not remember his native country, however, for while he was still an infant, the family had moved to a farm in Sedgwick County, Kansas, and there he was reared. Their farm was near Wichita, well-known as a Texas trail-herd terminus and a flourishing railroad hub that had developed into the third-largest settlement in the state.

On reaching manhood, McVicar took a job as a Wells-Fargo agent in Wichita and after working out of that office for several years, transferred to the Wells-Fargo agency in Cripple Creek, Colorado. Being from the cowtown of Wichita, notorious for its cowboy sprees, he was no stranger to violence; and in addition, in Cripple Creek it had once been necessary for his younger brother to kill a man in self-defense. To Emma, having been born in a foreign country and claiming a wicked city in far-off Kansas as a hometown (she may not have known that Wichita had a population of only 17,000) sounded exotic and very sophisticated.[81]

In addition, McVicar had a way of making Emma feel special. Though a man of few words, he would quietly toss off a casual statement to some male acquaintance, but within Emma's hearing, that left her glowing with pride. For example, a friend once chided McVicar for not having taken Emma to a ball on the previous evening. Coming to the defense of the man she loved, Emma replied that though she hated to miss the dance, she had no dress "fit" to wear. McVicar turned to her, eyed the slim form clad in a gray-silk, homemade dress, and then commented to his friend that if he had known Emma owned "the dress she had on," he certainly would have made it a point to escort her to the ball.

McVicar proposed to Emma and convinced her to sell the chicken farm and move to Bisbee, located in the southern part of the Territory not far from the Mexican border. On 1 September 1902, the couple traveled to Tombstone and obtained a marriage license. McVicar listed his age as thirty-three and his future bride's as twenty-five (probably what she had told him, though in reality she was almost thirty). The same day, the couple went to the home of a minister of The Christian Church in Bisbee (McVicar's choice, since Emma was Catholic) to be united in marriage. After a brief honeymoon in Mexico, the couple returned to Arizona, but once there, decided that because of McVicar's preference for urban life, they would move to San Francisco and with the proceeds from the chicken farm, open a small business.[82]

Emma, who was so much in love she was willing to do anything to keep "the city man" she had been fortunate enough to attract, attempted to adopt her husband's cosmopolitan ways: the train excursions, the drinking, the meals at international restaurants, or the relaxed oyster and beer suppers which "Al" so enjoyed. But in spite of her efforts, she seemed unable to shake the customs that had become ingrained during her years of mountain life. For one thing, she never lost her shyness; yet when a store clerk attempted to make a sale by feigning an interest in her, Emma mistook the salesmanlike gesture as an overture of friendship and began to blurt out to this perfect stranger some intimate detail of her personal life. Since she felt herself superior to no one, she regularly granted people who were serving her indiscriminate license. And she never succeeded in attaining any degree of comfort with modern contraptions that had been unavailable on the farm. If, for example, it became necessary for her to use a telephone while she was at some business establishment, she would first ask permission, but when it was granted, she would reply, "Perhaps the best way out of it, you telephone for me, I am not acquainted with the numbers." Even after months of exposure to life in a city of more than 340,000 population, Emma was still "mountain folk."[83]

Since neither Emma nor McVicar had ever operated a business, it is not surprising their small enterprise did not prosper. Nevertheless, McVicar made no effort to curtail his high style of living, and even more disturbing to Emma, when he had been drinking heavily–which was any time he had enough money to buy a flask of whiskey–he might become violent. Though separations between the couple occurred sporadically and Emma would temporarily stay with Daisy, a married sister who also lived in San Francisco, she was ashamed to reveal the nature of her problems to her family.

Each separation would eventually end in a reconciliation in which McVicar expressed his love for Emma and his desire to change his behavior. Each promise made, however, was soon broken, and eventually the inevitable occurred: the McVicars lost both their business and their home. Other than the Arizona mining claims, which were of questionable value, the couple found themselves penniless, and in addition, both were without employment.

Despite all of their troubles and despite the temporary anger Emma felt towards McVicar after he abused her, she was still in love with him and still willing to do whatever was necessary to keep him. Rather than seeking employment himself, he hit upon a quicker way of raising money. He would place Emma in a brothel. When she protested, he beat her into submission.[84]

Though her husband's scheme violated her own moral code, Emma had come to believe McVicar's judgment was superior to hers. Growing up as a member of a minority group considered peculiar in Amador County had done little for her self-esteem. Thus just as she had provided for her mother's family for so many years, Emma now felt obligated to embark on a life of degradation in order to provide for the man she loved. As attorney Crocker expressed it, "She cared so much for him that she prostituted her body for his gain." And though McVicar debased himself by being willing to live "upon money earned by her in that capacity," she continued to love him. Fortunately for her, this unsavory period of her marriage was short-lived. As usual, her husband was determined to live beyond their means, and one night when she tried to hold back sufficient funds for their living expenses, he severely beat her. After he had inflicted "violence upon her body," Emma later told her attorney friend, McVicar "appropriated everything in the way of money that she had" and "deserted her."

For the time being, Emma's love for her husband had turned to hatred. She now regarded his supposedly refined tastes as nothing more than "riotous living." He had not only gone through her entire fortune–one she was not likely to ever again accumulate–but in the process had also irreparably disgraced her. This shameful secret she had managed to conceal from her family, but she had a second secret she could no longer continue to hide. During the stressful months of prostitution, she had for the first time in her life conceived a child. After spending years caring for someone else's children, she had been robbed of the right to enjoy her own firstborn. At some future day when she would look into the infant's face, she would be tormented by a suspicion the babe in her arms was the seed of one of the men who had defiled her. Instead of a joy, the child would be a sorrow, a reminder of a past she wished to forget.[85]

Emma had no desire to punish the husband who had brought so much grief into her life, but in accordance with her longstanding weakness (a need to have a potential mate available at all times), she felt driven to replace the man who had deserted her. Since she was among strangers, was no longer beautiful, and was in addition pregnant, her choice of men was limited. But there was one man who over the years had been unable to forget her. Though he could not write himself, Jean LeDoux had sent Emma letters which he had dictated to a younger brother, letters expressing a continuing love for her and a loneliness without her.

Emma responded to Jean's letters and his brother read them to him, but if the brothers were at all perceptive, they must have been troubled by the message Emma seemed to be conveying. Though she wrote that she loved Jean and was always careful to say nothing that might hurt him, she provided broad hints the love she felt for him involved no passion. One letter, for instance, stated, "You have no truer friend in all this world than I am to you, and nobody would do more for you. I am always glad to see you." Another letter opened with to "My old sweetheart," but closed with "Ever your sweetheart and *sister* Emma." And in a third letter, in which she mentioned that at the present time they could not be together, she also wrote, "Glad to hear from my dear boy" and "sorry you were disappointed in not hearing from me," going on to admonish him to take care of himself and "be a good boy." But even if Jean realized Emma felt no passion for him, he had no way of knowing it was because she reserved such feelings only for the husband who had abandoned her.[86]

By the time Emma gave birth to twin boys in the fall of 1903, she had received a letter from McVicar, informing her he had obtained a divorce. Ignorant of legal matters–which attorney Charles Crocker had always handled for her–she did not question the fact that a court had granted the divorce without serving her any papers. Her main concern was the pain she was feeling over the loss of the man she still loved. Hopeful of winning him back some day, she tried to keep in contact with him, writing to him in Arizona, where he had gone to sell their mining claims, and even sending him gifts, such as an expensive leather suitcase he could pack should he choose to return. But McVicar did not choose to return, nor to answer her letters, and therefore Emma was free–or so she believed–to resume a relationship with Jean. From the time Emma and Jean had been sweethearts, he had remained her closest friend. Of course the former drawbacks to their marriage persisted: the platonic nature of her love for him, his poverty and unpromising future, and Mary's disapproval.

In addition, two new drawbacks had arisen. The first drawback was Emma now had two children whom Jean might not want. Second, at the San Francisco rooming house where she had remained after McVicar's departure, she had met a new friend, one who because of his occupation was more promising than Jean. Joe Healey (who would later become the key witness against Emma at her trial) operated a plumbing business with his father, earning sufficient money to conduct an impressive courtship. But after her bitter experiences with McVicar, Emma was leery of becoming involved with another man from the city. "I was foolish once," she wrote Jean, "but not any more." This time, she continued, "a city guy" will not "get any strings on me." Nevertheless, Healey continued to pursue her, and Emma continued to write Jean that she would feel "better"being with him than "the fellow" she was seeing.[87]

Emma's dilemma in choosing a man to replace a husband she still loved continued on into the year 1904. However her own pressing problems in selecting a satisfactory mate and providing for the twins did not cause her to abdicate her position as head of the former Cole family. When in February she received news that James Head had died and Mary was in financial distress, Emma immediately moved back to the Pine Ridge farm and once again assumed control. Three months later, her sister Daisy gave birth to a second child, and Emma had to return to San Francisco to care for the mother, the infant, and the older child, Harry, as well as to keep house for her brother-in-law. "Daisy is fine, considering," Emma wrote Jean, "but not able hardly to wait on herself at all. I am kept quite busy with that naughty little Harry. Oh! He is a bad one sure. When I told him uncle Jean wanted him to come up and go riding on the mowing machine and drive Jerry he said auntie lets you and Harry go up and see uncle Jean this afternoon. Most everything with him is this afternoon."[88]

When Daisy had regained her strength, Emma returned to Pine Ridge, which she now considered her permanent home. Though she had tried to adopt city ways to please McVicar, she was gradually coming to realize she preferred the rural life and culture. Rather than being ashamed of her mountain heritage, she now took pride in it, and while shopping in town would proudly inform the clerks waiting on her that she was "the head of a ranch."

After Emma's second departure from San Francisco, she and Joe Healey continued their relationship by mail, and in April, he followed her to the farm, spent a week installing plumbing in Mary's house, presented Emma with a diamond engagement ring, loaned her one hundred dollars so Mary would not have to sell the cattle in order to save the farm, and suggested a wedding date of April of the following year. Despite Healey's show of generosity and his declaration of intentions, he was forced to return to San Francisco alone. Emma remained at the farm, wore Healey's engagement ring, and wrote him faithfully, but it was neighbor Jean LeDoux she was seeing daily, and as Mary so astutely observed, it was Albert McVicar that Emma "always was talking about."[89]

Only three months after Joe Healey went back to the city, Albert McVicar returned to California and took work as a carpenter at the Rawhide gold mine near Jamestown, about forty miles southeast of Jackson. Emma, who was still keeping track of her supposed ex-husband as best she could, sent him a letter at the mine. This time he responded, thus initiating a correspondence that continued to the end of 1904. Then early in 1905, McVicar stopped writing. As far as Emma's plans were concerned, his timing could not have been worse. Her scheduled wedding to Joe Healey was but two months away, and she did not want to remarry if there was a chance for reconciliation with McVicar. Without revealing her purpose to her family, Emma rode to Sutter's Creek–where the drug store offered a telegraph ser-vice–and handed the druggist a note, requesting him to send it to A. N. McVicar in Jamestown. The message, the druggist noted, read, "What is matter? I have had no mail."

McVicar did not respond to the telegram, but Emma continued to wait as long as she could before proceeding with her wedding plans. When it was only six days before the ceremony and she still had not heard from McVicar, she took the train to San Francisco to be married. But on her arrival, Healey greeted her with the surprising news he was breaking off the engagement. His mother, he explained, had received an anonymous letter informing her the woman who was to become her daughter-in-law within a few days had once been "a common woman of the street." He agreed with his mother, Healey said, that Emma "was not a fit woman" for him to marry.

Her past with McVicar had caught up with Emma, preventing her from entering into a respectable marriage. Graciously, she accepted Healey's decision and returned to Amador County. As soon as she had departed, Healey sent her a letter, insisting she return the ring and also repay the one hundred dollars he had loaned her. He needed the ring immediately, he wrote, so he could prove to his mother that he had given up Emma and "would never have anything to do with her again."[90]

When Emma responded to Healey's letter, she promised to return the ring in person at some future date, but explained that for the time being she had no way to repay the money. Because of illness, she had not been able to practice her dressmaking trade for some time. Actually, she had not been in good health since the birth of her twins, and after suffering aban-donments from two men within a period of two months, she took to her bed. By July, Mary realized her daughter was worsening rather than im-proving and summoned medical help. The doctor who examined Emma stated her condition was so severe there was little hope of saving her.

Though Emma was too ill to make any final requests, Mary correctly surmised that in her final days Emma would want to see McVicar. When Mary proposed writing him, Emma replied, "Oh, I don't care," and Mary immediately had a letter delivered to the Rawhide mine, informing her former son-in-law that Emma "was very low, if he wanted to see her he better come." By the following day, McVicar was at the Head farm. It was the first time Mary had met McVicar, but under the circumstances, they had little time for conversation. He did, however, attempt to explain away the divorce to Mary, saying the couple "had a little trouble in San Fran-cisco, and she didn't go back to him."

As Mary observed McVicar hovering at Emma's bedside, she concluded "he seemed to think quite a good deal of her." Being a mother who found it difficult to accept the fact that for a second time her daughter had gone against her religious upbringing by obtaining a divorce, Mary watched how Emma and McVicar behaved when together, and in spite of their claim to be divorced, had the comforting impression that in actuality, they were still husband and wife.[91]

During McVicar's stay, Emma slowly began to recover. However she was suffering from a condition the doctor described as "retroversion, or an abnormal position of the womb which by pressure on certain nerves and by pulling on the structures which hold the womb in place cause this continuous dull pain." Even when she regained enough strength to be up and around, the doctor explained, the preexisting condition, and therefore the pain, would persist.

To allow her to get some sleep, the doctor provided her with morphine tablets, but left instructions "not to use them unless absolutely necessary." What the doctor did not realize was that Emma was already dependent upon the drug. As Mary later explained, her daughter had been taking morphine for four or five years: "She was sick and was taking it, and after that she has taken it whenever she felt bad. . . . We have always had it in the house, more or less, and she has always had it." This availability of morphine would prove to be Emma's undoing, as well as the undoing of the concerned man keeping the vigil at her bedside.[92]

As soon as Emma was lucid enough to hold a rational conversation, McVicar commenced begging her "to come back to him." When she declined to give her promise, he turned to Mary. "I wish you would coax her to come back to me," he said, "I will marry her and I will treat her right."

But Mary was hesitant to become involved. "Well, I don't know," she answered, "I don't like to talk to her."

For the time being, McVicar dropped the subject, but as he was preparing to return to the mine, he again broached the matter. "Mother, I wish you would coax Emma to come back to me," he repeated. "If she don't come back to me," he went on, "my life isn't worth living."

Moved by the sincerity in his voice, Mary replied, "Albert, I will do the best I can."[93]

After McVicar had gone, Mary relayed his message to Emma. Though her mother could not grasp the full significance of the promise "to treat her right" if she returned to him, Emma certainly could. They were the precise words she had been wanting to hear from him for three years. But when she wrote to tell him so, McVicar did not reply to her letter.

As in the case of the planned marriage to Healey, Emma was again under pressure to obtain a prompt answer from McVicar. Her one remaining male friend, Jean LeDoux, was growing weary of waiting, and with good cause. He had already waited for Emma for seven years, and throughout that period, watched her choose one man after another in preference to him. For the past two years, Jean had become impatient, hinting he might marry someone else, a girl who was more interested in him. By a strange coincidence, or so Jean claimed, the other girl who was willing to marry him without delay also happened to be named Emma. A more suspicious person might have been doubtful of this coincidence, but not Emma Cole Barrett Williams McVicar, as evidenced by a letter she sent Jean. "I will not be able to come up next Saturday for the picnic," she wrote, "and how I would like to of come up for Flemings Dance Saturday night for I am afraid you will make love to the other Emma and I will lose you."[94]

It also appeared she was losing McVicar. It had now been a month since he left the farm and returned to the Rawhide mine, and Emma had not received a single letter from the man who had promised to remarry her and treat her right. On August 24, she again hastened to Sutter's Creek drug store and handed the druggist a note to be sent to A. N. McVicar at Jamestown. The message was nearly identical to the telegram she had sent him in February: "What is the matter? No mail. E." And though telegraph records showed McVicar did receive the message, he reacted in the identical manner as he had in February, that is he did not even bother to respond to Emma's urgent plea.

This time, however, Emma would not wait so long for a return telegram, or perhaps it was Jean who would wait no longer. At any rate, in light of her fear of being without a man in her life, Emma's reaction was true to form; on 26 August 1905–after waiting only two days for a response from McVicar–she and Jean secretly traveled out of Amador County, across Sacramento County, and into Yolo County. There, in the county seat of Woodland, they appeared at the county clerk's office. Nearly a year later, the clerk could still recall the unusual visit.

"I was busy in the office and a gentleman and lady came in and I stepped up to the counter and asked them what they would like," the clerk related. "She said they wanted a marriage license; she done all the talking." When the clerk opened his register and asked for name, age, nativity, and residence, he noted that again "she" answered, providing all the data requested (and unbeknownst to the clerk, deducting six years from her own age so it would appear she was three years younger than Jean, rather than three years older). After recording the information Emma had provided for both parties, the clerk offered a pen and asked them to sign their names. "He cannot sign," Emma volunteered, indicating toward Jean. The clerk then instructed Emma to sign, but allowed the thirty-year-old illiterate to make "his mark," which the clerk and Emma witnessed. After the signing, Emma inquired where they might find "a man to marry them" and the clerk gave directions to a justice of the peace.[95]

The Woodland justice of the peace also remembered the couple entering his office. "I recognized of course the way they came in what was up," he recalled. Jean, whom he described as "a dark complexioned man, dark moustache and hair," and "rather a striking man in some respect," spoke no greeting, but instead held out a marriage license while Emma stated, "We wish to be married." With no other preliminaries, the justice proceeded with "the full ceremony," then pronounced them "husband and wife" and congratulated the couple. "I have a formula there which I always go through," the justice explained, "I don't think I vary at all without they might want to have a ring." But Emma and Jean had presented no ring, so no variation was necessary.

After the standard ringless ceremony, the justice certified there was "no legal impediment to the marriage" and filed the document with the recorder. Meanwhile, the apparently happy newlyweds departed for the LeDoux farm in Amador County, unaware they were leaving behind in Yolo County a document which would later be used against Emma, legal evidence she was guilty of bigamy.[96]

Because of Mary's opposition to the marriage, Emma and Jean lived at the LeDoux farm for the first month. But when it became obvious the Head farm would be lost through debt if Emma did not reassume control, Mary asked her daughter, new son-in-law, and twin grandsons to move in with her, and they did. Though Jean carried out his agreement to rent and farm Mary's fifty acres, she was critical of him, and it was true that he could be, or at least appear to be, sullen and that he occasionally drank too much.

The drinking problem had existed since Jean was a youth. In a quite tactful manner, Emma had once brought the problem to Jean's attention in a letter: "I feel it my duty to write you a few lines," she began. "My dear, you are mistaken if you thought I was mad at you last night. . . . Of course I knew you were drinking, but my dear, I never said a word about it to you, . . . and you had no right to go home in any such way as you did, and not come in and say good bye to me." But despite his discourteous behavior of the previous night, she added, "I am not mad at you. No, I could not get mad." Though Emma may not have become angry when Jean drank too much, Mary did. In fact Mary found his behavior so intolerable she rose from her sick bed, left the farm, and took a job as a home nurse.[97]

Later, Emma was able to restore peace between her husband and mother, and Mary returned to the farm. As they settled into a routine–Emma doing the housework and soliciting dressmaking, Jean farming and also hiring out as a teamster–it seemed that at last Emma had established a stable home for her mother and her sons, who were now almost two years old. But once again, McVicar intervened in her life. Nearly three months after receiving Emma's telegram, he finally decided to respond. Unaware she was now wed to another man, McVicar suggested a brief reunion so the former marriage partners could become reacquainted. He had asked for a nine-day vacation from the mine, he explained in his letter, and would like Emma to join him at Stockton. The meeting place would require a three-hour train trip for each of them, and they could spend the holiday together, staying at hotels and dining in restaurants.

Emma–now thirty-three years old, drab in appearance, and enervated by years of hardship–had an agonizing decision to make. She still loved McVicar, but after previous experiences was afraid of placing trust in him. In addition, she would not want to jeopardize the security of her sons and

Mary, nor to hurt Jean, merely to satisfy her own romantic yearnings. She had assured Jean a city man would never again get strings on her, but in reality she had never been able to sever the emotional ties binding her to McVicar. On receiving his invitation, she was as vulnerable as a moth fluttering in the glow of a candle flame. Against all odds, she held out hope the fire that had singed her on other occasions would not ignite her powdery wings this time. She decided to spend the holiday with McVicar.[98]

The meeting was kept secret from her family, and she returned from Stockton as though nothing had happened. But the Christmas holidays presented a strong contrast between the family gathering spent at the farm and the romantic tryst in Stockton. Meanwhile, her seeming reluctance to reunite with McVicar made it appear to him she had become less susceptible to his charms. He now became prompt with his letters, pressing her to return to him and live at the Rawhide mine. For three months, she resisted the urge to join him, delaying as long as possible so she could have time to consider such a weighty decision.

Then in early March, an ultimatum from McVicar arrived. It was "now or never," he warned her in a letter. Just as the threat had previously worked for Jean LeDoux, it now worked for McVicar. Not wanting to take the chance of losing him, Emma immediately began making plans to leave. Displaying the caution of one skilled in the battle for survival, she confided in Mary, but made no revelations to Jean, her husband of only seven months. Such a confession would have been equivalent to burning a painfully constructed bridge behind her, a bridge that must be left standing for the sake of the economic security of her family. If McVicar proved to be what he now claimed, a sober, responsible worker who saved his pay rather than squandering it, she could then send for the twins. And it would be much easier to explain the situation to Jean in a letter written from a distant location.[99]

In preparation for her departure, Emma made arrangements for temporary care of her two sons, offered a prepared excuse to Jean, and then on Saturday, March 10, commenced packing. Since she herself owned no luggage as fine as the leather suitcase she had sent as a gift to McVicar, she placed her possessions in a large wicker basket: her best dress, the gray silk; a few items of underclothing; and a heart-shaped box filled with powders and cosmetics. And, Mary noticed, Emma also slipped eighty dollars—which represented her entire savings—into a small purse and dropped it into the basket with the clothing. After tying shawl straps around the basket to cover the top, she laid out her traveling outfit: a black-silk suit and green-silk, hand-embroidered blouse.

On Sunday, March 11, (and dates and accompanying actions are now important because it was only two weeks until McVicar would be discovered in the trunk), Emma left the farm. Since there was no railroad to Jackson, she had to depart from Martell's Station, about four miles distant. Three hours later, she arrived at the Southern Pacific depot in Stockton, where

McVicar was waiting for her. He was pleased to see her, informing her that since he now had "profitable employment," he wanted "to make amends to her" for his previous "wrong." First on their itinerary, he announced, would be a shopping spree at Breuner's furniture store. Then they would leave for the City, the local name for San Francisco.[100]

The trial reunion seemed to be getting off to a good start, much like a second honeymoon. On Monday morning, the couple spent nearly two hours at Breuner's picking out furnishings for the cottage they would occupy at the Rawhide mine: lace curtains, a couch, a stove, a cupboard, and several other items. The bill amounted to nearly two months' salary for McVicar, but he made a down payment, ordered the purchases shipped to him in care of the Jamestown railroad depot, and promised to come back later to make the final payment. Then the second-honeymooners were off to the City, where they first rented a hotel room and then went out for, as in the old days, a supper of shellfish and beer.

After they had returned to their hotel room that night, McVicar became ill, complaining to Emma that he had "cramps" and was "sick at the stomach." When he commenced "retching," she became alarmed and hurried downstairs to get help. As the doctor entered the room, he noted McVicar was still vomiting in the slop pail and Emma "seemed very much concerned and worried" about her husband. They had been to a restaurant, McVicar explained, and "the damned food disagreed with him."[101]

After diagnosing the case as "an acute attack of indigestion," the doctor gave the patient several glasses of water, causing him to vomit again and "throw off the indigestible substance . . . taken for his supper." The doctor then sent McVicar to bed, administered two quarter-grain doses of morphine, and left two more grains of morphine to be taken as "needed for pain." As he was leaving, Emma mentioned "she was in the habit of taking the drug" and "could not sleep without it," so the doctor also provided her with a small vial of morphine tablets.

When he called at the hotel room on Tuesday morning to check on his patient, the doctor found him "resting in bed." McVicar reported he was feeling "weak" and "bad," (in addition to his stomach ache, he suffered from chronic back pain and a toothache), but still he stated he was "much more comfortable" than on the previous night. The doctor gave him a bottle of tonic, as an aid in rebuilding his strength, and then left. The narcotic prescribed on the previous visit allowed McVicar to get some rest that night, and by Thursday he was feeling well enough to travel.[102]

On March 15, he and Emma took the train to Jamestown, as close as they could get to the Rawhide mine by railroad, and spent the night at the Willow Hotel on Main Street of the old section of town. Despite the one glitch in their holiday–McVicar's illness in San Francisco–he was still behaving like a honeymooner. When he arose before dawn on Friday morning so he could report to work at the Rawhide by the starting hour, he showed special consideration for Emma by not waking her. Instead, he allowed Emma to sleep in, arise at her leisure, and spend the rest of the morning exploring the little mining village located at the base of the Sierra Nevada range.

Because Jamestown was fifty-eight years old, it was already considered a historic settlement. The 1848 discovery of a seventy-five-pound gold nugget on a creek that once wound through the very street on which their hotel stood had resulted in an influx of thousands of gold seekers. Now, however, the town had been reduced to some 3,000 inhabitants, but several of the renowned gold-rush businesses, such as elegant hotels and colorful saloons, were still operating. In spite of the decrease in population, the town was still important as a mining supply center and also for being the home base of the Sierra Railroad, on which Emma and McVicar had arrived.[103]

It would not take long to tour the entire town, and before noon Emma was ready for a carriage ride to the mine. Her driver–who was delivering groceries to the Rawhide company store–took a narrow road that meandered west through hilly country for about half a mile, then entered a flat that stretched out in front of them for another half mile, and at last turned right and wound up one of the foothills at the western slope of the Sierra to reach the mine. Emma now had the opportunity to view the typical mining plant which was to be her new home. In addition to a hoisting works, stamp mill, and chlorination plant, there were also an office, school, barns, a blacksmith shop, a combined general store and post office equipped with a telephone, a hospital, a company boardinghouse with nineteen sleeping rooms, and scattered beyond the boarding house, sixteen small cottages which married miners could rent. One of these cottages, McVicar had promised her, had been reserved for them.[104]

On her arrival at Rawhide, Emma was greeted by disappointment. When they had reached Jamestown the previous night, they had learned their furniture had not yet arrived. But that problem the mine superintendent had remedied by offering the couple a vacant room at the hospital and suggesting they take meals at the company boardinghouse. The second problem, however, could not be resolved by the superintendent since he himself was the cause. He had decided against making needed repairs to their cottage; the couple would have to accept it in its present rundown condition.

Emma, who was known for her tidiness but also for her agreeableness, left the unheated hospital room where they would sleep, walked to the dirty, dilapidated rental unit, examined it, and declared she would "like to stay there." The smallness of the community (twenty-five men living at the boarding house, the families in the cottages, and the cook and her husband occupying one room of the hospital) presented no problem for Emma, nor did the mine's remote location. Its buildings occupied about sixty acres, a little larger than the Head farm, and she was not only accustomed to remoteness, but also accustomed to living without such amenities as a store within walking distance. What she was not used to was the constant pounding noises emanating from the stamp mill — the deafening, round-the-clock stomping of the ore, taking place only 200 feet from their room at the hospital. The remoteness at Pine Ridge had at least been blessed by a peaceful silence.[105]

But Emma was not a complainer; it had always been her way to adapt to whatever circumstances presented themselves, and life at Rawhide provided what were in her eyes the best circumstances possible, the opportunity to be with the man she loved. He seemed to feel the same way about her. Among the possessions he moved to their room at the hospital were the letters she had written him over the years, arranged in neat bundles, tied with cords, and stored in the leather suitcase she had sent him. The couple's pleasure in being together again was obvious to all who observed them: McVicar's former roommate at the boardinghouse noticed that Mac "seemed to be quite happy" in his wife's presence; the blacksmith observed that Mac "felt pleased when his wife came"; and the woman who cooked for the boardinghouse and lived in the hospital agreed that "everything was pleasant and agreeable" between the McVicars.[106]

At some point during their reunion, Emma learned it would not be necessary for them to remarry. McVicar had not divorced her, and they were still husband and wife. In light of her marriage to Jean, the news must have come as a shock, but on the other hand, it also facilitated the breakup with him. When the time was right, she would write Jean, explaining that their marriage in Woodland could not be considered legal because she had still been married to McVicar. Since she and Jean were–as they had always been–best friends, he would understand when she explained to him how much she loved McVicar. As she confided to the cook, "I like McVicar so much" I will "never marry again if he dies." For a woman who had previously found it essential to have a fiancé or husband within quick reach, a vow not to remarry in the event of McVicar's death was probably the strongest concession, and therefore the strongest proof of love, Emma could imagine.[107]

McVicar seemed proud of his devoted wife and spent much time after work introducing her to friends. He was well liked at the Rawhide; coworkers admired his quiet confidence and wry sense of humor, and the mine superintendent respected him as an excellent worker. McVicar had previously alerted Rawhide residents Emma was coming, informing them when she got there, they must come by the cottage for "a good feed." He did not reveal to his friends that he and Emma had wed some years before, but instead claimed he had recently married a "grass widow" (a divorced woman) from Jackson. Interestingly enough, he had married a true widow, the widow of the deceased miner William Williams, but revealing his fascination with Emma's teenage divorce, McVicar chose to acknowledge only her marriage to young Charles Barrett. Other than this one small deception regarding Emma's previous marriage to Williams, the inheritance upon

THE KENNEDY GOLD MINE, including superintendent's mansion, as seen through the spokes of a huge tailings wheel. *Photo by F. E. Boswell*

Williams's death, and the bad months in San Francisco, McVicar seemed to be a changed man. In fact in the three months before Emma arrived he had been living so frugally he had not drawn any pay.[108]

For the first time in her thirty-three years of life, Emma was ready to declare her emotional independence from Mary. Even during "the best part of her married life," she told a clerk who waited on her at the store, "she had been staying with her mother, who was an invalid." But at last she had reached the conclusion she had "done her duty towards her mother long enough, and she was going to house-keeping with her husband, Mr. McVicar." Her mother could get along nicely without her; after all, she still had one son at home and owned "a nice ranch." "Nice" in comparison to what? In comparison to the farm the Coles had lived on before Mary married James Head, of course, but Emma's impressed listener had no way of knowing the basis of comparison.[109]

Despite Emma's resolve to put her own life first, when a letter from Jackson arrived at the Rawhide post office, she read it and realized she was incapable of abandoning her mother. Jean had gotten drunk and lost his teaming job, the letter from Mary stated, and without the teaming income, Mary would surely lose the farm. There was no question in Emma's mind that she must return to Pine Ridge, the question was whether or not she could persuade McVicar to return with her.

Emma was an intelligent woman, not manipulative, but as her letters reveal, persuasive. Still, the fact that McVicar did not turn a deaf ear to her persuasive argument shows the sincerity of his resolve to be a good husband this time around. When he agreed to give up his three-dollars-per-day carpenter job at the Rawhide and "assume control of the ranch" he was entering the bargain with eyes wide open. He had spent five days at Pine Ridge while Emma was sick and thus was fully aware of the limitations of the dwelling house and farm. Nevertheless, he wanted to be with Emma and was therefore willing to attempt the difficult task of extracting a living from the fifty acres of hay pasture and small fig orchard. To supplement their income, he calculated, he could earn as much as four dollars a day by using Mary's two workhorse teams and wagons to haul tailings from the Kennedy or Argonaut mines. But he did have one misgiving, he joked to his former roommate: "He didn't like to go over there on account of his mother-in-law, . . . didn't like to get mixed up with a mother-in-law."[110]

To this joking remark, Emma good-naturedly answered that Al "had no reasons to think that way, because he didn't know her mother." She was in a good mood, Rawhide citizens noted, elated because McVicar had so readily agreed to give up his job and relocate to the farm. For her, it was the impossible dream come true: to bring the city man, whom she felt she could not do without, back to live with her family in her beloved mountain home. She had arrived at Rawhide on March 16, a Friday, and only three days later, McVicar gave the mine superintendent notice to quit. On March 21, he went to the office to draw the three-months' wages due him. After subtracting bills run up at the dining room and company store, the owner handed McVicar only twenty dollars in gold coin and a check for seventy dollars.

Dressed in suit and tie and carrying the gold coin in his pocket, McVicar rode into Jamestown to cash the check, and while in town, bought the constable a cigar and had a drink at the Commercial Saloon.[111]

During McVicar's absence, Emma packed her things in the wicker basket; and in the leather suitcase she had given him, she packed his belongings: a pair of work overalls and work boots, an undershirt, two white shirts, two suit coats and a vest, a pair of dress shoes, eight collars, a bundle of neckties, a handkerchief, a shaving mug and a brush, and a packet of photographs. Since the suitcase was full, she put her husband's razor and jackknife into her own basket. There was no room left for her letters which McVicar had saved, so bundle by bundle, she burned them in the hospital stove. Despite the sentimental value of the correspondence, it would not have been wise to take it back to the farm and have Mary decipher secrets of the disgraceful San Francisco episode. While Emma was burning the letters–an act which would later be used in the murder case brought against her, as well as carrying a razor and knife in her basket–she confessed to the cook she had not really wanted to live in the rental cottage because it was "too dirty."[112]

When McVicar returned from Jamestown that evening, some of his friends dropped by the hospital to bid the departing couple farewell. Emma put on the gray-silk dress, but since it was impossible to entertain their guests in the small room and since a storm was brewing outside, the celebrators walked to the porch of the company store. There they chatted and shared a bottle of whiskey, which soon had them feeling very convivial. After only one drink from the bottle, Emma became quite bubbly, expressing regret she had not kept her husband's promise of a "good feed," but inviting any of them who happened to visit the Jackson area to stop by their ranch for a chicken dinner.

And when McVicar's roommate requested him to write, Emma said that "if Al didn't write, she would." It was dark by the time the couple was ready to leave, so one friend presented a lantern to the guests of honor as a gift. McVicar fastened it to the carriage dashboard to light their way, and with a chorus of well-wishing in the background, he and Emma climbed into the carriage. Within the circle of dim, flickering light given off by the lantern, the husband and wife setting out together on the stormy night made a rather handsome couple: a tall, well-built man in a dark suit, seated next to his slender, neatly groomed wife, who was wearing a hat, an ankle-length gray coat over the gray-silk dress, and on her lap, holding the wicker basket that contained a razor and knife which were concealed from sight by the shawl straps.[113]

That night they went only as far as Jamestown and slept again at the Willow Hotel. Time was counting down fast for McVicar. The couple spent March 22 in Jamestown and the next morning had their last breakfast together at Suey Lee's Chinese restaurant on old town's main street and then caught the Sierra Railroad train. Emma was wearing her traveling outfit, the same embroidered green blouse and black skirt she had been wearing when McVicar met her at the Stockton depot and they had begun a new life together. McVicar was wearing his best suit, a white collar, and tie. Tucked into his vest pocket was a half-pint of whiskey. By the time they arrived at the Stockton depot, the flask would be empty.[114]

About noon, they stepped off the train into a downpour of rain and headed directly to the California Hotel on Main Street, the hotel where they had stayed previously. On the third floor, they settled into Room 97, the same room they had occupied on the first night of their reconciliation. This room in which McVicar was to die was 8' x 12', had a window with a view of Main Street, and was furnished with a bed, bureau, small table and chair, washstand–set with two glasses, a basin, pitcher, soap dish, and towels–one rocking chair, and a commode hiding a slop pail. Two toilets, one each for ladies and gentlemen, were located down the hall.[115]

Leaving Emma in the room, McVicar walked to the Kirk Saloon to replenish his depleted whiskey stock. Then he returned and commenced consuming the contents of his second half-pint flask that day. When that flask was empty, there would a third, and by evening, a fourth flask. In light of these expenditures on alcohol, his habit of not drawing his Rawhide pay, but instead letting it accumulate, took on new meaning. Evidently he had changed his former bad habits simply by keeping money out of his own hands. Unfortunately, his pockets were now filled with what was left of the twenty dollars in gold coin received at the Rawhide, plus the seventy-dollar check cashed in Jamestown. And he was coming dangerously close to his former behavior in San Francisco during the early months of their marriage.

Nevertheless, the couple remained cordial. For the noon meal, he took Emma to the Bon Ton restaurant, located directly across from Stockton's renowned, three-story courthouse. And in turn, she stopped at a drug store and used her own money to buy him an expensive tonic called "Beef, Iron and Wine," so he could continue the course the San Francisco doctor had prescribed for building up his health following the recent illness. They also went to Breuner's furniture store, where McVicar instructed a salesman that the furniture he had previously purchased should be shipped to Martell's Station instead of Jamestown. In the evening, he took Emma out for an oyster and beer supper.

After eating, they returned to the hotel, but instead of preparing to retire for the night, McVicar informed Emma she could stay in the room while he enjoyed a night on the town.[116]

For hours she waited up for him. It was some time after midnight when he finally returned to their room with a male companion. The two men had a bottle of whiskey with them and were discussing their night of gambling. McVicar then advised Emma he expected her to perform the same service for his companion which she had previously performed for his gentlemen friends in San Francisco. Whether or not she complied remains a secret, for in describing the fateful night, Emma picked up the story at the point where she returned from the hotel toilet and found McVicar vomiting into the slop pail. He had taken two doses of the "knockout drops" Emma used to fall asleep when she was in pain and had no morphine, and as a chaser, he had taken some morphine tablets.

"I went to him and asked him if he was sick," she later related, and he replied, "I can't get my breath." Then he slipped off his shoes, unbuttoned his shirt collar, loosened his tie, and sat down on the bed. "I took a paper and went to fan him," Emma said, but "he fell over sideways on the bed. . . . I got a glass of water and tried to give it to him, but he couldn't drink it, it all ran down his face." Leaving him as he had collapsed on the bed, Emma undressed and climbed in beside him.

When she awoke on the morning of March 24, a Saturday, the husband stretched out beside her was dead. Following the despicable incident of the previous night, he had seemed despondent, and she felt certain he had purposely overdosed on morphine to end his life. But she was afraid authorities would not believe her, but instead blame her for his death. It took her hours to decide what to do. Since she could not bear to be in the same room with him, she dressed in her traveling outfit and stood in the corridor pondering the dilemma. Other hotel guests noticed her there, standing at the top of the circular staircase and gazing down, so lost in meditation she hardly seemed aware of them. Because she was in a state of shock at McVicar's death–made even more horrible because it had been at his own hand and also because she might be blamed–she could not think clearly.[117]

Leaving the hotel, she paced the streets of Stockton. She later told police, "I walked all around and down to the wharf." At one point, she encountered a policeman. "He stopped and looked at me and I stopped and looked at him," but "he said nothing and I said nothing. I was going to tell him, but I thought if I would tell him, he would put me in the calaboose."[118]

At last Emma decided what she must do. A few days earlier at Rawhide, during the glow of the happy reunion, she had vowed her undying love for McVicar, but he had betrayed her once again. He had not changed as he had promised. She must accept that this time he was lost to her forever. The practicality learned from years of struggling to survive on the farms of Amador County reminded her that what remained of her life was only an obligation to two small sons and an invalid mother, all three of them completely dependent upon her. The four of them could not survive without Jean's help, so he must never know she had intended to bring McVicar back to the farm to replace him. She decided to return home and resume her former life, just as though nothing had happened. Rather than notifying authorities of McVicar's death, she would take the remains back to Pine Ridge for burial. First, it would be necessary to obtain some sort of inexpensive coffin for McVicar.

At a hardware store, she bought a large trunk, placed it next to the bed, opened its lid, and rolled McVicar into it. As the body fell, a guest across the hall heard a "loud thud." Since his limbs were still supple, she was able to fold him into the small space, close the lid, and fasten the lock. With McVicar secure in his makeshift coffin, she proceeded on to other tasks which must be completed before she returned to the country. Later, she must go to San Francisco and keep her long-delayed promise to return Joe Healey's engagement ring, but first she must pay the balance of the furniture bill owed at Breuner's, and while she was in town, make some purchases, such as a new corset and a skirt to replace the black-silk one, which had become soiled with mud during the rainstorm.[119]

Clerks who waited on her as she was doing her shopping noted that Emma "was very quiet" but did not seem "nervous in any way." And as usual, she provided a few snatches of information about her private life: "I don't feel like spending any more money than I have to," or "I must take the next train to the City," and "I must meet a party in San Francisco."[120]

When the salesman at the furniture store took her payment, he asked if Mr. McVicar would be coming in also, and she replied, "No, I don't think that he will."

After she had attended to all her business in town, she hired an express man and his assistant to take the trunk down the two flights of hotel stairs, heft it onto their two-horse wagon, and deliver it to the Southern Pacific depot. But Emma was, as one reporter bluntly put it, "so ignorant as to not know" that luggage must be checked before shipping, and when a Southern Pacific employee found the heavy, unticketed trunk aboard the train which would soon be leaving for Martell's Station, he rejected it. Later, another employee dumped the rejected trunk in the baggage room.[121]

Unaware she was leaving McVicar's body in the Southern Pacific baggage room rather on the train for Amador County, Emma boarded the San Francisco-bound train and on arrival at the City, took a room at the Royal Hotel for the night. She had telegraphed Joe Healey she was coming. He was anxious to retrieve his ring, and she felt obligated to fulfill her promise, but in addition, she was hoping Healey might offer her advice or assistance.

The following morning, a Sunday, he invited her to a restaurant, but was so angry over her delay in returning the ring and her inability to repay his one hundred dollars, he would not speak; instead, he sat across the table glaring at her.

"Talk to me," she begged, "I am in trouble."

But Healey was unsympathetic. As he expressed it, he had "found out she was a married woman again" (meaning he had somehow learned of her marriage to Jean). Therefore Healey felt no obligation to assist her. He did, however, pass the afternoon with her while she was waiting for a train. They went for a walk in the Presidio, and at a refreshment stand, he bought them "soda water and cracked crab."

Healey also accompanied her on the trolley ride to the ferry depot, and then on a boat across the bay to Point Richmond. While they were on the wharf, he paid a nickel to have her weighed, and as the scales spit out a ticket listing her weight as 102 pounds, it also included her fortune. As Emma scanned the message, she trembled. The fortune read, "Your secret is safe for the present."

The eighty dollars Emma had brought with her from the farm was nearly gone, and she had to ask Healey to lend her ten dollars so she could get home. Begrudgingly, he handed her a five-dollar gold piece and then walked her to the train depot. But after helping her aboard the passenger coach, he bid her good-bye by saying, "I hope never to see you again."[122]

During the train journey from Richmond, Emma revealed an appalling ignorance of the geography of her native state by asking the conductor when they would reach Sacramento. She was familiar with the capital because she and Jean had passed through it on their way to Woodland to be married. When the conductor informed her they would not go through Sacramento at all, she wanted to know "what was the largest town we struck between there and Stockton."[123]

At the next stop, which was Antioch, she left the train and took a hotel room for the night, registering as Mrs. Jones. In the morning, even before she had time to eat breakfast, the constable's brother came to arrest her.

"If you want me," she told him, "I am here."

The constable's brother delivered his prisoner to the city marshal, T. P. Shine, who after bidding her good morning, stated, "I don't like to incarcerate you."

"I don't want to go to jail," she pleaded, "don't be hard to me. I don't want to be put in jail."

Agreeing the Antioch jail was "unfit to put a woman in," Marshal Shine decided to question the prisoner as they strolled the streets of town and the planked walks of the wharf. When asked afterwards why he had not brought the suspect before the town magistrate, Shine replied, "Well, I will tell you, I was a greenhorn in the business, didn't know much about it."

But evidently he did know enough about the business to realize if you want to get a woman to talk, you ply her with alcohol. At some point in the interrogation of the female suspect, the officers provided her with a glass of whiskey, (reminiscent of the blacksmith's suggestion that Vulcan Vedder should give Lucinda a drink to get information from her). The whiskey, especially on an empty stomach, did make Emma talkative, and though she spilled out the entire story of McVicar's death, including the man who had come back to the hotel room with her husband, she insisted she "had done nothing wrong." Eventually, Shine took the prisoner before the Antioch justice of the peace.[124]

The discovery of the corpse in the trunk was already dominating newspaper headlines, but upon Emma's arrest, she quickly became the focal point of the unfolding story. Each day reporters felt obligated to come up with a "new sensation" about the trunk murderess. Some were a little like British news reports on the trivialities of the queen's day: "She slept well last Tuesday night, and ate her meals to-day with as much relish as if she had been dining at a swell restaurant." However the reports lacked the complimentary nature which might have been accorded to royalty: "The woman has systematically 'worked' all of the men with whom she came in contact for every dollar possible, and it is evident that she wanted the money in McVicar's possession . . . and went to extremes to get it."

Each time authorities transported Emma to a different location, huge, unmanageable crowds surged about her to catch a glimpse of the "brazen" female killer who remained "cool and unconcerned in face of awful charge." To those who saw her, the biggest mystery of all was how such a small woman could have gotten the corpse into the trunk. The crowds, like the reporters, mistook Emma's stoic mountain philosophy, that is accepting one's fate without show of emotion, for the mark of a hardened criminal. Thus they were surprised to read that after her arrest, she had said, "I want my mother." Of course there was no way to contact Mary Head directly; the only possible means of getting a message to the Pine Ridge farm was to telephone attorney Charles Crocker and ask him to watch for Emma's brother and stepbrother passing on their way to Jackson. So Emma would have a wait before the devastating news could reach her mother.[125]

The prisoner was not allowed to read newspapers. The press presented the murder as the outcome of a classic love triangle, a tragic conflict between femme fatale Emma, and the two men who were so unfortunate as to love her: Jean LeDoux and Albert McVicar. Though reporters presumed Emma had not loved McVicar, after all she had killed him, they felt certain she had a "passionate love for LeDoux."

Some members of the press were disappointed when they first saw the beauty of Amador County, describing her as "not pretty but rather plain," "scrawny," and "sallow-complexioned." But one San Francisco correspondent could see traces of her "former beauty." Another reporter credited her with showing an intelligence equal to a college graduate, other than for her occasional use of rustic terms.[126]

Newspaper writers offered a variety of motives for her crime: "May have been revenge," or vowed to "play even" to a man who had deceived and lied to her, or "Robbery Probably Motive." But whatever motive assigned, Jean was always the man for whom she had committed the crime. It was assumed LeDoux was a dashing, romantic figure right up until the day authorities traveled to Amador County to question him. The interviewing officer was shocked to discover an "ignorant Frenchman" barely eking out a living on a hillside farm.[127]

While awaiting trial, Emma was to be incarcerated in the San Joaquin County jail in Stockton. On her entrance, the matron stated, "I took all her clothes off and searched them thoroughly." She also unpinned Emma's long, thick hair and ran her fingers through it in search of some hidden weapon. But during the entire search, the matron found nothing except "just her purse and seven dollars and twenty cents." (The wicker basket had been turned over to the Sheriff and district attorney for search.)

After being stripped and undergoing a body and hair search, Emma was locked in solitary confinement. Her tiny cell, she wrote, was "a dark room" with "dreadful sanitary conditions." That first night in jail, Emma did something which was rare for her; in the privacy of the darkness she wept. Unable to eat, she tried to fall asleep. "My bed," she stated, "consisted of a mattress on the floor, no pillow, and a soiled blanket. The place was infested with cockroaches, sewer rats and all manner of vermin."

No sooner had she retired, than the matron woke her, informing her the district attorneys had ordered her to come downstairs so they could question her.[128]

As Emma stepped into the interrogation room of the jail, the assistant district attorney greeted her with "an epithet" so crude it could not be repeated later in court. Stunned by the insult and unaware she should ask for an attorney, Emma obediently responded to each question asked and then upon request poured out her story for a second time. Feeding into the district attorney's theory that a male accomplice had lifted the corpse into the trunk, Emma included in her statement certain fabrications intended to shift blame to Joe Miller, the man McVicar had brought to the hotel room. But more important to her, the other fabrications in her story would prevent Jean from learning she had intended to resume her marriage with McVicar and bring him to the farm to assume Jean's role.

For their naivete, these false portions of her statement are easy to detect. For example, she claimed that Joe Miller (which may or may not have been the man's true name) had threatened her when she attempted to run to get help for the dying McVicar: "He took from his pocket a large knife which was sharp on both sides; he also had a six-shooter." And to cover her apparent callousness in going shopping after her husband's death, she also blamed Miller: "Your skirt is very muddy in the back," he said, and then "gave me ten dollars and told me to buy a new one."[129]

Her clumsy fabrications would do her great harm at the upcoming trial, but the information she so freely gave authorities made great copy for the newspapers. Not until April 18 did Emma have a respite from the news media frenzy. On that notorious date, the earth quaked under the city of San Francisco, buildings toppled, fire raged, and hundreds died.

Details about Emma's daily activities at the jail or revelations about her mysterious past were temporarily replaced by articles about "the wreck and ruin" of the cosmopolitan city on the bay, "the young and the old tottering along the debris-laden streets" with "what few pitiable belongings they could carry." Among the collapsed and burned buildings lay the "dead and dying," while "scores of half-starved dogs" roved the devastated hills, "gnawing and tearing at the corpses half-buried in the ruins; where only a leg or an arm protruded the dogs were digging for the rest of the body." Damage to property is estimated at "over forty million dollars," the rest of the world read, and "150,000 people are homeless."[130]

Only two days before the quake, Emma had astonished the public by having the temerity to refuse to plead guilty. The news should have come as no surprise, police insisted, because they had warned that Mrs. LeDoux would "be a hard prisoner to break down." The Coles' loyal friend from Jackson, Charles Crocker, agreed to represent Emma, but sought a more prestigious attorney to take the lead role in the defense. Finally, Crocker was able to engage Charles Fairall, described as "the well-known authority on criminal law" who had authored the book *Criminal Law and Procedure.*

While the defense was laying out a case that McVicar was a hard-drinking, abusive man who had committed suicide, prosecutors C. W. Norton and George McNoble claimed they had already lined up more than eight witnesses who would prove "a clear case of murder in the first degree." The Sacramento *Bee* summed up Emma's slim chances for acquittal with the line, "Public sentiment against the accused is a unit."[131]

On June 9 testimony commenced. That morning officers led Emma from her dark cell into the dazzling sunlight and escorted her the two blocks from the county jail to the courthouse where she was to receive justice. The massive granite structure, encircled by green lawn and situated directly opposite the Bon Ton restaurant–where Emma and her late husband had dined on his last day of life–was considered one of the most beautiful architectural achievements in the state. Its three stories were topped by an ornate, four-storied dome which lifted into the sky a large statue of a voluptuous female Justice, holding a sword at her side and with her right hand, raising to the level of her breast a set of perfectly balanced scales. Emma was optimistic enough to hope the scales would tip in her favor, but as the two defense lawyers realized, the extensive pre-trial publicity would greatly influence the quality of justice the accused woman could receive.

Judge William Nutter had set up special tables for the press and also added fifty chairs to his courtroom, but his preparations were woefully inadequate for the hundreds who at dawn commenced lining up at the courthouse door. "The crowd could not begin to get inside," the press reported. Those fortunate enough to be admitted—among them many women carrying small children—found themselves jammed together in a room "crowded almost to suffocation."[132]

From the moment the twelve men who formed the jury filed in, proceedings took on the atmosphere of a three-ring circus. Spectators attempted to listen to the prosecution's lengthy opening statement, promising the facts witnesses (pared down to only sixty-two individuals) would relate about Emma's crime, and at the same time keep an eye on Emma's reactions. But from the start, the center ring was occupied by attorney Charles Fairall, so impassioned by Emma's cause he could scarcely contain himself. The Judge was a stern man of a rather petulant nature, stringent with attorneys and abrupt with witnesses, and ordinarily he ruled his court with an iron hand. If, for instance, he feared a witness was preparing to elaborate on an answer, he would cut off the speaker with a comment such as, "We don't care what you remarked."[133]

But after the prosecution's opening statement (the defense made none), Fairall initiated a heated debate, and Judge Nutter quickly realized that controlling the flamboyant lawyer was going to be no easy matter. The Judge was determined to put up a good fight. Yet each time Nutter admonished the noted defense attorney, Fairall responded with, "Your Honor, we respectfully submit, but take exception to the Court's ruling," thus putting the Judge on notice the defense was reserving all possible rights for a future appeal of the case.

The main bone of contention between defense and judge was Fairall's insistence that before prosecutors brought on a parade of witnesses to testify that Emma was a murderess, they should establish a murder had indeed been committed. "First prove a death," Fairall argued, "second prove a death by criminal means, third connect the defendant with it."

But Judge Nutter responded that the Court would permit whatever "order of proof" the prosecution wished to follow.

"We object," Fairall persevered, "to any evidence which tends to connect the defendant with the alleged crime until they have established the corpus delicti. We think that is elementary." Otherwise, he contended, every statement which prosecution witnesses uttered would be "immaterial and irrelevant." When the Judge overruled this objection, Fairall responded with his usual, "Exception!"[134]

Nutter sputtered at such insolence and instructed the prosecution to proceed with their witnesses in whatever manner they saw fit. As the district attorney commenced direct examination of the first witness, a San Francisco correspondent noted, "spectators listened with breathless interest to every question and answer." It soon became obvious that nearly every witness called had previously stood in line to view McVicar's remains. Standard answers to "When was the last time you saw the deceased?" were "Several days after he was dead," or "In the morgue," or "I seen him Sunday morning and in the afternoon; I visited the morgue twice during Sunday."[135]

A reporter for the *Bee* noticed that at the defense table, the accused woman was "sitting quietly and thoughtfully listening to every word," and at times, she would make notes. Though Charles Crocker sat at her elbow and, for added support, Mrs. Crocker sat in the first row directly behind the defendant, Fairall was seldom close at hand. When a direct examination dragged on, it was not uncommon for the criminal-law authority to release his nervous energy by springing from his chair, prancing about the courtroom, posturing for the jury and audience, and tossing off plainly audible asides. Considering the Judge a rank amateur at courtroom procedures, Fairall was not above spouting out criticisms of the Court.[136]

At one point, Judge Nutter completely lost his temper. "Now this will stop," he advised Fairall.

"I am trying this according to my best light . . ." Fairall began.

But Nutter cut him off before he could finish. "You are trying this case, Mr. Fairall, by just walking around the room and interjecting remarks about these remarkable statements - that must stop in this case."

In an attempt to pacify the Judge, Fairall replied, "I hope we will have no unpleasant feelings."

"We will not," Nutter stated, "if you pursue the ordinary way of trying a case."

"We except to the remarks of the Court," Fairall answered, and there the matter ended for the time being.[137]

As Fairall got the opportunity to cross-examine each of the twelve prosecution witnesses who appeared on the first day, he demonstrated his famed skills. Any witness who attempted to spar with the adept lawyer usually ended up on the canvas in a daze. One of Fairall's techniques of handling a witness who appeared less than forthright was to stand and ponder the response for a moment and then ask, "You are quite positive in your opinion as to that?" or "You are prepared to testify to that?" When the witness reaffirmed his or her certainty, Fairall would quietly inquire, "Is that the answer you want to stand?" Frequently the evasive witness would experience a sudden change of heart, deciding not "to stand" on the answer, but instead to change it.

The supposedly stolid chief Baker–who had never before seen "a naked dead body" and who had left the autopsy when doctors slit open the cadaver–proved to be no match for the feisty defense lawyer. Under Fairall's persistent questioning, Baker became "greatly excited," the San Francisco correspondent noted, and left the stand "badly rattled."[138]

Fairall was able to expose the lack of credibility of several prosecution witnesses. For example when he asked one man how he had fixed the hour to which he testified during direct examination, the response was, "I guessed it." And when another witness was asked how he had been able to identify Emma on the train to Antioch, the man replied, "Just had a sort of intuitive knowledge."[139]

Fairall was also able to expose instances of minor perjury committed not to convict the defendant, but so the witness could save face in the community. For instance the owner of the California Hotel testified that after the McVicars vacated Room 97 on March 24, she had ordered the porter (who also served as the maid) to change the bed linens, and he had done so. And the hotelkeeper's son, also an employee at the hotel, took the stand and confirmed his mother's testimony regarding the standards of sanitation at the hotel. He personally had delivered the clean sheets to the male maid, the son testified under oath. However when Fairall questioned the male maid who had reportedly performed the linen change, quite a different picture emerged:

QUESTION BY ATTORNEY FAIRALL: What did you do in cleaning up the room?
ANSWER BY THEODORE DOHRMANN, PORTER AT CALIFORNIA HOTEL: Swept the room, and took everything out what was dirty, and fixed up the bed.
Q: Was there any change made of the bed clothing at that time?
A: No.
Q: You are sure of that, are you?
A: Yes, I am sure.
Q: It was not changed upon Saturday?
A: No, sir.
Q: May you not be mistaken about the change not being made?
A: I guess not.[140]
In a second instance, Dr. Southworth, the coroner, testified he had taken

custody of all specimens removed from McVicar's body during autopsy, placed them in glass fruit jars, sealed the lids with wax, wrapped the wax-sealed jars in a newspaper, and personally delivered the bundle to a chemist for testing. But when Fairall cross-examined the chemist who had received the specimens, the chemist stated there had been no wax, nor for that matter any other seal, on the jar lids. Instead, the chemist testified, Dr. Southworth had closed the jars with a "rubber band."[141]

In conjunction with doctors Hull and Latta, who performed the autopsy, Dr. Southworth committed additional perjury. All three doctors testified that during the dissection of the corpse, there was not "any odor or any smoke" in the autopsy room, thus enabling them to smell "different parts of the body to see if there was present any characteristic odors of any poisons or anything else." To discredit the three doctors' testimony, Fairall called to the stand a newsman who in the line of duty had observed the entire autopsy:

QUESTION BY ATTORNEY FAIRALL: Other corpses in the room was there?

ANSWER BY WILL DAVIS, REPORTER FOR *STOCKTON MAIL*: Yes, there were two more.

Q: Was there any odor around about?

A: All I can say it smelled bad, smelled corpsy and bad.

Q: Two more corpses. And the odor from the body, . . . The odor around there was very strong, as I understand you to say?

A: Well, it was too strong for me.

Q: Was there any smoking going on?

A: Yes. . . . The Coroner, as I remember, I think he came in with a cigar in his hand nearly gone, and he laid it down somewhere.

Q: How many did you smoke?

A: Well I smoked probably at least three, possibly more. . . . I smoked just as often as I could.

Q: On account of the odor?

A: Yes sir.[142]

The editor of the *Stockton Record*, another of the sixteen men present at the autopsy, confirmed the reporter's observations by testifying, "Well, there was considerable smoking, I presume half of the men there were smoking."[143]

But it was when autopsy performer Dr. Latta took the stand on June 11, that Fairall began a series of questions whose climax resounded through the courtroom like an exploding bombshell. At one point of the examination, Latta, who considered Fairall's questioning a useless formality and therefore took it lightly, turned to the jury and chuckled.

"You can laugh," Fairall chided, "but I am simply wanting the facts without any jokes here."

Before Fairall's two-day cross-examination would conclude, the doctor's smug smile would vanish:

QUESTION BY ATTORNEY FAIRALL: You, as a physician would want to determine whether the person was dead before you began your examination, wouldn't you?

ANSWER BY DR. S. E. LATTA: Yes, sir.

Q: What tests of death did you apply?

A: We felt of his heart . . . by laying our hands over his heart and feeling carefully; and of the pulse; watching for respirations.

Q: You didn't use a stethoscope?

A: No, sir.

Q: Will you explain what coma is? . . . Does not the heart action sometimes become very slow and feeble?

A: You can always feel the heart beat in coma.

Q: You think you can . . . hear it with your ear?

A: Yes.

Q: May not the heart's action be so feeble that even an experienced auscultator may fail to detect the sound?

A: No, sir.

Q: You think the ear is sensitive enough to detect the heart's action even in all cases? . . . Was there conversation going on in the room at the time of autopsy?

A: Oh, I suppose they were all talking; suppose they were talking, yes.

Q: Didn't take the temperature?

A: No, sir. . . . I said that it [the corpse] was warm inside.

Q: And you didn't use a thermometer, but simply your hand?

A: I did.

Q: Did you test the eyes with drugs to note whether the pupil would contract or dilate?

A: No, sir.

Q: What else did you observe about the eye?

A: Well, . . . that it was dull, and sunken in the head, dull look that the dead have.

Q: May not an eye lose its lustre and still life exist?

A: I have stated two or three different and separate times my reasons for believing that this man was dead.

Q: Did you apply any mechanical tests of death?

A: Yes, with the knife.

Q: And you never took the temperature of the body at any time?

A: The man was dead.

Q: You say he was dead? . . . I believe this is the first time you stated that. Now tell us upon what you base your conclusion that the man was dead at that time?

Witness, audience, and jurors sat stunned. Obviously Fairall was suggesting the unthinkable, that McVicar might have been in a coma when taken out of the trunk, that the doctors had commenced an autopsy upon a living individual, that the victim in this murder case might have been killed, not by the female defendant, but "with the knife" of the doctor when he severed McVicar's brain from his spinal cord.

Dr. Latta exploded in a flurry of self-defense: "We were around there for several minutes before we operated on that man. . . . I have stated these same things he is asking me, again and again and again. . . . I don't know what his object is unless it is to catch me, tie me up."[144]

After the doctor's emotional outburst, Fairall sedately turned to the Judge and made a motion to strike the part about "trying to catch him and tie him up."

"That part may go out," Nutter agreed, and Fairall resumed the grilling, keeping the distressed doctor on the stand the remainder of the day and requesting him to return the following morning.[145]

June 12 brought no letup for the doctor, with Fairall continuing to hammer away at the inadequacy of the autopsy in a series of scathing questions:

Q: Did you make a microscopic examination of the blood?
A: No, sir. . . . Because we didn't have time.
Q: Did you weigh the brain?
A: No, we didn't weigh the brain.
Q: What was the reason you didn't look for it [embolus] in the brain?
A: Because the idea never appeared to us that there was embolus in the brain. . . .
Q: Did you make any microscopical examination of the tissues of the heart?
A: No, sir.
Q: You didn't preserve any of . . . the contents of the gall bladder?
A: No, sir, we didn't.
Q: You allowed the contents to run away?
A: Yes, sir.
Q: Did it then run right off into the corpse, the gall?
A: I think it did, I can't say as to that.
Q: What was done with . . . fecal matter . . . in the bowel?
A: Well, it was emptied into a slop bucket.
Q: It was not saved for analysis?
A: No, sir.
Q: Don't some poisons get into the bowel or intestine?
A: Yes, sir.[146]

But the final blow to the doctor's competency came when he admitted he had made no notes of the autopsy. "You have preserved no notes, then, of this?" Fairall asked with disbelief, "didn't you consider it necessary, Doctor, to make notes?"

When Latta explained it was merely a "question of personal opinion," Fairall pressed the point.

"Wouldn't you consider it better if everything had been recorded so that there would not be any possibility of a mistake?" he persisted.

But McNoble (the Assistant District Attorney who had greeted Emma with an unrepeatable epithet when she entered the interrogation room) objected that the question was "not applicable to this case," and Judge Nutter sustained the objection.[147]

On the following day, however, Fairall doggedly took up the previously forbidden line of questioning with Coroner Southworth: "You think it is better to rely on memory in those things than to have it in writing?"

The coroner answered that he was opposed to note-taking at an autopsy (although a shorthand reporter was present) because "so many useless things are put down." "To a man who is capable," Southworth continued, "it is merely a matter of his observations and remembering them."

Evidently the district attorney's male stenographer held the same opinion about taking notes as the coroner and doctors did. Even though the stenographer was being paid to make a record of the doctors' findings, during the three-hour autopsy he made only the following notes: McVicar's "weight, the color of his hair and his eyes, and his moustache, and the number of bruises."[148]

In Fairall's continuing attack on the investigation into McVicar's death, he also took to task the chemist who had performed the tests on McVicar's specimens, soliciting from him testimony that the specimens were not labeled. Packed together inside one jar, the chemist said, were "some pieces of liver, a piece of pancreas, stomach, and another piece of some organ I didn't recognize, and some bloody serum." After "grinding" the "mixture of these organs and bloody liquid" into a viscera "soup," the chemist had performed his tests and concluded that McVicar had died of morphine poisoning.[149]

Judge Nutter's court followed the Biblical admonition to rest but one day out of seven, and throughout the month of June, the sessions continued six days a week. In spite of his firmness, Nutter followed the democratic procedure of permitting jurors the opportunity to ask questions of any witness. And though the Judge attempted to curb Fairall's theatrics as much as possible, he did at times allow the attorney considerable latitude during cross-examination. So that in addition to the ineptness of the autopsy and laboratory work, Fairall was able to reveal that from the moment of Emma's arrest, her rights had been consistently violated. One of the most glaring violations was the failure to inform her of her right to an attorney. The aging Sheriff Sibley had testified that his "purpose" in regards to the statement he had taken from Emma was "to find out who committed this, and how it was done, and all about it."

QUESTION BY ATTORNEY FAIRALL: Your object was to get her to talk?
ANSWER BY W. F. SIBLEY, SHERIFF OF SAN JOAQUIN COUNTY: My object - well, yes.
Q: Did you inform her of her right to have an attorney?
A: No, I didn't inform her of her right to an attorney.

And when T. P. Shine (the Antioch marshal who had admitted on the stand to being a "greenhorn in the business") was asked if the Antioch justice of the peace had informed Emma of "her right to counsel," Shine asked, "Her right to what?"[150]

In addition, Sheriff H. E. Kay of Emma's home county testified that in response to a communication from Sheriff Sibley, he had conducted an illegal search and seizure in Mary Head's home. Gradually, Fairall drew out a description of Kay rummaging through drawers of a commode and bureau to find Emma's personal letters and photos, which were then delivered to Sheriff Sibley.

"Never at any time secured a warrant to search the premises, or any authority from any Court to do this?" Fairall asked Kay.

The Amador Sheriff responded, "No, sir."

Though Nutter allowed Kay's admission of the illegal search and seizure into the court record, the Judge then added his own opinion on the issue of whether or not the police procedure had been legal: "I don't think it is very material." Nutter's attitude toward obtaining evidence was summed up with this statement, "I don't care how he [Kay] got it."[151]

Like the Judge, the jurors weren't particularly concerned about such technicalities as the defendant's rights. As the prosecution paraded witness after witness, jurors heard the damaging information that at the time of Emma's arrest she had been carrying a razor and jackknife in her basket, that she was guilty of bigamy, that shortly before the murder she had burned every letter she had written to McVicar, and that not long after murdering her husband, the callous country seamstress had gone on a shopping spree, blithely purchasing a fifty-cent corset and a five-dollar silk underskirt while she boasted to clerks about being "the head of a ranch" and having to "see a party in San Francisco." Witnesses identified her by her "large, dark eyes," her "prominent cheek bones," her "slight" figure, her green-silk embroidered blouse, black-silk skirt, and basket with shawl straps.[152]

Jurors were most riveted by the testimony of star witness Joe Healey, Emma's ex-fiancé. He claimed that during their conversation at the San Francisco restaurant on the day after the murder, she had told him McVicar was dead and then asked him to store the deceased man's property. By property, Healey insinuated, Emma might have meant the trunk containing the corpse. Even more damaging was a reported telephone conversation ten days before McVicar's death. Healey testified Emma had called and informed him McVicar was going to die soon.

"Healey gave his testimony with dramatic effect," wrote the Sacramento *Bee* reporter, "and it caused quite a sensation in Court." Healey's testimony was sensational, of course, because it provided convincing evidence that Emma had committed the murder with premeditation.[153]

The climax of the trial was expected to be Emma's appearance on the stand. She was anxious to testify, and both jurors and spectators were anxious to hear the sound of her voice and observe her demeanor, especially under cross-examination. On the day appointed for her to take the stand, the courtroom was even more crowded and suffocating than usual, and as the audience waited, the atmosphere in the room grew increasingly tense.

Before calling Emma to the stand, however, Fairall wanted to enhance her credibility with a series of witnesses who had not only encountered her at the San Francisco brothel, but also had been aware of the fact it was her own husband who had urged this degradation upon her. In a society which placed such high value upon "respectability," it was no easy matter to find a man who was willing to admit in court that he had visited a brothel, but the able defense attorneys had managed to locate three such witnesses.

As Fairall commenced questioning the first man willing to bare his soul to the court, a farmer from Madera County, District Attorney Norton objected. "I can anticipate what is coming," he said to Nutter. But over the District Attorney's protestations, Nutter allowed Fairall to explain why the farmer's testimony was relevant:

"I want to prove this defendant was in a house of prostitution," Fairall said, "with the full knowledge and consent and approbation of the deceased person who was at that time her husband, and that she cared so much for him that she prostituted her body for his gain; that he lived upon money earned by her in that capacity. . . . I want to go back . . . and trace the relationship of the parties from date to date. . . . I want to show it continued up to the very last day before his death."

"That is wholly irrelevant, - irrelevant and immaterial," Nutter ruled. "It is absolutely, in the opinion of the Court incompetent testimony. . . . The deceased is not on trial."[154]

Thus the jury would not learn of the year of abuse Emma had suffered from McVicar. Fairall had hoped to gain sympathy for the accused by presenting an image of McVicar as a husband who, when drinking, not only beat Emma, but also sank to the level of acting as a pimp for his own wife. Instead, jurors were allowed to retain the image offered by the press:

The murder victim came from a wealthy, highly respected family of Scotch Canadians who had emigrated to Kansas. He was survived by his widowed mother, Caroline McVicar, age seventy; several prominent siblings; and an uncle, Albert Newton Sullivan, a judge who despite his advanced age and debilitating grief had come all the way to Stockton to testify at the trial and to escort the coffin of his deceased namesake back to Kansas for burial. In life, Albert Newton McVicar had been a "quiet, industrious" gentleman, "one of the best workmen" ever, and a gifted artisan who "could turn his hand at everything." And, "he was not a drinking man."[155]

Judge Nutter's ruling to bar testimony regarding Emma's battery and forced career of prostitution left Fairall with only one remaining line of defense, attempting to prove her contention that McVicar had committed suicide. Bringing in a series of impressive authorities, Fairall was able to establish that the victim may have died from a combination of alcohol, "knockout drops," and morphine, and that Emma had probably not caused the bruises and blood on the corpse. The expert witnesses explained that head and facial bruises could have been caused immediately after death, when the express men tumbled the trunk down two flights of hotel stairs. While the bleeding from the nose could have occurred after death through force of gravity, namely while the trunk was standing on end, and the corpse was positioned with legs up and head down, knees pressing against chest.[156]

But the expert testimony made little impression upon the jury. McVicar was dead from morphine poisoning, jurors reasoned, and Emma had admitted placing his body in the trunk and attempting to dispose of it. In addition, Joe Healey claimed that Emma had inadvertently given him one week notice of her intent to commit murder. Fairall was a master at rattling witnesses, pointing up inconsistencies in their testimony, and exposing their bias. And he could convince jurors that parts of the investigation had been inept and that some of Emma's legal rights had been violated. But Emma's fate depended on whether or not he had been able to convince the jury there was a reasonable doubt the accused woman had poisoned her husband.

After listening for hours to the prosecution's closing argument, delivered on June 23, a Saturday, the twelve men of the jury retired to deliberate in a large, windowed room of the courthouse. From across the street, newsmen wrote, they were "closely watching the jurymen with glasses." At the first ballot, all twelve men voted "guilty," but an argument broke out over the recommendation of sentence. Hours of quarreling followed. Then exactly six hours from the time they had entered the deliberation room, the jurors adjourned and departed for the courtroom.

"Mrs. LeDoux," the San Francisco correspondent observed, "was sitting in front of the Judge's bench when the announcement was made that the jury was coming in. She did not give any indication of excitement, but calmly awaited her fate." The crowd, however, heard the announcement concerning the jury's return and "surged into the room and almost forced people off their feet."

As the jury foreman handed the court clerk the verdict, the defendant and her attorneys rose to their feet, and the audience hushed. Keeping his eyes on Emma, the correspondent noted that she stood "with her head high."

Breaking an almost eerie silence, the clerk read, "We, the jury . . . find the defendant, Mrs. Emma LeDoux, guilty of murder in the first degree" with no recommendation of sentence to the Court. Still watching Emma, the correspondent saw that "there was not even a movement of the muscles of her face except that a faint smile played over her features," in fact, "she was by far the most composed person in the room."[157]

On the morning of August 7, Emma appeared before Judge Nutter for sentencing. The same correspondent who had observed her at the trial wrote that she was "attired in a neat suit of black." When called upon "to stand and receive sentence," she "slowly stood erect, and, facing the Judge, never took her eyes from him" as he sentenced her "to be hung by the neck until dead" on the San Quentin gallows between the hours of eight A.M. and noon on 19 October 1906. The condemned woman received her "death sentence without a tremor." Only "her face changed slightly as the blood rushed to her cheeks," but "she remained calm and sat down."

Following the sentencing, a deputy sheriff escorted Emma back to her cell amidst "a large crowd that had assembled on the lawn and along the streets." After she had been locked in her cell, she asked to see her mother and a priest, but when the two requested visitors arrived at the jail, both were denied entrance.[158]

Soon after the trial, Fairall produced two witnesses who swore in court that a juror "had declared to them during the trial that he would hang the defendant." Rather than questioning the accused juror, Judge Nutter responded to the testimony of the "colored" man and the "youth" by finding them "guilty of contempt of court" for speaking to a juror. Nutter fined each man one hundred dollars (approximately two month's salary) and sentenced both to two days in jail. Following this punishment for reporting juror prejudice, no further witnesses came forth.[159]

Fairall appealed the case, but it took the California Supreme Court three years to make a decision. While Emma waited to learn if and when the death sentence would be carried out, she was kept in solitary confinement in the same dark, unsanitary cell where she had awaited trial. She was allowed no medicine to alleviate the constant pain from her displaced womb, and the months of darkness caused a deterioration in her eyesight, leaving her nearly blind. During her months of solitude, Emma lived with the painful knowledge that Sheriff Kay had foreclosed on Mary's farm. A second agony was the future of Emma's twin sons. Though Emma's younger sister Liddie–who had married Louis LeDoux and lived in Oregon–had allowed the twin boys to reside in her home, the couple held Emma financially responsible for their care. Naturally she had no income and thus no assurance that Louis LeDoux would let the twins remain under his roof.[160]

Not until the May session of 1909 did the California Supreme Court at last reverse the decision of the superior court. Revealing the full extent of

ALBERT MCVICAR, as photgraphed after his death. Infamous trunk can be seen at top of picture. *Courtesy California State Library*

his previously exposed bias, Judge Nutter personally petitioned the justices of the Supreme Court to reverse their own decision. Meanwhile, Emma was denied any contact with her attorneys. During a barrage of visits in which District Attorney Norton, Sheriff Sibley, and the jail matron joined forces to wring a confession of guilt from Emma, she refused to sign the prepared statement, insisting it would be morally wrong to sign a confession of guilt when she was in fact innocent.[161]

For days she remained under pressure from the same three visitors. They advised her that the only way to escape the gallows was to plead guilty; should she submit to a second trial, it would surely result in an irreversible hanging sentence and, in addition, cost the state of California money it could not afford. When Emma held firm, the matron reminded the prisoner that her health had already deteriorated to the point where she "could scarcely walk alone," and it would be impossible for her to survive the ordeal of a second trial. But if Emma would only sign the document they presented, Judge Nutter would show "clemency" and "they would have her out within six (6) months."

Not realizing her letters were not being delivered, Emma vainly continued writing to advise her attorneys she needed to seek their advice. When no replies came, she concluded her counsel had abandoned her. "I have no recollection of signing any such paper, neither do I believe I did," Emma wrote. Nevertheless, on what would be his last visit, District Attorney Norton emerged from Emma's cell with a signed confession in hand.[162]

On 2 February 1919, Emma entered the women's section of San Quentin prison. During admittance to the small, high-walled "hen house," as the women's facility was called, the infamous trunk murderess was issued the standard blue uniform and assigned inmate number 24077, the number she would bear for the rest of her life. As soon as she had regained her strength, she assumed the job of sewing uniforms for male inmates. Her daily routine within the high walls was confined to a tiny cell, the sewing room, the dining hall, and a concrete pit which served as an exercise yard.[163]

It was several months before she learned she had entered not for a six-month term, as she had been promised, but with a life sentence. When the pardon failed to arrive, she wrote to authorities at Stockton, but received no answer. Not until Sheriff Sibley learned of her plight did she receive any help. Sibley, whose health was declining rapidly, vowed he would have her out of prison within three years, but before he could accomplish his mission, he died. On his deathbed, Sibley had made a final plea to authorities to honor their pledge to Emma, but still no pardon was forthcoming.

Emma quickly adapted to prison life, being described by prison officials as an "exemplary" inmate. During Emma's second year of incarceration, the matron selected her as trusty of the women's department, and she served in that capacity for eight more years. Because of Emma's trustworthiness and her fairness to inmates under her supervision, the matron not only issued her a set of keys, but even relied upon her to manage the facility in the matron's absence. During a general riot in 1916, Emma performed a heroic act which earned her praise from the President of the Board of

Prison Directors. While "windows were broken with flat irons, furniture was destroyed," and the matron was attacked, Emma was also "knocked down and kicked" until she was bleeding and injured. Yet she managed to rise to her feet, escape her attackers, and bring help. "Mrs. LeDoux," the Board President wrote, "went to the rescue of the Matron of the Women's Department when the latter was being attacked . . . and saved the life of the Matron when all the rest of the Prisoners just looked on."[164]

Though she was able to function well within the prison walls for ten years, apparently Emma's ordeals had left her unfit for life on the outside. She twice received a work-release parole, and though individuals working closely with her during her periods of parole described her as "a very sympathetic person" and "a dear sweet little lady," both paroles were revoked for an infraction of rules.[165]

Following Emma's return to San Quentin, Jean, who continued to love her and had refused to seek a divorce, informed Charles Crocker that "he would help her and even take her back," but his sisters had "threatened to put him out on the street and disown him" if he did "anything on her behalf." Because of his financial dependence upon his sisters, with whom he now lived, Jean eventually gave in to their demands and in 1921 divorced Emma. Twenty years later, she died in prison at age sixty-nine, leaving in her file one last plea for release on a work permit: "I wish to go out and do something constructive and useful," she wrote in this final request. The letter is marked "Denied."[166]

Question of Emma's Guilt

Until her dying day, Emma contended she had not poisoned McVicar. And all evidence against her was circumstantial, but the prosecution's main witness, Joe Healey, convinced the jury Emma had not only poisoned McVicar, but also planned the crime ten days in advance. The problem with this theory is it fails to take into account Emma's intelligence. Reporters who interviewed her in the Stockton jail stated that despite her limited education, she appeared to have the intelligence of a college graduate. Based on this opinion, it seems plausible that if the crime were premeditated, she could have formulated a much better plan. To explain away this apparent flaw in the prosecution's case, one rather chauvinistic male reporter theorized that the cunning murderess had actually formulated an ingenious plan, however, at the last moment, "her woman's nerve" had let her down and she had abandoned it.[167]

But the main flaw of the prosecution's case was not the lack of intelligent planning before the murder, but as Fairall pointed out at the trial, the lack of proof that McVicar was indeed murdered. A third flaw was the heavy reliance upon Joe Healey's testimony. Cross-examination revealed that the ex-fiancé was a biased witness and a rather unstable person, thus making his testimony suspect. While on the stand, Healey revealed a slight paranoia, describing how on occasion he employed a "true-blue friend" to tail him in case he should happen to need a witness to any of his actions. Also, he demonstrated a strong hostility, even announcing plans to bring a law suit against one newspaper for defaming his character. In the early stages of investigation, he explained, Stockton police had taken him into custody as a possible accomplice in McVicar's murder, and the press had reported his arrest. But even more than the newspaper, Healey blamed Emma for damage done to his reputation. As he put it, "She dragged my name into this case."

Also, when Fairall questioned Healey about the one hundred dollars he had loaned Emma to save the Head farm, Healey replied, "I advanced her that money for two months and I am waiting for it yet."

In addition to his bitter feelings toward his ex-fiancee, his general hostility, and his anxiousness to cooperate with the prosecution in order to clear his own name, Healey may have inadvertently provided false information. When he testified that Emma had telephoned him before the murder to inform him McVicar would soon die from miners' consumption and that the doomed man planned to spend his final days in Arizona, he may have been confusing statements Emma had once made about her second husband, William Williams.

But most condemning in Healey's testimony is a contradiction that raises doubts about the existence of the alleged telephone call from Emma ten days prior to the murder, the single piece of evidence that suggests premeditation. Healey claimed that during this telephone conversation, Emma had stated, "Poor Al, Al McVicar hasn't long to live." Then during their restaurant meal in San Francisco on the day after the murder, Emma said, "Poor Al has died," to which Healey responded, "Al who?"[168]

The occurrence of this second conversation between Emma and Healey at the restaurant was not disputed, and since Fairall did not challenge its contents, in all likelihood Healey reported it accurately, that is while they were at the restaurant in San Francisco, Emma did tell him McVicar had died. However there is no such corroborating evidence for the first conversation, allegedly held by telephone. And Healey's response of "Al who?" during the second conversation–the one that is not in doubt–suggests he did not know who Al was. Yet he claimed to recall that in a conversation held ten days earlier Emma had identified the man who was going to die as Al McVicar.

Emma's defense attorneys doubted the veracity of Healey's testimony. And both Crocker and Fairall believed that Emma loved McVicar deeply. Both lawyers also believed she was innocent. When the prosecution had first presented its theory that Emma murdered her legal husband because of "a passionate love" for Jean, Fairall hopped out of his chair and in his usual abrasive manner and brutally blunt language shouted, "She didn't love LeDoux. She could not love that pop-eyed wood chopper who could neither read nor write."

Fairall was convinced that even if Emma had wished to kill McVicar–and because of his repeated abuse she had sufficient motive–she would have been unable to carry out the crime because she loved her abuser too much.[169]

Likewise, Emma's lifetime acquaintance Charles Crocker believed she had loved McVicar too much to kill him. In Crocker's analysis composed twelve years after the trial, he conceded only "that Mrs. Le Doux put the corpse in the trunk" and that fact "does not make her guilty of murder." In Crocker's opinion, the single feature of the case "which tended to influence the minds of the jurors in rendering the verdict was the fact that his body was found in a trunk."

Crocker understood Emma well, and he reasoned that since she had previously been living as Jean LeDoux's wife and knew it would be necessary to resume that relationship after McVicar's death, she did what many individuals would have done "under similar circumstances." "Imagine for a moment," he continued, "a married person, male or female, occupying a room with other than their husband or wife and discover that your bed-fellow is a corpse - is it not natural that she would try to shield herself from publicity and keep the fact of her liaison from her husband."

But as Crocker made clear in the letter, his contention that Emma was innocent was only a personal opinion. "As to whether Mrs. Le Doux took the life of McVicar or he committed suicide is a fact known to no one but herself," he concluded.

In addition to the suicide theory, Fairall suggested during the trial the second possibility (also espoused by Mary Head) that McVicar had accidentally taken a fatal combination of drugs. Being inebriated at the time, he may have unintentionally overdosed on the sleeping drops and morphine. But whatever occurred in Room 97 of the California Hotel in the first hours of 24 March 1906, Emma took the secret to the grave.[170]

It may have been a secret she concealed even from herself. Though she felt it was morally wrong to sign a confession of guilt, she may have been refusing to acknowledge certain realities concerning her role in the crime. On the previous occasion when McVicar had become ill and commenced retching–while they were in the hotel room in San Francisco on March 12–Emma had been so concerned she fled the room and returned with a doctor so speedily that her husband was still kneeling over the slop pail.

But on the second occasion he became ill–at the California Hotel in Stockton on the final night of his life–Emma did not summon help for him. And on the following morning when she awoke, saw her husband's body in the same position in which he had fallen on the bed, and assumed he was dead, she did not, in a desperate hope some flicker of life might remain in his body, rush to find a doctor. Instead, she was apparently willing that McVicar should die.

Whether she gave her husband the morphine, or whether he himself took it, will never be known conclusively. But had Emma been allowed to speak to the priest she summoned after hearing her death sentence, she might have received some enlightenment regarding her own guilt.

Emma was in a position similar to Chester Gillette, another well-known murderer of the day who was at that very time awaiting execution. Theodore Dreiser based his novel *An American Tragedy* on the case of Gillette, who was accused of drowning his pregnant fiancee while boating on Big Moose Lake in upper New York state during the summer of 1905. On circumstantial evidence, Gillette was convicted of the crime and later electrocuted. In Dreiser's novel, a minister asked the condemned man if he had wanted to save his fiancee when she fell from their boat. After deep thought, the young man awaiting the electric chair stated he had tried to save her and he felt sorry when he could not. But then he added that he had also felt rather glad to be free of her, and after further soul-searching, went on to admit he really had not wanted to save her from drowning.

The minister responded, "In your heart was murder then." It appears that on the night of 24 March 1906 Emma LeDoux also had murder in her heart.[171]

Perhaps she had come to realize, if only subconsciously, that it would be better for her if her husband were dead. In her many years on the farm, the time had always come when it was necessary to sacrifice the lovingly nurtured livestock so the family could survive, and now the time had come to let go of her love for McVicar, for the sake of her own integrity and for the survival of her children and mother. Despite her refusal to display any emotion, this human sacrifice had not been easy for Emma to make. In fact at the trial, she could not bear to look at McVicar's displayed clothing, and when prosecutors rolled the blood-stained trunk into the courtroom, Emma had to turn her face away.

Afterword to LeDoux Story

Modern social scientists might regard the theories of Berthine Adair, pioneer woman doctor who for years treated battered wives, as simplistic. Yet Adair's contention that the causes of the wife battery she had treated were liquor, lust, and bad laws does not seem to be a bad summary of the Emma LeDoux case. As Hester Griffith, an officer in an early women's organization, wrote in 1918, if Emma had been a man, she would not have been left in jail for life for killing her mate. "Men," Griffith argued "are favored who seem to have committed more atrocious crimes."[172]

And in a letter written in 1921, an international banker who had become interested in Emma's case pointed out the basic unfairness of her being sent back to prison after parole for allegedly "taking one drink of liquor" while serving alcohol to others at a party, especially since her accuser operated a still on his own property. This accuser responsible for the revocation of Emma's parole was her own brother-in-law, the wealthy fruit dealer for whom she had once kept house while her sister Daisy was re-covering from a difficult childbirth. Daisy's husband became the employer who under terms of the prison work release had to pay Emma ten dollars a month for services he had previously received from her free of charge. As the banker who criticized Emma's return to prison stated, among the du-ties the brother-in-law demanded of Emma was picking the fruit which he used in making brandy in his private still.[173]

But returning to Dr. Adair's theories about injustices suffered by fron-tier women, Emma LeDoux's adult life–starting with McVicar's abuse; in-cluding the conspiracy of a district attorney, sheriff, and judge to deprive her of her rights to contact her lawyers or have a new trial; and ending with her brother-in-law's success in sending her back to prison because she supposedly sipped the alcohol she was serving and therefore was "a menace to the public safety"–is an illustration of abuse that included a husband's immoderate use of alcohol, forced sexual submission, and if not unjust laws, at least a lack of justness on the part of officials entrusted with administering them.[174]

Retrospect on Domestic Tragedies

Stockton's prestigious Haggin Museum still preserves the infamous LeDoux trunk in a storage room. The city's ultra-modern, multi-million-dollar court-house proudly displays the same statue of Justice that presided over Emma's trial; and the decaying, spindly-legged headframe of the Kennedy mine still soars to a height providing a view of the acres of tailings which McVicar had planned to haul away with Mary Head's four workhorses. But the story of the trunk murder has been nearly forgotten. However the basic problem involved in the murder, that is domestic abuse, lives on.

A woman's loving a man too much has been a universal problem. Long before the domestic tragedies of Lucinda Vedder of Nevada City and Emma LeDoux of Amador County, the mythological Medea, princess of Colchis, loved Jason too much, so much she committed a crime against her own royal house in order to be with him. Afterwards, when in Jason's land the pair had married, assumed the throne, and had two children, he betrayed her. Her passionate love for him turned to uncontrollable hatred and Medea retaliated by sacrificing Jason's two sons. She had killed the children, she explained, not because she loved them less, but because she loathed Jason more.

Though Emma LeDoux was certainly not born a princess, she was more judicious than Medea in fitting her actions to her emotions, that is in di-recting her wrath at the perpetrator rather than at two innocent children. More than Emma loathed McVicar, she loved her twin sons, and in the hope of being able to return to them, she either killed the man who once again had induced her to betray herself, or else she stood by and waited as he died. But in the end, her crime had the same result as Medea's: Emma also lost her two beloved sons.

The society that condemned her had provided no help during her difficult marriage to an abusive husband, nor little justice after she committed her crime. And following her coerced confession, authorities did not keep their promise to free her in six months and allow her to reunite her broken family: the twins, Mary, and Jean, who still loved her.

The LeDoux-McVicar murder case was a Western tragedy. Tragedy, of course, is a form of drama in which the main character undergoes a moral struggle, but a struggle which eventually concludes in disaster. And in Greek tragedy, the main character must be a person of high birth, so that the concluding disaster affects not only one individual, but an entire kingdom as well, thus lending the story great significance.

The second portion of the definition notwithstanding, the life of Emma LeDoux–a commoner of the Old West whose entire existence was a struggle to preserve family–is no less tragic than Euripides's drama about Medea. The tragic element which is common to both stories is a use of violence, violence which destroyed a family. And the argument could be made that Emma's story is also of national significance: since the family is the basic unit of a nation, as the family goes, eventually, so goes the nation.

IV

Epilogue

As the stories related in this volume reveal, an external force sometimes destroyed frontier families, as in the case of the Whitman-Sager household. But in some instances, an erosion from within occurred: the children, a wife, or a husband experienced physical or psychological maltreatment within the home. And, as evidenced by the stories of Elvina Apperson, Mary Allen, Lucinda Vedder, and Emma LeDoux, family maltreatment could escalate to the level of homicide. Probably, as in today's society, those cases of family violence which were reported were merely the tip of the iceberg, but they are sufficient to affirm theories which contemporary psychologists now advance regarding domestic violence. For example, what better description of the marriage of the knife-wielding John Vedder and his wife Lucinda than "Terrifying Love," the title of Lenore Walker's 1989 book. And when child-abuse expert Andrew Vachss, both attorney and author, writes that "emotional abuse scars the heart and damages the soul," he is summarizing the emotional experience of Matilda Sager, who stated that no matter how long she lived, she would never forget "the indignities, and cruelty" she suffered as a child.[1]

In regard to domestic violence and the courts' attempts to deal with the problem, similar patterns of behavior are found in the Old West and the modern era. The concept of the sanctity of the home makes it difficult to curb violence within a family. And on occasion the judicial system charged with protecting victims from abuse is capable of revictimizing. In 1854 an Oregon judge agreed to grant custody of fifteen-year-old Matilda Sager to her abuser, the county clerk. And in 1995, an Oklahoma County judge revictimized another fifteen-year-old girl, who like Matilda, was unwilling to testify against her accused abuser, her adopted father. Charging the teenage girl with contempt of court, the Oklahoma judge sent her to the county jail overnight. The following morning, the girl was returned to court wearing leg shackles and handcuffed to another criminal defendant. Appalling as the Oklahoma judge's tactics may seem, for poor judgment they do not surpass the ruling of the California judge who incarcerated Agnes Vedder in the Sacramento County jail when she was not yet two years old.[2]

Another similarity between then and now is found in the characteristics of the principals: both perpetrators and victims. As do abused children of the present day, some frontier children attempted to explain away their abuser's conduct, such as J. B. Hoss, who stated that in administering whippings with "the first thing handy," his father "probably meant well." And like today, frontier children could attempt to turn their accumulated hostility back on the abusive care giver, as when J. W. Blakely searched for his foster father, so he could "beat Downing within an inch of his life." And like modern youngsters who feel themselves unworthy of having loving parents and a secure home, Matilda Sager came to accept her repeated beatings as being "inevitable" as "the winter rain."

The battered wives of both eras display low self-esteem, self-blame, an appreciation of attractive qualities of an abusive husband, a readiness to forgive his violent acts, a tendency to forget bad portions of the marriage and treasure good memories, a desire to reconcile, and a continuing love for the abusive husband. And battered wives, such as Elvina Apperson and Lucinda Vedder, place their lives in grave danger when they try to escape an abusive marriage.

The wife batterers of both past and present display possessiveness, jealousy, a need to control, an obsession for the wife, a fear of abandonment, a bifurcated personality of congeniality in public and chronic hostility at home, a phase of contrition after releasing rage upon the wife, a belief in male supremacy, and a tendency to deny guilt.

But there also differences between early and modern domestic violence. In the frontier family, factors such as the prevailing reluctance to discuss any behavior regarded as scandalous, a resulting lack of knowledge and awareness of the problems of domestic violence, and a frequent isolation from other members of society combined to provide an ideal setting for abuse. And since the rights of frontier women and children were limited, and since society condoned the punishment of children and wives, both groups were especially susceptible to all forms of abuse, while their abusers were apt to escape censure or punishment.

It is likely that the foregoing stories of frontier families provide some insights for present-day society. Narcissa Whitman, for example, was an individual wholly committed to the highest plane of human existence, yet she found it impossible to summon feelings of tenderness for an emaciated orphan infant and her six older brothers and sisters simply because they were not her "natural" children.

Narcissa Whitman's admission probes the root of the problem. And her behavior as a parent proves that compassionate individuals can, under certain circumstances, revert to abusive behavior. Child abusers are not necessarily the aberrants of society; instead, they may be individuals with high moral standards who on occasion employ violence as a means of accomplishing their goals.

Violence, of course, is a part of the American heritage. Our nation was born through violence, our westward expansion was accomplished through violence, our union of states was preserved through violence, and as a leader in the international community we sporadically employ violence in various parts of the world. The violence of our nation's past is passed on to future generations.

Thus it is not surprising that the violence practiced and glorified on the national level is also practiced at lower levels. Severe discipline in the home is condoned even by the scriptures. The violence in our modern schools–students armed with knives or guns, student attacks upon each other or teachers, and corporal punishment administered to students–is not new; we have the precedents of Wesley Hardin stabbing a classmate, students of frontier schools ejecting teachers through a window, and the teacher at Wailatpu administering cruel whippings to the Sager orphans. The desperadoes of the Western gold camps were forerunners of contemporary street gangs, and Montana vigilantes a model for white-supremacist groups.

This is not to condemn our American heritage, for it also includes a constant struggle for reformation and improvement. Gold miners in Montana's Alder Gulch, for example, extended their jurisdiction beyond settling mining claims in order to punish a miner who was abusing his wife and children. And early schoolteacher J. D. Matlock made the amazing discovery that "You do not have to use a club to control children." Despite the brutality inherent in the frontier experience, most pioneers exhibited a love for a peaceful society. Our ancestors who settled the West were both dreamers and creators; and perhaps from their example, we can draw the inspiration to accomplish as much as they did.

And to what better accomplishment could present-day society aspire than reversing the accelerating trend toward crime in the streets, breaking the cycle of family violence, or seeking alternatives to the habit of resolving problems with an immediate application of violence, such as slapping an infant's exploring hand or firing a gun at an antagonist. An immediate application of violence was the solution Wesley Hardin chose when he shot the white ox that was attempting to join his herd, that John Grannis chose when he struck his wife for disagreeing with him, and that X. Beidler chose each time he slipped a noose over the head of an untried suspect.

These are times when describing home life as "heavenly"–as did the early primer–might seem quaintly amusing or overly sentimental. Yet inspired by the courage and daring of the Western pioneers' dream of establishing a better life for their families, we might in these cynical times show the courage to formulate daring plans to create more nurturing homes, rear more responsible families, conduct more stimulating school classes, and, as should follow, create a stronger nation. We might individually and collectively adopt the dream of passing on to future generations the heritage of an orderly, yet non-violent culture.

About the author

Ruth Elsie Mather was herself a child of the frontier. Her parents were Western settlers whose home was lit by kerosene lamps and heated by burning the sagebrush and greasewood being uprooted and cleared away to make the new land arable.

She is a retired college instructor and a genealogist whose own family tree includes Cotton Mather, Abraham Lincoln, Daniel Boone, and William Clark of Lewis and Clark. Over the past decades she has contributed articles on Western history to numerous magazines, journals, and encyclopedias, and has with coauthor F. E. Boswell written four mining-frontier histories, all published by university or other scholarly presses:

Hanging the Sheriff: A Biography of Henry Plummer
John David Borthwick: Artist of the Gold Rush
Gold Camp Desperadoes
Vigilante Victims: Montana's 1864 Hanging Spree

Her Western studies have earned her a listing in *Who's Who in the South and Southwest*, *Who's Who in America*, *Who's Who in the World*, *Dictionary of International Biography*, and *Outstanding People of the 20th Century*.

Her first novel, *The Cottonwood Murders: Unsolved*, is scheduled for publication in December 1998.

Notes

I: Child Abuse on the Western Frontier

1. *Oregon Journal* (Portland), 17 March 1922.
2. Jesse A. Applegate, *A Day with the Cow Column* (Fairfield, Washington: Ye Galleon Press, 1990), 136.
3. *Oregon Journal*, 23 October 1930.
4. Ibid., 17 March 1922.
5. Fred Lockley, "Emma Perkins Hembree," *Conversations With Pioneer Women* (Eugene, Oregon: Rainy Day Press, 1981), 4; Applegate, 144.
6. Frank Myers, *Soldiering in Dakota Among the Indians in 1863-4-5* (Fairfield, Washington: Ye Galleon Press, 1975), 15-16.
7. Ibid., 11; Fanny Wiggins Kelly, *Narrative of My Captivity Among the Sioux Indians*, in Myers, 37.
8. I. D. Ferguson, "Helpless Women and Children Massacred," *Frontier Times* 10 (July 1938) 15:458-62.
9. J. Marvin Hunter, "Mr. And Mrs. John Riggs Killed by Indians," *Frontier Times* 1 (October 1937) 15:1-3.
10. Myers, 28.
11. *Oregon Journal*, 26 May 1925.
12. Granville Stuart, *Prospecting for Gold* (Lincoln: University of Nebraska Press, 1977), 146-47.
13. Ibid., 23-25; Fred Lockley, "Andrew Smith," *Conversations with Bullwhackers* (Eugene: Oregon: Rainy Day Press, 1981), 77.
14. John David Borthwick, *The Gold Hunters* (New York: International Fiction Library, 1917), 67; Michael McLatchy, "From Wisconsin to Montana and Life in the West 1863-1889: The Reminiscences of Robert Kirkpatrick" (Dissertation, Montana State University, 1961), 159; *Oregon Journal*, 23 May 1925.
15. Isabella Bird, *A Lady's Life in the Rocky Mountains* (Sausalito, California: Comstock Editions, Inc., 1987), 62, 44.
16. Applegate, 154-44.
17. *Oregon Journal*, 23 May 1925.
18. In the early decades of the twentieth century, newspaperman Fred Lockley conducted more than 10,000 interviews with pioneers. These interviews appeared in Lockley's *Oregon Journal* column for nearly twenty years. Collections of these interviews have been published in two books: *Conversations with Pioneer Women* and *Conversations with Bullwhackers*, both listed in the bibliography.
19. *Oregon Journal*, 25 December 1921.
20. Catherine, Elizabeth, and Matilda Sager, *The Whitman Massacre of 1847* (Fairfield, Washington: Ye Galleon Press, 1981), 10, 152.
21. Ibid., 10.
22. Ibid., 11.
23. Edward Evans Parrish, *Diary of Rev. Edward Evans Parrish: Crossing the Plains in 1844* (Fairfield, Washington: Ye Galleon Press, 1988), 8.

24. Ibid., 10.
25. Sager, 13-15, 184.
26. Ibid., 14-15, 184.
27. Parrish, 26; John Minto, "Reminiscences of Experiences on the Oregon Trail in 1844," *The Quarterly of the Oregon Historical Society* 2 (1901) 2:163.
28. Sager, 187.
29. Ibid., 16.
30. Ibid., 17, 108; Parrish, 35-36, 38.
31. Narcissa Whitman, *The Letters of Narcissa Whitman* (Fairfield, Washington: Ye Galleon Press, 1986), 182.
32. Narcissa Whitman, *My Journal* (Fairfield, Washington: Ye Galleon Press, 1982), 7.
33. Ibid., 15-46.
34. Ibid., 15, 16, 18, 20; Whitman, *Letters*, 11, 13.
35. James B. Marsh, *Four Years in the Rockies or the Adventures of Isaac P. Rose* (New Castle, Pennsylvania: W. B. Thomas, 1884), 156.
36. Whitman, *Journal*, 22.
37. Whitman, *Letters*, 37-38.
38. Ibid., 37-38.
39. Ibid., 40.
40. Ibid., 46, 93.
41. Ibid., 49, 47.
42. Ibid., 47, 55.
43. Ibid., 74, 80, 83.
44. Ibid., 79, 83-84.
45. Ibid., 85.
46. Ibid., 85-87.
47. Sager, 19-20.
48. Ibid., 21; Whitman, *Letters*, 200; *Oregon Journal*, 5 July 1923.
49. Sager, 22; Whitman, *Letters*, 201.
50. Sager, 91; *Oregon Journal* 24 and 25 July 1923.
51. Sager, 108-109; *Oregon Journal,* 24 December 1921.
52. Whitman, *Letters*, 187, 200; Sager, 109, 112, 22.
53. Whitman, *Letters*, 186-87; Sager, 101.
54. Sager, 27, 31; Whitman, *Letters*, 188, 212.
55. Sager, 30; Whitman, *Letters*, 187.
56. Sager, 23, 25.
57. Sager, 30, 23, 25; Whitman, *Letters*, 187.
58. Whitman, *Letters*, 201-02; Sager, 25.
59. Henry H. Spalding, Letter to Stephen Prentiss, 6 April 1848, in Whitman, *Letters*, 230-35; Whitman, *Letters*, 218.
60. Whitman, *Letters*, 82-83, 218.
61. Spalding, 230-35; Sager, 87-88.
62. Sager, 60-62, 68, 102-03, 119.
63. Sager, 68, 81-82, 90, 103, 118-19; *Oregon Journal*, 6 September 1923; Spalding, 231.
64. Sager, 128-29, 90.
65. Ibid., 103-04.
66. Ibid., 132-37.
67. Ibid., 131-32; *Oregon Journal*, 24 December 1921 and 13 July 1927; *Seventh*

Census of U.S.: 1850 Population Schedule of Washington County, Oregon Territory; Whitman, *Letters,* 212.

68. *Seventh Census of U.S.: 1850 Population Schedule of Washington County, Oregon Territory;* Whitman, *Letters,* 212; *Oregon Journal,* 24 and 25 December 1921.

69. Sager, 125; *Oregon Journal,* 24 and 25 December 1921.

70. *Oregon Journal,* 24 and 25 December 1921; Sager, 144-46.

71. Sager, 103.

72. Whitman, *Letters,* 48, 47; *Oregon Journal,* 19 and 20 October 1922.

73. *Oregon Journal,* 22 October 1922.

74. Ibid., 19 November 1927.

75. Ibid., 26 May 1925.

76. *The Gospel Primer* (author, publisher, and date unknown), 18.

77. Lockley, "Captain Ed Carr," *Conversations with Bullwhackers,* 295, 299, 301.

78. *Register and Descriptive List of Convicts Under Sentence of Imprisonment in the State Prison,* California State Archives, Sacramento; R. E. Mather and F. E. Boswell, *Gold Camp Desperadoes* (San Jose, California: History West Publishing Company, 1990), 175-79.

79. James Williams, "Statement," Handwritten MS, Bancroft Library, University of California, Berkeley. (An unidentified contemporary of James Williams added the commentary to the bottom of the Statement and then initialed it.)

80. *Eighth and Ninth Censuses of U.S.: 1860 and 1870 Population Schedules of Scotland County, Missouri;* Tom Horn, *Life of Tom Horn* (Norman: University of Oklahoma Press, 1964), 3.

81. Horn, 4, 6, 8.

82. Ibid., 8, 9.

83. Joseph William Moch, Letter to History West Publishing Company, 25 October 1994; Horn, 256.

84. *Oregon Journal,* 24 July 1931.

85. Sager, 90.

86. James F. Meline, *Two Thousand Miles on Horseback* (New York: The Catholic Publication Society, 1872), 268-69.

87. John Wesley Hardin, *The Life of John Wesley Hardin* (Norman: University of Oklahoma Press, 1961), 5.

88. *Eighth Census of U.S.: 1860 Population Schedule of Trinity County, Texas;* Hardin, 5-6, 12-16, 38, 40-42.

89. Hardin, 8-10.

90. Ibid., 7, 12-14, 16.

91. Ibid., 29, 34, 35, xv, xvii. For a discussion of inaccuracies in Hardin's autobiography, see Rick Miller, *Bloody Bill Longley* (Wolfe City, Texas: Henington Publishing Company, 1996), 25-27.

92. Hardin, 6.

93. Margaret Ronan, *Frontier Woman: The Story of Mary Ronan* (Missoula: University of Montana, 1973), 6, 1.

94. Ronan, 23-24, 13-15, 19.

95. Lew L. Callaway, *Montana's Righteous Hangmen* (Norman: University of Oklahoma Press, 1982), 108; Ronan, 24.

96. Ronan, 24-25.

97. Ibid., 23; Thomas J. Dimsdale, *The Vigilantes of Montana* (Norman: University of Oklahoma Press, 1953), 205. For a discussion of Dimsdale's possible membership in Vigilantes, see R. E. Mather and F. E. Boswell, *Vigilante Victims* (San Jose,

California: History West Publishing Company, 1991), 175.

98. *Oregon Journal*, 23 March 1929.

99. Ibid., 19 December 1927.

100. Ibid., 11 April 1920.

101. Lockley, "George Turner," *Conversations with Bullwhackers*, 133.

102. John Evans Brown, *Memoirs of an American Gold Seeker* (Fairfield, Washington: Ye Galleon Press, n.d.), 8.

103. Bird, 202.

104. *Boise News* (Boise, Idaho), 26 March 1864. Reprinted from *Times* (Aurora, Nevada), n.d.; Michael Leeson, *History of Montana 1739-1885* (Chicago: Warner, Beers & Company, 1885), 265; Bird, 166; Mark Twain, *Roughing It* (New York: Holt, Rinehart and Winston, 1966), 250-54.

105. Applegate, 96, 147-48, 54.

106. Ibid., 182, 202-03.

107. *Oregon Journal*, 24 December 1921.

108. "The Diary of a Frontier Preacher," *Frontier Times* 11 (August 1939) 16:499, 501.

109. Lockley, "George Turner," 133; Horn, 8.

110. *Oregon Journal*, 19 November 1927.

111. J. Goldsborough Bruff, *Gold Rush, The Journals* (New York: Columbia University Press, 1949), 247.

112. Clare V. McKanna, Jr., "The Origins of San Quentin," *California History*, March 1987, 54.

113. *Oregon Journal*, 24 December 1921.

II: Spousal Battery on the Frontier

1. Charles Ferguson, *A Third of the Century in the Gold Field* (Chico, California: M. A. Carson, 1924), 96; John David Borthwick, "Mining Life in California," *Harper's Weekly*, 3 October 1857, 635; Bird, 65; Dimsdale, 18.

2. *Oregon Journal*, 24 April 1934; Stephen Crane, "A man said to the universe," *Poems of Stephen Crane* (New York: Thomas Y. Crowell, 1964), 49.

3. Lockley, "Benjamin Franklin Bonney," *Conversations with Bullwhackers*, 20-22.

4. Whitman, *Letters*, 78, 119.

5. Borthwick, "Mining Life in California," 633.

6. Louise Amelia Clappe, *The Shirley Letters* (San Francisco: T. C. Russell, 1922), 326.

7. Lockley, "Berthine Adair," *Conversations with Pioneer Women*, 29-30.

8. Dimsdale, 18; John Grannis, "Diary," SC. 301, Montana Historical Society Archives, Book I, 11.

9. Alva J. Noyes, *Dimsdale's Vigilantes of Montana: A Contemporary History of the Treasure State* (Helena, Montana: State Publishing Co., n.d.), 220.

10. *Nevada Journal* (Nevada City, California), 10 March 1854; *History of Nevada County, California* (Berkeley: Howell-North, 1970), 65.

11. McLatchy, 137-38.

12. Lockley, "Elvina Apperson Fellows, *Conversations with Pioneer Women*, 65.

13. Elizabeth Geer, "Diary, 1847," *Transactions of the Oregon Pioneer Association, 1907*, in Lillian Schlissel, *Women's Diaries of the Westward Journey* (New York: Schocken Books, 1982), 165.

14. *Nevada Democrat* (Nevada City, California), 21 April 1860.

15. Stuart, 174.

16. Elizabeth B. Custer, *Tenting on the Plains* (New York: Charles L. Webster, 1887), 412.

17. Grannis, I:2; Trial Records of The People of the State of California vs. Henry Plumer in Nevada County in 1857, California State Archives, Sacramento; *The Evening Bee* (Sacramento), 21 June and 4 August 1906.

18. Ann Eliza Young, *Wife No. 19* (Hartford, Connecticut: Dustin, Gilman & Co., 1875), 402-10; Mather and Boswell, *Gold Camp Desperadoes*, 175-79; Grannis, II:6.

19. Court Records, Laramie County, Wyoming; *Owyhee Avalanche* (Silver City, Idaho), 26 October 1994.

20. Lockley, "Elvina Apperson Fellows," 65; *Oregon Journal*, 25 December 1921.

21. *Nevada Democrat*, 4 December 1866.

22. Grannis, I:2.

23. *Seventh Census of U.S.: 1850 Population Schedule of St. Joseph County, Indiana*; Grannis, I:2, II:26-27.

24. *Eighth Census of U.S.: 1860 Population Schedule of Arapahoe County, Kansas Territory*; Grannis, I:1-2.

25. Ibid.; *Ninth Census of U.S.: 1870 Population Schedule of Jefferson County, Montana Territory*.

26. Grannis, I:2.

27. *Eighth Census of U.S.: 1860 Population Schedule of Arapahoe County, Kansas Territory*.

28. Grannis, I:2; Helen F. Sanders, ed., *X. Beidler: Vigilante* (Norman: University of Oklahoma Press, 1957), 21.

29. H. Sanders, 72; Grannis, I:3.

30. Grannis, I:3, 8, 26.

31. Ibid., I:3-5.

32. Ibid., I:6, 26.

33. Ibid., I:6-8; Ronan, 15.

34. Grannis, I:6-8.

35. Ibid., I:8-9.

36. Ibid., I:9-10; Ronan, 15; Meriwether Lewis and William Clark, *The Journals of Lewis and Clark* (New York: New American Library, 1964), 221.

37. Ronan, 17.

38. Grannis, I:10-13.

39. Ibid., I:2.

40. Ibid., I:10.

41. Ibid.; H. Sanders, 22.

42. Grannis, I:13.

43. H. Sanders, 32-33.

44. Grannis, I:11-13.

45. H. Sanders, 27, 22.

46. Grannis, I:13-14, 26.

47. Ibid., I:14-16.

48. Ibid., I:16-17, 19-21.

49. Ibid., I:19; Lockley, "Captain Ed Carr," 299.

50. Grannis, I:19-24.

51. H. Sanders, 32.

52. Wilbur Sanders, "The Story of George Ives," in H. Sanders, 72.

53. Ibid., 71-73; Grannis, I:23; *Daily Oregonian* (Portland), 13 April 1864.

54. Grannis, I:23-24.

55. Ibid., II:1-2.

56. Ibid.

57. Ibid., II:2.

58. Ibid., II:10.

59. Ibid., II:3, 5.

60. Ibid., II:8-9.

61. Ibid., II:9-20.

62. Ibid., II:16, IV:7; Bird, 44.

63. Grannis, II:16-21.

64. *Montana Post* (Virginia City, Montana), 27 August 1864.

65. Grannis, II:19.

66. Ibid., II:17-18, I:26.

67. Ibid., II:19, 21-26.

68. Ibid., II:26.

69. Ibid., II:27-28.

70. Ibid., III:2, 9.

71. Ibid., III:3.

72. Ibid., III:1-6.

73. Ibid., III:7-10, 13-15.

74. Ibid., III:22, IV:1, 3.

75. Ibid., III:20, IV:3-4, 6, 9.

76. Ibid., IV:10-14, 15-17.

77. Ibid., IV: 11, 13, 16-17.

78. Ibid., IV:18.

79. H. Sanders, 128-32; *Montana Post*, 2 September 1866; Grannis, IV:19.

80. Callaway, 5; Nathaniel Pitt Langford, *Vigilante Days and Ways* (New York: A. L. Burt Company, 1912), 90, 538.

81. Grannis: IV:21.

82. Ibid., II:27.

83. Ibid., II:2, I:2.

84. *Ninth Census of U.S.: 1870 Population Schedule of Jefferson County, Montana Territory.*

85. Schlissel, 98, 56, 78.

III: Domestic Tragedies on the Frontier

1. Lockley, "Elvina Apperson Fellows," 63-64.

2. Ibid.; *Seventh Census of U.S.: 1850 Population Schedule of Washington County, Oregon Territory.*

3. Lockley, "Elvina Apperson Fellows," 64.

4. Ibid.

5. *Seventh Census of U.S.: 1850 Population Schedule of Washington County, Oregon*

Territory; Oregon Journal, 25 December 1921.

6. Author's note: I do not know the source of this tale, but when I was young, I heard it told for the truth.

7. McLatchy, 159; *Oregon Journal,* 25 December 1921.

8. *Oregon Journal,* 25 December 1921.

9. *Seventh Census of U.S.: 1850 Population Schedule of Sacramento County, California;* Marriage Records of Sacramento County, California; Trial Records of The People of the State of California vs. Henry Plumer in Nevada County in 1857 and Trial Records of The People vs. Henry Plummer in Yuba County in 1858, California State Archives, Sacramento.

10. Plumer Trial Records of Nevada County; Plummer Trial Records of Yuba County.

11. Plummer Trial Records of Yuba County.

12. Ibid.

13. Death Records of Sacramento County, California.

14. *Morning Transcript* (Nevada City, California), 2 November 1860; *History of Nevada County, California,* 12.

15. Plumer Trial Records of Nevada County.

16. Borthwick, "Mining Life in California," 634.

17. *Nevada Democrat,* 8 July 1857; Plummer Trial Records of Yuba County.

18. Plumer Trial Records of Nevada County and Plummer Trial Records of Yuba County.

19. Ibid.

20. Ibid.

21. Ibid.

22. Ibid.

23. Ibid.

24. Ibid.

25. Ibid.

26. Ibid.

27. Ibid.

28. Ibid.

29. Ibid.

30. Ibid.

31. Ibid.

32. Ibid.

33. Ibid.; Governor's File on Henry Plummer, California State Archives, Sacramento.

34. *Nevada Journal,* 16 October 1857. Information rewritten from *Sacramento Bee,* n.d.

35. Death Records of Sacramento County, California; Plumer Trial Records of Nevada County.

36. Alfred Barstow, "Statement of Alfred Barstow, A Pioneer of 1849," MS., H. H. Bancroft Collection, Bancroft Library, University of California, Berkeley.

37. *Morning Transcript,* 15 October 1860; *Nevada Daily Transcript* (Nevada City, California), 21 November 1862; *Nevada National* (Grass Valley, California), 10 March 1860.

38. *Eighth Census of U.S.: 1860 Population Schedule of Sacramento County, California.*

39. *Alta California* (San Francisco), 14 July 1851. Reprinted from *Sacramento Times & Transcript.*

40. David Pierce Barstow, *Recollections of 1849-51 in California* (Inverness, California: Press of Inverness, 1979), 21; *Mountain Messenger* (Downieville, California), 6 May 1871.

41. *Mountain Messenger*, 6 May 1871.

42. Ibid.

43. Ibid.

44. D. Barstow, 22.

45. Borthwick, "Mining Life in California," 633.

46. Ibid.

47. Paul Hightower, "Texas Execution," *Deja News, Inc.*, 1 February 1998. For complete story of lynchings of Luduska Hill and her daughters see Mark Dugan, *Tales Never Told Around the Campfire* (Athens, Ohio: Swallow Press/Ohio University Press, 1992), 3-13.

48. *The Evening Bee,* 5 and 15 June 1906; *San Francisco Chronicle*, 10 July 1906.

49. *San Francisco Chronicle*, 19 July 1906.

50. Ibid.; Trial Records of the People of The State of California vs. Emma LeDoux in San Joaquin County in 1906, California State Archives, Sacramento, 13-14.

51. LeDoux Trial Records, 13, 86, 101.

52. *San Francisco Chronicle*, 26 March 1906; LeDoux Trial Records, 767, 103-07.

53. LeDoux Trial Records, 104.

54. Ibid.

55. Ibid., 142-43.

56. Ibid., 144-45, 124.

57. Ibid., 123, 145, 248, 158.

58. Ibid., 146-47.

59. Ibid., 150, 252-54, 261.

60. *San Francisco Chronicle,* 25, 26, and 31 March 1906.

61. LeDoux Trial Records, 637, 575-77.

62. *San Francisco Chronicle*, 27 March and 11 July 1906.

63. Ibid., 26 March 1906.

64. Rose Eva Schultz, Letter to Governor William D. Stephens, 22 November 1921, Governor's File on Emma LeDoux, California State Archives, Sacramento.

65. Charles Crocker, Letter to Hester T. Griffith, 8 January 1918, Governor's File on Emma LeDoux.

66. Application for Executive Clemency, Governor's File on Emma LeDoux; *San Francisco Chronicle*, 26 March 1906; Elinor Wylie, "Let No Charitable Hope," *Collected Poems of Elinor Wylie* (New York: Alfred A. Knopf, 1938), 65.

67. Application for Executive Clemency; LeDoux Trial Records, 868-69; *San Francisco Chronicle*, 26 and 28 March 1906; *Tenth Census of U.S.: 1880 Population Schedule of Amador County, California*; Borthwick, *The Gold Hunters*, 130-31.

68. Borthwick, *The Gold Hunters,* 144, 255-56.

69. *Tenth Census of the U.S.: 1880 Population Schedule of Amador County, California.*

70. *San Francisco Chronicle*, 26 March 1906; Emma LeDoux, Letter to Jean LeDoux, 30 May 1904, LeDoux Trial Records, 892-94.

71. Crocker Letter; *San Francisco Chronicle*, 26 and 28 March 1906.

72. *San Francisco Chronicle*, 28 March 1906; *The Evening Bee,* 27 March 1906.

73. *Register and Descriptive List of Convicts; San Francisco Chronicle* 28 March 1906; Crocker Letter; Emma LeDoux, Letter to Jean LeDoux, 30 May 1904.

74. Crocker Letter.

75. Ibid.; *San Francisco Chronicle*, 26 March 1906; LeDoux Trial Records, 782.

76. *Tenth Census of U.S.: 1880 Population Schedule of Amador County, California;* Emma LeDoux, Letters to Jean LeDoux, 4 and 20 January 1903, LeDoux Trial Records, 879-80, 892, 869-72; *San Francisco Chronicle,* 28 March 1906.

77. LeDoux Trial Records, 872, 892-94; *San Francisco Chronicle,* 28 and 30 March and 8 August 1906; Emma LeDoux, Letter to Jean, 30 May 1904.

78. Crocker Letter; *San Francisco Chronicle,* 26 and 27 March 1906.

79. *San Francisco Chronicle,* 26 and 27 March 1906.

80. Ibid.; Emma LeDoux, Letter to Jean LeDoux, 20 January 1903; LeDoux Trial Records, 142, 104, 219.

81. *Ninth Census of U.S.: 1870 Population Schedule of Sedgwick County, Kansas; The Evening Bee,* 27 March 1906; LeDoux Trial Records, 765.

82. Crocker Letter; Marriage Records of Cochise County, Arizona Territory; LeDoux Trial Records, 629-36, 784.

83. LeDoux Trial Records, 481, 552, 722; *San Francisco Chronicle,* 28 March 1906.

84. Crocker Letter; LeDoux Trial Records, 925-26; Emma LeDoux, Letters to Jean LeDoux, 4 and 20 January 1903.

85. Crocker Letter; LeDoux Trial Records, 925-26; Application for Executive Clemency.

86. Emma LeDoux, Letters to Jean LeDoux, 4 and 20 January 1903 and 20 April 1904; LeDoux Trial Records, 881, 890-92.

87. LeDoux Trial Records, 797, 892-94, 677-78; Crocker Letter; Application for Executive Clemency; Emma LeDoux, Letter to Jean LeDoux, 30 May 1904.

88. Emma LeDoux, Letter to Jean LeDoux, 30 May 1904.

89. LeDoux Trial Records, 481, 674, 1020.

90. Ibid., 859, 681; *San Francisco Chronicle,* 27 March 1906.

91. LeDoux Trial Records, 1016-21.

92. Dr. L. L. Stanley, Letter to Warden J. A. Johnston, 6 October 1914, Governor's File on Emma LeDoux; LeDoux Trial Records, 928-30, 1014.

93. LeDoux Trial Records, 1016-21.

94. Ibid., 893; Emma LeDoux, Letter to Jean LeDoux, 30 May 1904.

95. LeDoux Trial Records, 859, 642; Marriage Records of Yolo County California.

96. LeDoux Trial Records, 647-49; Marriage Records of Yolo County, California.

97. Emma LeDoux, Letter to Jean LeDoux, 20 April 1904; *San Francisco Chronicle,* 26 March 1906.

98. LeDoux Trial Records, 865.

99. Ibid., 705.

100. Crocker Letter; LeDoux Trial Records, 806-07, 809.

101. LeDoux Trial Records, 807.

102. Ibid., 977-80; *San Francisco Chronicle,* 30 March 1906.

103. LeDoux Trial Records, 688.

104. Ibid., 688-90.

105. Ibid., 689, 746, 763.

106. Ibid., 784, 706, 762.

107. Ibid., 748.

108. Ibid., 783; *San Francisco Chronicle,* 26 March 1906.

109. LeDoux Trial Records, 866.

110. Ibid., 705-06, 709.

111. Ibid., 743.

112. Ibid., 74, 130, 746.

113. Ibid., 704-08, 782.

114. Ibid., 743.

115. Ibid., 743, 25, 44.

116. Ibid., 66-67, 73, 544, 606.

117. Ibid., 478; Crocker Letter.

118. LeDoux Trial Records, 582, 605-12. NOTE: Emma's statement to police regarding the events of 24 March 1906 is riddled with falsehoods intended (1) to remove blame from herself and place it on Joe Miller, the man McVicar brought back to the hotel room (or at least the name Emma used for him) and (2) to keep Jean from learning she had intended to continue her marriage to McVicar and bring him back to the farm. Therefore, the only portions of her statement that can be accepted are those corroborated by one of four sources: witnesses who observed the McVicars together in Stockton (pp. 29-91 of LeDoux Trial Records), witnesses at Rawhide who heard the McVicars state their plans (pp. 697-803), Charles Fairall's statement to Judge Nutter regarding testimony of witnesses he had secured (p. 926), or the Charles Crocker Letter.

119. LeDoux Trial Records, 510, 523, 669.

120. Ibid., 512, 515.

121. Ibid., 814, 456, 558; San Francisco Chronicle, 26 March 1906.

122. LeDoux Trial Records, 611, 654, 656-59, 680.

123. Ibid., 719.

124. Ibid., 577-78, 589-94.

125. San Francisco Chronicle, 27 and 29 March 1906; The Evening Bee, 27 and 28 March 1906.

126. San Francisco Chronicle, 28 March, 10 June, and 6 August 1906.

127. Ibid., 26 and 30 March and 10 June 1906; The Evening Bee, 27 March and 25 June 1906.

128. LeDoux Trial Records, 1029; Emma LeDoux, Letter to Governor William D. Stephens, 27 December 1921, Governor's File on Emma LeDoux.

129. LeDoux Trial Records, 1040, 607, 609.

130. The Evening Bee, 20 April 1906; San Francisco Chronicle, 25 April 1906.

131. San Francisco Chronicle, 16 April 1906; The Evening Bee, 5 and 21 June 1906.

132. The Evening Bee, 5 June 1906; San Francisco Chronicle, 21 June 1906.

133. LeDoux Trial Records, 1008.

134. Ibid., 29, 33.

135. Ibid., 52, 701, 541.

136. San Francisco Chronicle, 15 June 1906; The Evening Bee, 21 June 1906.

137. LeDoux Trial Records, 874-75.

138. Ibid., 163; San Francisco Chronicle, 10 June 1906.

139. LeDoux Trial Records, 555,567.

140. Ibid., 55-56. (The passage quoted represents only a portion of the testimony Dohrmann gave on this topic.)

141. Ibid., 306.

142. Ibid., 285, 1004-07. (The passage quoted represents only a portion of the testimony Davis gave on this topic.)

143. Ibid., 1009.

144. Ibid., 158-205. (The selection of questions and answers is extracted from Latta's cross-examination and represents only one issue covered.)

145. Ibid., 178.

146. Ibid., 169, 203, 206, 209, 231, 234. (The selection of questions and answers is extracted from Latta's cross-examination and represents only a sampling of

issues covered.)

147. Ibid., 177, 201.

148. Ibid., 289, 153.

149. Ibid., 306-07, 312.

150. Ibid., 620, 593.

151. Ibid., 1010-11.

152. Ibid., 465, 479, 510.

153. Ibid., 640-50.

154. Ibid., 925-26.

155. *The Evening Bee*, 26 and 27 March 1906; *Tenth Census of U.S.: 1880 Population Schedule of Sedgwick County, Kansas.*

156. LeDoux Trial Records, 928-94.

157. *San Francisco Chronicle*, 24 June 1906.

158. LeDoux Trial Records, 1056; *San Francisco Chronicle*, 8 August 1906.

159. *San Francisco Chronicle*, 11 July and 4 August 1906.

160. LeDoux Trial Records, 1010; Application for Executive Clemency.

161. "Supreme Court-April Term 1909," *California Reports*, CLV:535.

162. William Vacher, Letter to Governor William D. Stephens, 15 October 1921, Governor's File on Emma LeDoux; Emma LeDoux, Letter to Governor William D. Stephens.

163. *Register and Descriptive List of Convicts*; Emma LeDoux, Letter to Governor William D. Stephens.

164. C. L. Neumiller, Letter to Governor William D. Stephens, 31 October 1921, Governor's File on Emma LeDoux.

165. Testimony of Deputy Parole Officer R. E. Langworthy at Meeting of Board of Prison Directors Held at San Quentin Prison on 22 October 1921; Nellie Dolph, Letter to Governor William D. Stephens, 2 December 1921, Governor's File on Emma LeDoux.

166. Charles Crocker Letter; Emma LeDoux, Letter to Board of Prison Terms and Paroles, 8 December 1933, Governor's File on Emma LeDoux.

167. *San Francisco Chronicle*, 26 and 28 March 1906.

168. LeDoux Trial Records, 624-38, 654-57, 672-82.

169. *San Francisco Chronicle*, 8 August 1906; LeDoux Trial Records, 926.

170. Crocker Letter.

171. Theodore Dreiser, *An American Tragedy* (New York: Boni and Liveright, 1925), 389-90.

172. Hester T. Griffith, Letter to Governor Hiram Johnson, 25 May 1906, Governor's File on Emma LeDoux.

173. Vacher Letter.

174. J. H. Grande, Letter to Ed Whyte, 2 July 1921, Governor's File on Emma LeDoux.

IV: Epilogue

1. Lenore Walker, *Terrifying Love* (New York: Harper & Row, 1989); Andrew Vachss, "You Carry The Cure In Your Own Heart," *Parade*, 5, in *The Sunday Oklahoman* (Oklahoma City), 28 August 1994.
2. *The Sunday Oklahoman*, 5 February 1995.

BIBLIOGRAPHY

BOOKS

Applegate, Jesse A. *A Day with the Cow Column.* Fairfield, Washington: Ye Galleon Press, 1990.

Armitage, Susan and Elizabeth Jameson, eds. *The Women's West.* Norman: University of Oklahoma Press, 1987.

Barstow, David Pierce. *Recollections of 1849-51 in California.* Inverness, California: Press of Inverness, 1979.

Billington, Ray Allen. *The Far Western Frontier 1830-1860.* New York: Harper & Row, 1956.

_____, ed. *The Frontier Thesis: Valid Interpretation of American History?* Huntington, New York: Robert E. Krieger Publishing Company, 1977.

Bird, Isabella. *A Lady's Life in the Rocky Mountains.* Sausalito, California: Comstock Editions, Inc., 1987.

Borthwick, John David. *The Gold Hunters.* New York: International Fiction Library, 1917.

Brown, Dee. *The Gentle Tamers: Women of the Old Wild West.* Lincoln: University of Nebraska Press, 1958.

Brown, John Evans. *Memoirs of An American Gold Seeker.* Fairfield, Washington: Ye Galleon Press, n.d.

Bruff, J. Goldsborough. *Gold Rush, The Journals.* New York: Columbia University Press, 1949.

Callaway, Lew L. *Montana's Righteous Hangmen.* Norman: University of Oklahoma Press, 1982.

Caughey, John and Laree. *California Heritage: An Anthology of History and Literature.* Los Angeles: Ward Ritchie Press, 1962.

Clappe, Louise Amelia. *The Shirley Letters.* San Francisco: T. C. Russell, 1922.

Crane, Stephen. "A man said to the universe." *Poems of Stephen Crane.* New York: Thomas Y. Crowell, 1964.

Custer, Elizabeth B. *Tenting on the Plains.* New York: Charles L. Webster, 1887.

Dimsdale, Thomas J. *The Vigilantes of Montana.* Norman: University of Oklahoma Press, 1953.

Dreiser, Theodore. *An American Tragedy.* New York: Boni and Liveright, 1925.

Dugan, Mark. *Tales Never Told Around the Campfire.* Athens, Ohio: Swallow Press/Ohio University Press, 1992.

Earp, Josephine Sarah Marcus. *I Married Wyatt Earp.* Tucson: University of Arizona Press, 1976.

Ferguson, Charles. *A Third of the Century in the Gold Field.* Chico, California: M.A. Carson, 1924.

French, Joseph Lewis, ed. *The Pioneer West: Narratives of the Westward March of Empire.* New York: Garden City Publishing Co., Inc., 1937.

Gabriel, Ralph Henry, ed. *Sarah Royce, A Frontier Lady: Recollections of the Gold Rush and Early California.* New Haven: Yale University Press, 1932.

Geer, Elizabeth. "Diary, 1847." *Transactions of the Oregon Pioneer Association,* 1907.

In Lillian Schlissel. *Women's Diaries of the Westward Journey.* New York: Schocken Books, 1982.

Gentry, Curt. *The Madams of San Francisco.* Sausalito, California: Comstock Editions, 1964.

Georgi-Findlay, Brigitte. *The Frontiers of Women's Writing: Women's Narratives and the Rhetoric of Westward Expansion.* Tucson: University of Arizona Press, 1996.

The Gospel Primer. No Author. No Publisher. n.d.

Griswold, Robert L. *Family & Divorce in California, 1850-1890: Victorian Illusions & Everyday   Realities.* Albany: State University of New York, 1983.

Graulich, Melody. "Violence Against Women: Power Dynamics in Literature of the Western Family." In Susan Armitage and Elizabeth Jameson, eds. *The Women's West.* Norman: University of Oklahoma Press, 1987.

Hacker, Margaret Schmidt. *Cynthia Ann Parker: The Life and The Legend.* El Paso: The University of Texas at El Paso, 1990.

Hardin, John Wesley. *The Life of John Wesley Hardin.* Norman: University of Oklahoma Press, 1961.

Hine, Robert V. and Edwin R. Bingham, eds. *The Frontier Experience.* Belmont, California: Wadsworth Publishing Company, 1963.

Hirsch, Miriam F. *Women and Violence.* New York: Van Nostrand Reinhold Company, 1981.

History of Nevada County, California. Berkeley: Howell-North, 1970.

Horn, Tom. *Life of Tom Horn.* Norman: University of Oklahoma Press, 1964.

Kelly, Fanny Wiggins. *Narrative of My Captivity Among the Sioux Indians.* In Frank Myers. *Soldiering in Dakota Among the Indians in 1863-4-5.* Fairfield, Washington: Ye Galleon Press, 1975.

Klasner, Lily. *My Girlhood Among Outlaws.* Tucson: The University of Arizona Press, 1972.

Lacour-Gayet, Robert. *Everyday Life in the United States before the Civil War.* New York: Frederick Ungar Publishing Co., 1969.

Langford, Nathaniel Pitt. *Vigilante Days and Ways.* New York: A. L. Burt Company, 1912.

Leeson, Michael. *History of Montana 1739-1885.* Chicago: Warner, Beers & Company, 1885.

Lewis, Meriwether and William Clark. *The Journals of Lewis and Clark.* New York: New American Library, 1964.

Lockley, Fred. *Conversations with Bullwhackers.* Eugene, Oregon: Rainy Day Press, 1981.

_____. *Conversations with Pioneer Women.* Eugene, Oregon: Rainy Day Press, 1981.

Luchetti, Cathy. *'I Do!': Courtship, Love and Marriage on the American Frontier.* New York: Crown Publishers, Inc. 1996.

Marsh, James B. *Four Years in the Rockies or The Adventures of Isaac P. Rose,* New Castle, Pennsylvania: W. B. Thomas, 1885.

Mather, R. E. and F. E. Boswell. *Gold Camp Desperadoes.* San Jose, California: History West Publishing Company; 1990.

_____. *Hanging the Sheriff: A Biography of Henry Plummer.* Salt Lake City: University of Utah Press, 1987.

_____. *John David Borthwick: Artist of the Gold Rush.* Salt lake City: University of Utah Press, 1989.

_____. *Vigilante Victims.* San Jose, California: History West Publishing Company, 1991.

Meline, James F. *Two Thousand Miles on Horseback.* New York: The Catholic Publication Society, 1872.

Miller, Rick. *Bloody Bill Longley.* Wolfe City, Texas: Henington Publishing Company, 1996.

Moynihan, Ruth B., Susan Armitage, and Christiane Fischer Dichamp, eds. *So Much to Be Done: Women Settlers on the Mining and Ranching Frontier.* Lincoln: University of Nebraska Press, 1990.

Myers, Frank. *Soldiering in Dakota Among the Indians in 1863-4-5.* Fairfield, Washington: Ye Galleon Press, 1975.

Myres, Sandra L. *Westering Women and the Frontier Experience 1800-1915.* Albuquerque: University of New Mexico Press, 1982.

Noyes, Alva J. *Dimsdale's Vigilantes of Montana: A Contemporary History of the Treasure State.* Helena, Montana: State Publishing Co., n.d.

Parrish, Edward Evans. *Diary of Rev. Edward Evans Parrish: Crossing the Plains in 1844.* Fairfield, Washington: Ye Galleon Press, 1988.

Peavy, Linda S. and Ursula Smith. *Women in Waiting in the Westward Movement: Life on the   Home Frontier.* Norman: University of Oklahoma Press, 1994.

Petrik, Paula. *No Step Backward: Women and Family on the Rocky Mountain Mining Frontier.* Helena, Montana: Montana Historical Society Press, 1987.

Reese, Linda Williams. *Women of Oklahoma, 1890-1920.* Norman: University of Oklahoma Press, 1997.

Riley, Glenda. *Building and Breaking Families in the American West.* Albuquerque: University of New Mexico, 1996.

_____. *The Female Frontier: A Comparative View of Women on the Prairie and the Plains.* Lawrence, Kansas: University Press of Kansas, 1988.

_____. *Frontierswomen: The Iowa Experience.* Ames: Iowa State University Press, 1994.

_____. *A Place to Grow: Women in the American West.* Arlington Heights, Illinois: Harlan Davidson, Inc., 1992.

_____, *Women and Indians on the Frontier.* Albuquerque: University of New Mexico Press, 1984.

Robertson, Janet. *The Magnificent Mountain Women: Adventures in the Colorado Rockies.* Lincoln: University of Nebraska Press, 1990.

Ronan, Margaret. *Frontier Woman: The Story of Mary Ronan.* Missoula: University of Montana, 1973.

Sager, Catherine, Elizabeth, and Matilda. *The Whitman Massacre of 1847.* Fairfield, Washington: Ye Galleon Press, 1981.

Sanders, Helen F., ed. *X. Beidler: Vigilante.* Norman: University of Oklahoma Press, 1957.

Sanders, Wilbur. "The Story of George Ives." In Helen F. Sanders, ed. *X. Beidler: Vigilante.* Norman: University of Oklahoma Press, 1957.

Schlissel, Lillian. *Women's Diaries of the Westward Journey.* New York: Schocken Books, 1982.

Shirley, Gayle C. *More Than Petticoats: Remarkable Montana Women.* Helena, Montana: Falcon Press Publishing Company, Inc., 1995.

Spalding, Henry H. Letter to Stephen Prentiss. 6 April 1848. In Narcissa Whitman. *The Letters of Narcissa Whitman.* Fairfield, Washington: Ye Galleon Press, 1986.

Sprague, William Forrest. *Women and the West: A Short Social History.* New York: Arno Press, 1972.

Stewart, Elinore Pruitt. *Letters of a Woman Homesteader.* Lincoln: University of Nebraska Press, 1961.

Stratton, Joanna L. *Pioneer Women: Voices from the Kansas Frontier.* New York: Simon & Schuster, 1981.

Stuart, Granville, *Prospecting for Gold.* Lincoln: University of Nebraska Press, 1977.

Twain, Mark. *Roughing It.* New York: Holt, Rinehart and Winston, 1966.

Walker, Lenore. *Terrifying Love.* New York: Harper & Row, 1989.

Welch, Julia Conway. *Growing Up With Ghosts: Memories of Silver City, Idaho.* Caldwell, Idaho: The Caxton Printers, Ltd., 1984.

Whitman, Narcissa. *My Journal.* Fairfield, Washington: Ye Galleon Press, 1982.

_____. *The Letters of Narcissa Whitman.* Fairfield, Washington: Ye Galleon Press, 1986.

Wright, Louis B. *Life on the American Frontier.* New York: G. P. Putnam's Sons, 1971.

Wylie, Elinor. "Let No Charitable Hope." *Collected Poems of Elinor Wylie.* New York: Alfred A. Knopf, 1938.

Young, Ann Eliza. *Wife No. 19.* Hartford, Connecticut: Dustin, Gilman & Co., 1875.

Zanjani, Sally. *A Mine of Her Own: Women Prospectors in the American West, 1850-1950.* Lincoln: University of Nebraska Press, 1997.

ARTICLES AND NEWSPAPERS

Alta California (San Francisco). 1851.

Boise News (Boise, Idaho). 1864.

Borthwick, John David. "Mining Life in California." *Harper's Weekly,* 3 October 1857, 632-34.

Daily Oregonian (Portland). 1864.

"The Diary of a Frontier Preacher." *Frontier Times* 11 (August 1939) 16:499-501.

The Evening Bee (Sacramento). 1906.

Ferguson, I. D. "Helpless Women and Children Massacred." *Frontier Times* 10 (July 1938) 10:458-62.

Hightower, Paul. "Texas Execution." *Deja News, Inc.,* 1 February 1998.

McKanna, Clare V., Jr. "The Origins of San Quentin." *California History,* March 1987, 49-54, 73.

Minto, John. "Reminiscences of Experiences on the Oregon Trail in 1844." *The Quarterly of the Oregon Historical Society* 2 (1901) 2:119-67, 209-54.

Montana Post (Virginia City, Montana). 1864-66.

Morning Transcript (Nevada City, California). 1860.

Mountain Messenger (Downieville, California). 1871.

Nevada Daily Transcript (Nevada City, California). 1862.

Nevada Democrat (Nevada City, California). 1857-66.

Nevada Journal (Nevada City ,California). 1854.

Nevada National (Grass Valley, California). 1860.
Oregon Journal (Portland). 1921-38.
Owyhee Avalanche (Silver City, Idaho). 1994.
San Francisco Chronicle, 1906.
The Sunday Oklahoman (Oklahoma City). 1994-95.
Vachss, Andrew. "You Carry The Cure In Your Own Heart." *Parade*, 4-6. In *The Sunday Oklahoman* (Oklahoma City). 28 August 1994.

UNPUBLISHED MATERIAL

Barstow, Alfred. "Statement of Alfred Barstow, A Pioneer of 1849." MS., H. H. Bancroft Collection, Bancroft Library, University of California, Berkeley.
Crocker, Charles. Letter to Hester T. Griffith. 8 January 1918. Governor's File On Emma LeDoux, California State Archives, Sacramento.
Dolph, Nellie. Letter to Governor William D. Stephens. 2 December 1921. Governor's File on Emma LeDoux, California State Archives, Sacramento.
Grande, J. H. Letter to Ed Whyte. 2 July 1921. Governor's File on Emma LeDoux, California State Archives, Sacramento.
Grannis, John. "Diary." 4 books. SC. 301, Montana Historical Society Archives, Helena.
Griffith, Hester. Letter to Governor Hiram Johnson. 25 May 1906. Governor's File on Emma LeDoux, California State Archives, Sacramento.
LeDoux, Emma. Letter to Board of Prison Terms and Paroles. 8 December 1933. Governor's File on Emma LeDoux, California State Archives, Sacramento.
_____. Letter to Governor William D. Stephens. 27 December 1921. Governor's File on Emma LeDoux, California State Archives, Sacramento.
_____. Letters to Jean LeDoux. 4 and 20 January 1903, 20 April 1904, 30 May 1904. Trial Records of The People of California vs. Emma LeDoux in San Joaquin County in 1906.
McLatchy, Michael. "From Wisconsin to Montana and Life in the West, 1863-1889: The Reminiscences of Robert Kirkpatrick." Dissertation, Montana State University, 1961.
Moch, Joseph William. Letter to History West Publishing Company. 25 October 1994.
Neumiller, C. L. Letter to Governor William D. Stephens. 30 October 1921. Governor's File on Emma LeDoux, California State Archives, Sacramento.
Schultz, Rose Eva. Letter to Governor William D. Stephens. 22 November 1921. Governor's File on Emma LeDoux, California State Archives, Sacramento.
Stanley, Dr. L. L. Letter to Warden J. A. Johnston. 6 October 1914. Governor's File on Emma LeDoux, California State Archives, Sacramento.
Vacher, William. Letter to Governor William D. Stephens. 15 October 1921. Governor's File on Emma LeDoux, California State Archives, Sacramento.
Williams, James. "Statement." Handwritten MS., Bancroft Library, University of California, Berkeley.

PUBLIC DOCUMENTS

Arizona. Cochise County Marriage Records.

California. Application for Executive Clemency. Governor's File on Emma
     LeDoux, California State Archives, Sacramento.

_____. Governor's Files on Emma LeDoux and Henry Plumer. California State
     Archives, Sacramento.

_____. Register and Descriptive List of Convicts Under Sentence of Imprison-
     ment in the State Prison. California State Archives, Sacramento.

_____. Reports. Supreme Court Term 1909. Volume CLV. State Law Library,
     Sacramento.

_____. Sacramento County Death and Marriage Records.

_____. Testimony of Deputy Parole Officer R. E. Langworthy. At Meeting of
     Board of Prison Directors Held at San Quentin Prison on 22 October 1921.
     In Governor's File on Emma LeDoux, California State Archives, Sacra-
     mento.

_____. Trial Records of The People of the State of California vs. Emma LeDoux in
     San Joaquin County in 1906, The People of the State of California vs. Henry
     Plumer in Nevada County in 1857, and The People vs. Henry Plummer in
     Yuba County in 1858. California State Archives, Sacramento.

_____. Yolo County Marriage Records.

Wyoming. Laramie County Court Records.

U.S. Bureau of the Census. Seventh Census of U.S.: 1850 Population Schedule.

_____. Eighth Census of U.S.: 1860 Population Schedule.

_____. Ninth Census of U.S.: 1870 Population Schedule.

_____. Tenth Census of U.S.: 1880 Population Schedule.

Index